Prisms of the People: Power and Organizing in
Twenty-First-Century America *(coauthor)*

How Organizations Develop Activists:
Civic Associations and Leadership in the
Twenty-First Century

Groundbreakers: How Obama's 2.2 Million
Volunteers Transformed Campaigning in America
(coauthor)

Moved to Action: Motivation, Participation,
and Inequality in American Politics

UNDIVIDED

UNDIVIDED

THE QUEST FOR RACIAL SOLIDARITY IN AN AMERICAN CHURCH

HAHRIE HAN

Alfred A. Knopf

New York • 2024

THIS IS A BORZOI BOOK
PUBLISHED BY ALFRED A. KNOPF

Copyright © 2024 by Hahrie Han

All rights reserved. Published in the United States by Alfred A. Knopf,
a division of Penguin Random House LLC, New York, and distributed
in Canada by Penguin Random House Canada Limited, Toronto.

www.aaknopf.com

Knopf, Borzoi Books, and the colophon are registered trademarks of
Penguin Random House LLC.

Library of Congress Cataloging-in-Publication Data
Names: Han, Hahrie, author.
Title: Undivided : the quest for racial solidarity
in an American church / Hahrie Han.
Description: First edition. | New York : Alfred A. Knopf, 2024. |
Includes index.
Identifiers: LCCN 2023043406 (print) | ISBN 978-0-593-31886-7 (hardcover) |
ISBN 978-0-593-31887-4 (ebook)
Subjects: LCSH: Racial justice—United States.
Classification: LCC HT1561 .H36 2024 (print)
LC record available at https://lccn.loc.gov/2023043406

Jacket photograph by LaylaBird/E+/Getty Images
Jacket design by Eli Mock

Manufactured in the United States of America
First Edition

For the entire Undivided family,

in Cincinnati and beyond

There is never time in the future in which we will work out our salvation. The challenge is in the moment, the time is always now.

—James Baldwin

Let justice roll down like water, and righteousness like an ever-flowing stream.

—Amos 5:24, New Revised Standard Version

There is no final struggle. Whether you win or lose, each struggle brings forth new contradictions, new and more challenging questions.

—Grace Lee Boggs

CONTENTS

AUTHOR'S NOTE

This is a work of nonfiction. The stories shared here are based on incidents I personally observed and things people told me. When I did not observe something firsthand, I sought multiple interviewees who could describe the same incident to me and consulted any available photographs, videos, notes, and documentation to ensure the greatest accuracy possible. Thoughts (and dialogue I did not observe firsthand) were described to me and fact-checked with sources. I interviewed all named characters (as well as many of the unnamed characters), with the exception of Sergeant Harris and Patricia. I did not use their real names because I was not able to track down the sergeant, and Patricia declined to participate in the project. I relied on first names to minimize exposure for most characters (except for some public figures) because of the appalling record of violent threats aimed at people fighting for racial justice. To add additional privacy protections for one character, whom I call Sandra, I used a pseudonym and omitted certain details.

UNDIVIDED

UNLIKE *ANYTHING* I'VE EVER SEEN

I first heard about Undivided when I was researching a Cincinnati, Ohio, campaign dedicated to passing a 2016 ballot initiative for universal preschool education. The campaign won an
improbable victory during a particularly divisive election. That
year, the presidential race between Donald Trump and Hillary Clinton shredded the dangling remnants of a Band-Aid of
politeness that obscured racial conflict in America. Although the
country had never properly reckoned with its sordid history of
enslavement, racial oppression, and state-sanctioned violence
against communities of color, we liked to pretend that we had.
Unlike most candidates who tried to disguise their racism, Trump
spoke openly about his beliefs that Mexicans were "rapists" and
criminals, that Muslims were terrorists, and that Black communities were unmitigated dens of self-inflicted unemployment, poverty, and violence. When a former grand wizard of the Ku Klux
Klan endorsed Trump, the candidate refused to renounce him.

According to the U.S. Census, Cincinnati had gone from being
88 percent white and 12 percent Black in 1940 to 50 percent white
and 40 percent Black in 2022. During that period, the scythe of
deindustrialization sliced across the economic fortunes of both
Black and white communities in Cincinnati. As often happens,

scarcity fueled racial resentment. Many white Cincinnatians who struggled to attain the picket fences and matching living room sets they coveted blamed Black communities. Yet in 2016, a supermajority of Black and white residents passed a ballot initiative to raise their own taxes to fund universal preschool education with targeted resources for poor—mostly Black—communities. The initiative passed by the largest margin of any new education levy in Cincinnati history.

People kept telling me about one church that had sent a steady stream of volunteers to support the initiative. Two young women, one white and one Black, had organized large, racially diverse groups of volunteers to phonebank for the ballot initiative. The campaign manager, a hardened operative who had been part of many bitter political fights throughout the Midwest, said their ardent volunteerism was "unlike *anything* I've ever seen."

The volunteers came from a Protestant evangelical megachurch called Crossroads—technically a multiracial church, but unequivocally white dominant in both numbers and culture. I had assumed the volunteers were left-leaning Unitarians willing to raise taxes on themselves to provide for the neediest children in the city, not notoriously conservative white evangelicals. Throughout the 2016 election, white evangelicals had been one of Trump's staunchest voting blocs, staying loyal to him even after he bragged on tape about grabbing women by the pussy. I wondered how these evangelicals became so animated in their support for a policy designed to benefit the Black community.

～

I spent election night 2016 in California, where I was living at the time. Riveted by the presidential returns, I forgot to follow the results for the preschool initiative in Cincinnati. The next morning at six thirty, my husband and I left for a long-planned trip abroad, leaving my parents to babysit our children. Just before we left, I informed my dad, who had gone to bed early, that Trump won. The unexpected election outcome still felt raw, and the country (Trump's campaign included) was scrambling to make sense of his victory. My dad, who still spoke English as a second language, was puzzled by the pervasive sense of disarray. He sent me a text at the airport: "Sometimes we may feel [sad]. But every time we find a wise solution. We will be alright." I thought about the arc of history my dad had witnessed in his lifetime. His parents fled south from North Korea during the Korean War. Carving the country into two arbitrary pieces forever separated my grandfather from his own mother. The new society my grandparents' generation built in the ravaged remains of South Korea enabled my parents to immigrate to the United States as graduate students in the early 1970s. They originally anticipated returning to Korea after my dad earned a PhD, but by the time he had completed his degree, my brother and I had started elementary school, and my parents decided they would rather raise us in the United States. South Korea was a nascent democracy at the time, and protection of human rights and opportunities for economic and educational advancement still felt fragile.

My parents moved us to Houston, Texas, where my dad found a job. We lived in a racially diverse middle-class neighborhood in southwest Houston alongside immigrants from all over the world. Violent fights between competing ethnic cliques dominated the social landscape in the local public schools. Our next-door neighbor's son and his friends once robbed our home. In a reflexive effort to shield my brother and me from this milieu, my parents sent us to a parochial school that happened to be largely white. They gamely learned to make small talk with white parents at school events to help our family fit in as much as possible. "Korean people don't chit-chat like that," they would chuckle.

Despite, or perhaps because of, everything he witnessed across these fractured worlds, my father maintained hope—which got me thinking about Issue 44, the Cincinnati ballot initiative. The leaders of the preschool campaign had been so optimistic before the election. After we boarded the plane, I looked up Hamilton County, Ohio, on my phone to find the election results. Even though Trump won the state by eight percentage points, Clinton beat Trump by ten percentage points in Hamilton County—a Democratic enclave within Ohio, where Cincinnati is the county seat. Yet the same voters approved Issue 44 by twenty-four percentage points! Thousands of voters who supported Trump must have also supported Issue 44. I wanted to learn more.

I discovered that the Crossroads volunteers had all been part of Undivided, a six-week program on racial justice their megachurch had developed and piloted in early 2016. Hundreds of these volunteers claimed that Undivided had propelled them to commit to Issue 44 with unusual ardor. Yet when people described Undivided to me, it sounded a lot like the diversity, equity, and inclusion (DEI) training programs that pervaded corporate America. Given the documented ineffectiveness of such programs, I could not understand how Undivided had the impact people claimed.

I reached out to volunteers and leaders with Undivided to understand more about the program, its history, and how it worked. Over the next seven years, I sat through multiple six-week sessions of the curriculum. I followed the trajectories of dozens of people, white and nonwhite, who had been through the program, engaging in hours of conversation with them over many years. We talked in their homes, in coffee shops and restaurants, at the church, in their workplaces, over the phone, in Zoom rooms, on social media, and in cars. I worked with a colleague to gather survey data cataloging the experience of over a thousand participants in the program. I generated reams of field notes, trying to understand what brought people to the program, how it affected them, and how it emerged and flourished in a church community often characterized by its infamous commitment to whiteness.

At each turn, the people I got to know seemed to be rewriting the script.

Here was a multiracial group of people doing more than putting up yard signs and buying tote bags in their effort to agitate for racial justice in America. The story of so many twenty-first-century social change efforts begins with outrage and ends with a whimper. The supposed racial reckoning that began after the murder of George Floyd in 2020 was no exception. Dubbed the "Great Awokening," the movement propelled millions of Americans into the streets in the middle of a global pandemic, grasping for ways to close the yawning gap between the society we pretended to be and the society we were constantly revealed to be. Books instructing white people how to become antiracist soared to the top of bestseller lists. Public opinion polls showed that support for the Movement for Black Lives was reaching its highest point ever, increasing by almost fifteen percentage points from the start of 2020. Corporations, universities, nonprofits, churches, small businesses, and other organizations scrambled to demonstrate their commitment to rooting out racial injustice. The volume, speed, and scale of this response prompted multiple headlines asking whether this time was different. The killing of George Floyd was hardly the first (or the last) time that a Black person had been brutally murdered at the hands of the state, but the public response felt different—was white America finally prepared to reckon with its complicity in racial subjugation?

Perhaps unsurprisingly, the answer was closer to no than yes. One year later, many of the promises that corporations and other organizations had made to take action in the summer of 2020 remained unfulfilled. Corresponding analysis of public opinion data showed that support for the Movement for Black Lives remained high among racial and ethnic minorities a year after the summer of 2020. Among white Americans, however, support for the Movement for Black Lives had plummeted *below* the baseline level of support prior to the killing of George Floyd. Bitter fights over the teaching of any curricula related to racial justice in schools began to emerge, and the brutal pattern of racially motivated violence against Black people continued unabated. Throughout American history, the struggle for Black freedom has been marked by patterns of progress followed by backlash, and this time was no different.

Political scientists Jennifer Chudy and Hakeem Jefferson argued that for too many Americans, the journey toward antiracism "started in a bookstore and ended on their couch." Even among many white liberals who professed support for racial justice, opinion did not translate into action. As they had throughout history, Black Americans continued to lead the struggle for Black freedom, turning pain into action. In contrast, for many white Americans—even those who were racially sympathetic toward Black people and other minorities—pain became stasis. Many people were still angry, but they didn't know what to do to effect durable change. What should liberal white people angry about racial disparities do besides march, vote every couple of years, donate money, and support companies and organizations that shared their views? Many resorted to buying swag that allowed them to emblazon their views on their clothes and tote bags. Support for the Black freedom struggle among white Americans seemed to be vapid at best, and volatile at worst.

Somehow, our politics had morphed to the point that most people, even those angered by injustice, behaved like consumers, choosing between political actions the same way they selected cereals at the grocery store. Against this backdrop, the people I got to know through Undivided distinguished themselves because of their commitment to sustained work together. They were figuring out how to fight for racial justice in ways that went beyond consumerism. They built relationships across race that spurred them to action and sustained them when it got hard. Undivided was just the spark. None of them described stories of dramatic transformation through the six-week program, but for many, going through that experience catalyzed a journey that shaped their behavior in the weeks, months, and years to come. Each of them, Black and white, struggled. None of them followed the formula that best-selling books offered about the "right" way to tackle racism in their own lives. Their journeys were each complex, unpredictable, and confounding in their own way.

Undivided also rewrote the script by focusing on structural injustice within white Christian evangelicalism. In 2016, when the program first began, focusing on racial justice beyond mere interpersonal reconciliation was unusual for any white evangelical megachurch, and it only became more so as evangelicalism went into crisis during the Trump years. For centuries, scholars argued, many (but not all) white Christian churches had provided refuge for white supremacy. Scholars like Anthea Butler and Jemar Tisby argued that white supremacy was built into evangelical theology itself. A nationally representative study of congregations across America found that in 2018–19, only 22 percent of predominantly white congregations had a "group meeting, class, or event" to "discuss race relations" in the past year. Even fewer, 9 percent, reported having one specifically regarding "race and the police," and only 7 percent had an "organized effort, person, or committee whose goal was increasing racial or ethnic diversity." The Baptist megachurch near my parents' home in Texas ran a school that refused to honor Martin Luther King Jr. Day. When the Southern Baptist Convention developed its own program in 2018 in response to fierce debates within the organization about how their faith should address questions of race, they focused it entirely on interpersonal reconciliation, which is typical of white evangelical groups. (They called the program Undivided, prompting the head pastor of Crossroads to say, "They stole it from us. We had the name and the program first.") By focusing on structural patterns of injustice, Undivided tried to break the mold.

Crossroads was a church that liked breaking the mold, unlike any faith institution I had ever encountered. It deliberately upended church conventions to try to draw more people into its community. In many ways, it seemed to be working. When I first started researching Undivided, Crossroads had about 22,000 people per week attending church, and the numbers were rapidly growing. Their approach to Super Bowl Sunday exemplified their philosophy. In most churches, that day saw some of the lowest church attendance of the year. To compensate, Crossroads decided to host an annual "Super Bowl of Preaching."

Like all of Crossroads' weekly services, it was quite a production. The church's most popular pastors assembled teams to compete through four "quarters" of competitive preaching. Each quarter, they drew a silly phrase out of a hat and delivered a sermon that incorporated that phrase. The more smoothly they worked it into the sermon, the more points they got. The event also had its own referees, commentators (including some former National Football League players), penalty flags, and all the trappings of the real Super Bowl. They even put on a glitzy halftime show and produced their own commercials, which alternated between advertisements for Crossroads events ("Come explore your relationship with God at Woman Camp!") and snarky spots rivaling *Saturday Night Live* in quality and humor. Nothing about the day's events felt like a traditional church.

I watched one Super Bowl of Preaching with my then seven-year-old, who had been raised attending weekly Buddhist meditations. My child watched the performance intently, and when it ended, turned to me and solemnly declared, "Mommy, I think I might be Christian."

Crossroads beat the trend of declining attendance. The Super

Bowl of Preaching got so popular that by 2021, the National Football League told them they could no longer use the trademarked name "Super Bowl." By working harder to be hip than holy, Crossroads hoped to create a church welcoming of all people. What better way to maximize growth and bring more people to God? From its earliest days, the church adopted the motto "Belonging comes before belief." A culture of radical hospitality replaced any kind of purity test.

When I first got to know Crossroads, I was worried its leaders and congregants might be suspicious of me and unwilling to talk. I was a college professor, a member of the purported coastal elite that the media liked to pit against Midwestern evangelicals. I was neither white nor Black, but Asian, occupying a liminal category of race in America. And I was a lapsed Catholic. I had attended eleven years of Catholic school in Texas as a child. We had schoolwide mass every Wednesday and started every Friday with a prayer service in the school gym. I began to chafe against Catholicism in high school, however, when I couldn't reconcile things my classmates and teachers said in theology class with things they did.

Crossroads, however, welcomed people not in spite of their flaws, their differences, their ignorance, or their odious pasts, but because of them. True to their culture, the people I met approached me with warmth and welcomed me into their experiences with kindness and generosity. When I first got to know them at the start of the Trump era, it was a church that seemed to hold people with opposing viewpoints together, even in a polarized nation. Instead of the politically conservative, fundamentalist, Bible-thumping older white men who dominated public images of evangelicalism, Crossroads had a younger and more racially, ideologically, and socially diverse congregation.

~

As I spent more time with the people who had gone through Undivided, I learned that neither the journeys of the individuals nor the program itself would be linear. I witnessed in real time the hard, unpredictable, unrelenting path that emerges for a group of people committed to individual and social transformation. Sometimes it was inspiring, sometimes it was just drudgery. Here were people committed to doing something about racial injustice, when most others felt stymied. Here were people who stood up for what they knew in their hearts they had to do, even though their friends, family, neighbors, and even clergy disagreed.

The Crossroads congregants who participated in Undivided represented a group of people who did not have a social home in America—too conservative for many left-leaning groups and too liberal for many right-leaning groups. They agitated for their sense of justice, even as the home they found for their work kept changing. Sometimes Crossroads embraced them and their work, and at other times it actively pushed them away. The church tried to straddle the two sides.

When Chuck Mingo, the Black pastor in Crossroads who co-founded Undivided, first preached about his need to act on racial injustice in early 2015, the church defended him. Brian Tome, the white head pastor, used his sermon the next week to make explicit his commitment to Chuck.

"I love what Chuck had to say last week," Brian said. How could a Black man living in Cincinnati not want to confront the issue of race? he asked. He acknowledged the pushback he and Chuck had received the past week, and the "storm" that would come with speaking more about race. "I know there are Black people in our midst that are like, 'Why don't y'all talk more about this?' And there are whites in our midst who are saying, 'Whoa, wait, is he implying . . . is he saying . . . whoa.'" Brian comically mimicked the expressions of concern that could come from either side, drawing laughter from the crowd. But then he dismissed people's concerns.

"I'm getting emails. He's getting emails. 'I can't believe you said that.' 'You don't support our police.' 'I'm leaving Crossroads.'" Brian sputtered in mock disbelief. Then he was unequivocal. "But if you think talking about the way things really are is difficult, you got to leave." Brian paused in the middle of the stage and looked directly into the camera. He waved one hand. "Bye, bye," he said, exaggerating his enunciation of each syllable. He drew applause. "See ya. Wouldn't want to be ya." Brian paused for effect, then concluded in one definitive breath. "When Chuck speaks, he speaks for me. He speaks for me and he's my friend, and he's got a calling from God."

Some people in the congregation clapped and whooped in affirmation. Others sat on their hands. The divided reaction in the cavernous auditorium of the Crossroads Church that week exemplified the church's constant attempt to sit at the confluence of competing currents in evangelicalism—among those who wanted their church to focus on converting more souls instead of changing society, those interested in building Christian political power in America, or those concerned with realizing Jesus's quest for justice. Crossroads sometimes seemed unsure about how to balance the tension between leading their community versus merely acting as a mirror for people's existing views.

When Brian later reflected on the church's handling of issues of race, he was very clear: "You can never win. No matter what we do, we hear it from both sides."

A few years later, one white woman who had become inspired by Undivided to advocate for racial justice met with one of the campus pastors at Crossroads to ask him what he was going to do as the epidemic of police brutality toward Black Americans continued unabated. The pastor shrugged.

"It's just not something we're going to focus on," he told her bluntly. Crossroads enabled Undivided but did not necessarily share its goals.

This confounding relationship between Undivided and Cross-roads was not unlike the confounding journey that many people within Undivided had to take.

This book traces those stories. Their quests were audacious, uncertain, filled with tension—and unfinished. Each of the characters I've chosen to focus on—one white woman (Jess), one Black woman (Sandra), one white man (Grant), and one Black man (Chuck)—participated in Undivided and began to see old things with new eyes. They formed new friendships and broke off old ones. They switched jobs, confronted racism in their personal relationships, got discouraged by the work, and renewed their courage to act, again and again. None of their journeys formed a straight line from complicity to justice. But none of them were sitting on their couches, either.

Their stories do not reveal that Undivided has cracked a secret code or developed a perfect model that everyone else lacks. Undivided is one program in a vast landscape of both faith-based and secular programs dedicated to antiracism. Critics argue that it's too corporate or too superficial; that it grew out of a white-dominant community, ignoring the long legacy of Black churches and Black faith leaders who have been doing the work for much longer; that it's too biblical; that it's not biblical enough; that, given the demographics of Crossroads, it focuses too much on the Black-white divide, ignoring other communities of color. These debates are real, and necessary. They push a field of leaders, programs, and organizations working on antiracism to be better. But to most of the thousands of participants taking one night a week out of their busy lives to give Undivided a try, those debates felt remote. Undivided was not perfect, and the experiences participants had were hardly uniform. But it had the great advantage of being available to people who were craving something from their church: it gave them a chance to struggle in concrete ways with the question of what it meant to respect and fight for the dignity of all, to enact in concrete ways their belief that everyone is a child of God.

All of the participants in Undivided were taking a risk, and the work remains incomplete. Only by taking these risks did these four people begin to pursue a different possible world emerging at the seams of the existing one. In a moment when the nation is struggling to realize a vision of a multiracial America, this story offers glimmers of the enormity of what real change might demand.

PART ONE

AGITATION

CHAPTER ONE

PODUNK WHITE PEOPLE

Sandra lurched into her parking space, nervous about the evening ahead. Her backpack, a Pandora's box of parenting gear, spilled its contents onto the floor of her Mazda minivan: toys for her two-and-half-year-old; games for her seven-year-old; extra layers of clothing for fickle Cincinnati springs; healthy snacks for the kids; and a few special treats squirreled away in obscure pockets. She believed that no one gave Black boys (and their Black mothers) much latitude, so Sandra was always ready with a quick bribe to make her sons behave. Her husband, who was white, told her she imagined the dirty looks people gave her when her boys acted out. But Sandra knew it wasn't in her head.

For the toddler, she still carried at least one change of clothes and another for herself—accidents could happen at any time—and organic wipes for general cleanup. Her parents mocked her organic purchases. "Why are you paying extra? That's just Democratic mumbo-jumbo," her dad said. He was a Republican. Following her father's lead, Sandra had been the only Black student in the Young Republicans club in college. Now, in 2016, she wasn't sure what she believed.

She had arrived at the Oakley campus of the Crossroads Church in Cincinnati. In 2016, Crossroads was among the fastest-growing megachurches in America (by 2022, it was the country's fourth-largest church, had an annual budget of $68 million and a weekly in-person attendance of more than 35,000 people, and had increased its weekly online audience during the 2020 coronavirus pandemic to half a million people). Like most nondenominational evangelical megachurches, Crossroads was a multisite church—spread across nine physical campuses in southern Ohio and northern Kentucky—that projected one weekly service into all of its physical campuses and to digital viewers elsewhere. Oakley was the mother-ship campus. Originally a big box store called Home Quarters that Crossroads bought and renovated, the building now featured a 3,500-seat auditorium and a large parking lot to match. There was an Olive Garden and Kroger in the shopping plaza across the street, and Starbucks and Condado Tacos on the corner behind Sandra. The Oakley campus looked more akin to a strip mall than a traditional church. Crossroads' leaders liked the fact that it didn't feel like a traditional church.

Sandra was at Oakley for the first night of Undivided, the racial justice program Crossroads was piloting. She had asked her husband to sign up, too, but he refused, volunteering to stay home with the children instead. She tried to ignore her creeping discontent with his decision and focus on the rare feeling of being unencumbered by her children's constant requests. Sandra reapplied her ChapStick as she glanced at her reflection in the rearview mirror. She was a petite Black woman with large, wide-set eyes and a broad smile that often animated her pretty face. At thirty-one years old, she had spent many years honing a habit of smiling to put at ease people discomfited by her long dreadlocks.

As Sandra walked across the parking lot, she passed by a line of fifteen skinny parking spaces for motorcycles near the church's front door. Crossroads' head pastor, Brian Tome, was an avid motorcyclist with an edgy sense of humor, and in front of each space was a tongue-in-cheek sign that sounded like something

Brian would say: "Motorcycle Parking Only: All Others Will Be Crushed and Towed."

Undivided started because of an unexpected outpouring of support that Chuck Mingo received the prior year when he preached about a calling he felt from God to act on issues of racial injustice. Chuck was the highest-ranking Black pastor at Crossroads (at the time, the campus pastor for Oakley) and one of the most popular preachers in the entire community. "I want to be a voice in our city for race relations," he had declared. At the time, levels of partisan polarization were at a historic high in the United States, and they would only grow. Protests over police shootings of unarmed Black men had launched the Black Lives Matter movement into the forefront of national politics. The continued, relentless rhythm of officer-involved shootings of Black men around the country kept it there. Racism had never been quiescent in America, but these shootings foregrounded some of its most acute consequences. In Cincinnati, the 2015 killing of Samuel DuBose by a white police officer brought the national debate to Undivided's backyard.

Cincinnati had historically been an aspirational destination for enslaved people fleeing the South before the Civil War. The National Underground Railroad Freedom Center now sits on the banks of the Ohio River downtown, maintaining a stony vigil over the waters that symbolized freedom for enslaved people—and economic prosperity for the city. Henry Wadsworth Longfellow memorialized Cincinnati's booming nineteenth-century economy in an 1854 poem, dubbing it the "Queen of the West." Its industrial economy collapsed in the twentieth century, however, as did that of other Rust Belt communities. As the city's economic prowess declined, white flight drove many white Cincinnatians to the surrounding suburbs in Hamilton County. Multiple Fortune 500 companies like Procter & Gamble and Kroger now have headquarters in Cincinnati, but their largesse is not evenly distributed.

Census data from 2020 shows that one in four residents lives below the poverty line, but Black people in Cincinnati are almost twice as likely to do so as white people. The worlds of Black and white residents are so distinct from each other that it is almost like there are two cities using one moniker.

Sandra was pleased—and surprised—when she heard Chuck preaching, but worried he was taking a risk by speaking out about race. Crossroads was 80 percent white (with a nonwhite population that was mostly Black), and Sandra knew that a lot of those people—including her husband—objected to Chuck's declaration. They thought that Chuck was being divisive simply by bringing up race.

Sandra and her husband had gotten married in 2012, after he had pursued her for over a year. When they first met, Sandra could not imagine dating him. He was a white man with crooked teeth, and she was just getting her life back together after a divorce. Having grown up in a Black, conservative Christian family, Sandra initially felt ashamed about being a divorcée and a single mom. When she left her first husband, she had returned to her parents' home in California with an eight-week-old baby in her arms. As she tried to rebuild her life, she found a church near her parents' house that was run by a Hispanic couple she liked. They were different from the fundamentalist pastors of her youth. "Come as you are," they said.

For the first time, she began to develop a real relationship with God. Even though her parents had dragged her to some kind of church "every single day" of her childhood, she realized she had simply been going through the motions. In this new church, she felt like she did not have to be perfect, which allowed her to face up to truths, like her divorce, that some other churches would condemn. She began to understand a God who was more benevolent than controlling. *God, if I can develop a real relationship with you, I know I can get through this period,* she prayed.

After two years in California, Sandra's life stabilized. Her son was two years old, she had developed an independent relationship with God, and she felt like she was ready to move back to Cincinnati, where her son could maintain a relationship with his father.

She moved into a Cincinnati neighborhood near her ex-husband, enrolled in a master's program in business and theology at Cincinnati Christian University, and worked odd jobs to make money. The Oakley campus of the Crossroads Church was near her new home. *I'll just go there,* she thought. It seemed like the most practical option. Crossroads' approach to culturally current communication and its edgy humor reminded her of the church she had been attending in Sacramento. It didn't feel "judgy" and strict like the church of her youth; instead, she felt like she could grow there.

Common friends at Crossroads introduced Sandra to the man who became her second husband, inviting them to the same social gatherings. Despite her initial skepticism, she softened toward him when she once overheard her son asking him, "Are you my dad?" Sandra felt like she had to give him a chance.

At the time, he had been attending church only sporadically. "If we are going to date," Sandra said, "you have to go to church." He started attending Crossroads regularly. "And we can't have sex before marriage," Sandra said. She had rushed into her first marriage and didn't want to make the same mistake again. She demanded that they date for a full year before they considered any next steps. He agreed to all of Sandra's stipulations. His steadfast persistence over the next year won Sandra's heart.

After the wedding, they took a honeymoon to Florida. That week, national controversy erupted when an unarmed Black seventeen-year-old high school student, Trayvon Martin, was killed in Sanford, Florida. Martin was walking home from the convenience store with a pack of Skittles in his pocket and a hoodie over his head when George Zimmerman, a neighborhood watch coordinator, shot and killed him. Sandra and her new husband were driving home from their honeymoon when they got into a heated debate about Martin in the car. The amorous sheen of their nuptials quickly eroded as her husband kept trying to defend Zimmerman's innocence.

Sandra was dumbfounded. She assumed that her husband would react to the shooting of an unarmed Black child just like she did. How could she and her husband see the same facts and interpret the situation so differently? Sandra felt hurt. Fear of deepening the hurt, of jeopardizing her second marriage, of speaking a truth she wasn't ready to articulate caused Sandra to remain silent.

For the next five years, they mostly avoided conversations about race in their family. Having two more children together made it easy. Bleary-eyed from lack of sleep, they closed themselves off from the outside world. Yet pain slowly carved subterranean fissures in their marriage.

Undivided was the first opportunity Sandra found to examine those fissures. There, she could explore her questions about racism in America while still bringing the fullness of her faith in God to the discussion. Until Undivided, Sandra felt like Crossroads was not a place where she could talk about race. The polarization of the issue in America and the increasing affinity of white evangelicals, the Republican Party, and white supremacists meant that bringing up race could generate controversy Sandra wanted to avoid.

∿

It had not always been a foregone conclusion that white evangelicalism would entrench itself in conservative partisan politics. In 1974, the most prominent white evangelical leader of the twentieth century, Billy Graham, helped organize Lausanne I: The International Congress on World Evangelization in Switzerland.

It was the largest, most diverse meeting of global evangelical leaders at the time, and it cast a bold vision for a globalized faith. The question of how involved evangelicals should be in social justice and social action was a topic of fierce debate. Some leaders, like Ecuadorian theologian C. René Padilla, passionately argued for a vision of evangelicalism that would directly engage with Jesus as a social justice leader. He received a standing ovation when he argued Western evangelicals were "selling a cheap brand of Christianity" based on a "[white] American way of life." Padilla argued that without tackling questions of justice head-on, "The racist can continue to be a racist, the exploiter can continue to be an exploiter."

But not everyone at Lausanne agreed. Historically, "evangelicalism" had been an umbrella term for what historian Molly Worthen called a "definition-defying" amalgamation of Christians. In the early twentieth century, the advance of Darwinism and the ascendance of Enlightenment traditions of secular rationalism throughout Europe and the United States forced many Christians to grapple with questions of how they wanted to define themselves. Worthen argued that even if they did not always agree on the answers, contemporary evangelicals united around a set of three animating questions: how to reconcile spiritual and rational knowledge, how to assure salvation through Jesus, and how to live publicly with faith in a secular world. At Lausanne, Padilla and other leaders brought conflicts about whether evangelicals should be involved in social action and social justice into the open. Padilla's opponents argued that evangelicalism should focus on gaining more converts through individual transformation rather than social transformation.

The 1974 meeting ended with the Lausanne Covenant, which expressed a commitment to social justice by offering "penitence both for our neglect and for having sometimes regarded evangelism and social concern as mutually exclusive." Multiple scholars have documented the ways white evangelicalism—and indeed, much of white Christianity—had been founded on principles of exclusion. Many white Protestants, among the first European settlers in America, had long been staunch defenders of the country's racial order. The Southern Baptist Convention, the largest evangelical denomination in the country, was founded as a splinter organization in 1845 when southern slaveowners could not coexist with northerners who refused to condone slavery. The Lausanne Covenant recognized the need to atone for evangelicalism's historic injustices, but some historians argued that it tried to take both sides. The covenant asserted that "reconciliation with other people is not reconciliation with God, nor is social action evangelism, nor is political liberation salvation," and that "we affirm that evangelism and socio-political involvement are both part of our Christian duty."

From a global perspective, evangelicalism after Lausanne became a multiracial faith, with the prominent rise of nonwhite churches and leaders. Now, fifty years later, the largest evangelical churches in the world are outside the United States. As of 2023, the three largest megachurches in the world were in Seoul, South Korea (the Yoido Full Gospel Church with 480,000 attendees); Lagos, Nigeria (the Living Faith Church with 275,000 attendees); and Hyderabad, India (the Calvary Temple Church with 225,000 attendees). In America, however, it took until the late twentieth and early twenty-first centuries for many churches (including Crossroads) to become more diverse. In 2000, 21 percent of megachurches reported being multiracial—defined as having no one racial group constitute more than 80 percent of the congregation. In 2020, 58 percent of megachurches reported being multiracial.

But many of these churches addressed diversity without confronting injustice. In 2008, Korie Edwards, a Black sociologist at Ohio State University, undertook a study of multiracial faith institutions, hoping to find models of racially just faith communities. She concluded, however, that the challenge of building authentically integrated churches in America remained an "elusive dream." Despite efforts at diversification, racism remained pervasive in the pews. According to 2018 polling data from the Public Religion Research Institute (PRRI), white Christians were more likely than any other demographic group in America to hold racist views when it came to topics like the appropriate use of Confederate symbols, racial inequality, Black economic mobility, treatment of Black people in the criminal justice system, and general perceptions of race and racism. The pollsters constructed a racism index that ran from zero (least racist views) to one (most racist views) and found that the general adult population in the United States scored 0.57. White evangelicals scored 0.78, white Catholics scored 0.72, and white mainline Protestants scored 0.69. Robert Jones, the president of PRRI, concluded, "If you were recruiting for a white supremacist cause on a Sunday morning, you'd likely have more success hanging out in the parking lot of an average white Christian church—evangelical Protestant, mainline Protestant, or Catholic—than approaching whites sitting out services at the local coffee shop."

Even though megachurches like Crossroads had more nonwhite faces interspersed into their congregations, they remained effectively white dominant, unable to share power. They scorned the scourge of racism in people's hearts, but ignored the way racial subjugation was entangled in American life and the way it molded people's social interactions, their dreams, their judgments of those who fail, and the workplaces, prisons, schools, communities, and social systems they inhabited.

For many years, Sandra felt removed from these fights about diversity, racism, and injustice in the church. In her mind, nameless people were debating abstractions, weaving stories that did not feel like her story. Sandra changed diapers, healed boo-boos, and spent time searching for belonging. She found it in Crossroads, where she could pray in community with people who believed in the same God she had gotten to know after her divorce. She went out to dinner with friends and joined activities organized by the church. Even if she was sometimes the only Black person in the group, she gravitated to kindness where she could find it.

Yet Sandra's heart knew what she needed before her head. When Chuck made his declaration to act on racial injustice in Cincinnati, he spoke from the Crossroads main stage. Sweat glistened on his freshly shaved head, and the tails of his pink button-down shirt spilled over the waistband of his jeans. He gesticulated vigorously, shifting his entire body weight to indicate arguments on the one hand, and then on the other. Forty years old at the time, Chuck was five feet, nine inches tall, with high cheekbones and expressive eyes that somehow managed to make his face look simultaneously chiseled and warm. These characteristics seemed emblematic of his personality. He was skilled at taking the edge off tense situations and made his audience feel like he was embracing them with his energetic preaching.

Watching Chuck speak and feeling her heart pounding in her chest, Sandra realized she had a yearning she had never admitted. Her oldest son was growing up and would soon become a Black boy much of society automatically feared. Her marriage was contorting itself around issues of race she could not discuss with her husband. Her backpack, stuffed with toys, wipes, and special treats for her Black children, became armor in a world that was not made for them. Sandra craved a church that would help her understand that world, that would speak to her experience as a Black woman, that would recognize her pain and express it when she could not.

Some people raised their hands or stood up in joy when Chuck made his declaration. Sandra could hardly contain her excitement.

Oh my God, she thought. *That is what I've been needing.* But as people applauded, Chuck became somber.

"I feel fear," he said. "Fear of failure, perhaps, fear of conflict, fear of rejection, fear of being wrong and having misheard God. Fear that this will be a rabbit trail that doesn't produce anything of lasting value for the Kingdom. Fear that I'll only attract and therefore preach to the choir, and it won't change anyone already deeply entrenched in their racial biases."

Sociologist Wes Markofski has argued that many Christians were like Sandra—they believed the core theological tenets of evangelicalism, but explicitly or implicitly rejected the right-wing politics associated with it. He called them the "other evangelicals" and estimated that they were scattered throughout evangelical churches in America. Many younger evangelicals and people of color fell into this category, which Markofski estimated could be as large as 35 percent of evangelicals—if "evangelical" was defined as those who believed in the theology. Some may not self-identify as evangelical in the public sphere because of the political con-notations of the term, yet they actively participated in evangelical faith communities. They also remained deeply conflicted about how to reconcile their theological commitments with political convictions they didn't like or understand.

By committing to antiracism, Undivided threw a lifeline to the "other evangelicals" in the Crossroads community. Prompted by the speed and scale of the response Chuck received after his declaration to act on racial injustice, Chuck's boss assembled a planning team of leaders from within Crossroads and the Cincinnati community to figure out next steps. At its core, the group had three Black women, one Black man, two white men, and one white woman. People in the group had ties to some of the most powerful institutions in the city, including Crossroads, Procter & Gamble, U.S. Bank, Cincinnati Children's Hospital, the nonprofit sector, and the grassroots organizing sector. They each had experience navigating the messy process of change in complex organizations.

They also had a healthy dose of skepticism about the work they were undertaking. Troy Jackson, a white man on the planning team, was a former evangelical pastor who had become a community organizer, working in a tradition of faith-based organizing with long historical roots. He knew that Crossroads was a white-dominant church, and he had seen how entrenched whiteness was in most evangelical churches, so he dubiously joined the planning team. Crossroads' sheer size made it an important player in Cincinnati, and he didn't want to miss the chance to influence the work.

"When I walked into that first meeting . . . I was as cynical as you could be that this would be a watered-down, me-and-my-friend-of-color experience that tries to keep everything as noncontroversial as possible," Troy said.

Lynn Watts was a Black woman on the Crossroads staff who became one of the cofounders of Undivided with Chuck. She had spent her career in sales in major companies like IBM and Microsoft and started her own business focused on diversity, equity, and inclusion (DEI) trainings when she left corporate America. She knew that decades of research on the intermittent anti-bias, prejudice-reduction, and diversity trainings showed they were often ineffective. In too many cases, they checked boxes but remained disconnected from the organizations they sought to change. She put it bluntly: "Those short, one- or two-day trainings? They don't work."

The idea of anti-bias or prejudice-reduction programs first emerged in the 1960s. Organizations—including corporations and government agencies—originally developed them in response to societal pressure stemming from the civil rights movement. The training was based on the assumption that creating racially diverse organizations depended on making people aware of their own prejudice and then counting on them to extinguish it from their hearts. The programs were either naive or willfully blind to the fact that racism—a carefully constructed edifice of social rules, practices, habits, structures, and laws—was not so easily dislodged.

Despite their vacuity, DEI trainings improbably became more ubiquitous, in part because policy fights around things like affirmative action and employment discrimination heated up in the 1970s and 1980s. Organizational lawyers favored "diversity training" as a strategy for legalistically warding off charges of discrimination. Pretending to solve the problem was apparently more important than actually solving it. In 2021, Betsy Levy Paluck, a psychologist at Princeton University, led a team of people analyzing more than four hundred experiments seeking to reduce prejudice and concluded that the body of evidence on the effectiveness of this work was "ill-suited to provide actionable, evidence-based recommendations for reducing prejudice." Nonetheless, nearly all big companies still have some form of diversity training, even if two-thirds of the HR professionals who run them report that they are ineffective.

The futility of expecting any six-week program to completely root out the insidious tentacles of prejudice and racial injustice is obvious. But hopelessness was also a form of surrender to the status quo. Chuck could no longer stay on the sidelines. Lynn, who had been on the Spiritual Growth Team at Crossroads, committed to working with Chuck because she appreciated the opportunity to apply her professional experiences in the context of her faith. *Maybe Jesus will be in the work,* she thought. Chuck, Lynn, and the other members of the planning team made a commitment to one another to try to build a program that not only addressed interpersonal reconciliation, but also structural injustice. They had to find a way.

They met weekly for a year, debating ideas, examining options, and planning their strategy. They finally launched the inaugural session, which Sandra attended, on a Monday night in February 2016. Twelve hundred other congregants joined Sandra. A cohort of volunteers greeted people at the sets of double glass doors, meeting their varying levels of curiosity, ardor, and hesitance with unrelenting cheer. Some people were exchanging hugs and high-fives as they greeted one another. Sandra felt apprehensive. Could a white evangelical church do anything meaningful on antiracism?

She slipped past the greeters at the door and checked in at the registration table. The volunteer gave her a number that denoted her small group. Because twelve hundred people could not fit into one room, the small groups were spread across two meeting rooms. Sandra found her group in the bigger room, which had the feel of a cavernous college gymnasium. It could easily have been the shipping and receiving center of the big box store that originally occupied the space. Along one wall was a large metal contraption that could be pulled up like a garage door, creating a passageway large enough for delivery trucks and forklifts to move in and out. Folding chairs were arranged in small circles of six to eight throughout the room. Large numbered placards denoted each circle, and welcome packets sat on the chairs. Video screens hanging from the ceiling projected a live video feed of the stage into both rooms.

Each small group was supposed to have one white and one nonwhite facilitator and a roughly even balance of white and nonwhite people. A few no-shows meant Sandra's group merged with another, yielding seven people: two young Black women (including her), another young white woman, and two white couples— one younger couple and one older couple.

Sandra had never met any of them before. She noticed the young white man making small talk with the Black woman next to him. He had clean-cut brown hair, glasses, and a small mustache and goatee. She could see tattoos peeking out from the edge of his shirt. His wife was sitting next to him. She overheard them saying they were from a small town about forty-five minutes outside Cincinnati. Sandra had spent enough time in rural parts of Ohio to know there were not a lot of Black people there. *What are these podunk white people doing here?* she wondered. She didn't say anything out loud, but she started to feel dismissive. She doubted that one program could be simultaneously meaningful for her, a Black woman, and these "podunk white people." *Who is this program for?* she thought to herself.

CHAPTER TWO

POLISHED CONCRETE

The inexorable force of social sanctioning meant Jess's parents never detected any contradictions in the entangled relationship between the Ku Klux Klan and their childhood churches. People in their circle told them that integrating white supremacist politics with their faith in God was normal, and they never thought to question it. Jess recalled hearing stories about her parents attending Baptist services in Florida (for her mom) and Southern California (for her dad) on Sunday morning, then staying for a potluck lunch. As people digested their sandwiches and coffee, the men would participate in a Klan meeting. Women socialized and children played while men sat around in their Sunday church clothes discussing ways to advance an agenda of white supremacy. Pursuing an agenda of white power thus felt natural to Jess's father. He tattooed the word *White* in a large scripted font on the back of his left triceps and the word *Power* onto his right triceps. He deliberately wore muscle shirts and tank tops in public to ensure everyone could see the words.

Like all children, Jess turned her head like a sunflower toward the light of her parents' love, even if it was darkened by shadows of hate. Throughout her childhood in Florida then Ohio, her father worked assiduously to instill a fear of being alone with

Black people in Jess and her sister. "They will murder you, they'll beat you up, they'll rape you," he would say.

When Jess was around eight or nine years old, she asked the pastor at her family's church what would happen to her Catholic friends when they died. He told her they would go to hell. It scared Jess. She was learning a social order that put white Protestants on top and condemned everyone else. Her pastor did not preach explicit white supremacy—in the 1990s, it would have been socially taboo for him to claim that Black people (or non-white people in general) were going to hell because of their skin color. "Old-fashioned racism," as some scholars called it, was out of vogue. It had been built on "beliefs in the biological inferiority of Blacks," a "desire for social distance between the races," and support for "policies insuring racial segregation and formalized discrimination." But over the course of the twentieth century, social norms around race changed so dramatically that explicit support for old-fashioned racism seemed to disappear.

In 1945, pollsters asked Americans, "Do you think Negroes should have as good a chance as white people to get any kind of job, or do you think white people should have the first chance at any kind of job?" Fifty-five percent of respondents thought employers should prioritize hiring white people. By 1972, after the civil rights movement, 97 percent of whites said Blacks should have as good a chance as whites in seeking employment. White Americans, in other words, came to almost uniformly express support for equal treatment in employment. The racism embedded in people's attitudes and beliefs did not, however, disappear. It had just taken on different forms.

As Jess described it, unlike her "we hate Black people" family, most white American families were more likely to say they didn't see color. Claiming the mantle of color blindness allowed whites to justify their dominance in employment, wealth, education, and other domains not by biological superiority, but by a commitment to a set of superior "American" values and behaviors, such as "individualism and self-reliance, the work ethic, obedience and discipline." Some scholars called this "laissez-faire" or "unconscious" racism because of its submerged nature. White Americans like Jess's pastor could have it both ways: they could claim racially egalitarian ideals by rejecting notions of biological inferiority based on race, but also resist change in the racial status quo by blaming any lack of upward social mobility among Black Americans on poor values.

Jess thus learned a complex architecture of judgment and reward that carefully parsed different groups of people to maintain the racial order. Hierarchy was the rule, God was the judge, and hell was the stick. As a child, Jess felt like deviating from the social order would send her to hell.

But it confused Jess. Her family could not afford to live in the suburban enclaves that enclosed families in a wrapper of whiteness. The working-class neighborhoods where they lived and the schools Jess attended were always racially and religiously diverse. Catholics, Blacks, and Latinos were her friends, classmates, and teachers. They weren't scary or undisciplined or lazy like adults told her they would be. But she put her confusion into a box and tried, as much as possible, to bury it, focusing instead on being a decent kid.

In high school, Jess became addicted to opioids and heroin. It wasn't until she became sober in prison that she dug up that box of confusion and reconsidered questions of social order. In the Ohio state penitentiary where Jess served her time, she befriended a racially mixed group of women. She began to ask questions. *Why,* she wondered, *did the guards force the Black women but not the white women to shave their heads?*

To rethink her orientation toward race and racism in America, Jess first had to reconsider her orientation to God. She had to let go of the idea that upholding a racialized social order was part of being Christian. Could she differentiate between belief in God and belief in the social institutions—the churches—that taught her about God?

~

In late 2011, Jess was serving a prison sentence in Clermont County, Ohio, just to the east of Hamilton County, where Cincinnati sits. She had been sentenced to four years in state prison for burglary and forgery, a by-product of the daily quest for money she undertook to feed her addiction. She got clean in prison, but was in limbo, because she was still wanted for two additional crimes in Brown County.

Jess did some research into sentencing policies in Ohio and realized that, according to Ohio's Fast and Speedy Trial Act, any person incarcerated in an Ohio correctional facility could request the speedy disposition of any untried charges pending against them. Jess filed her paperwork and was soon called to court in Brown County.

She showed up in the courtroom wearing a green and white prison uniform, with handcuffs shackling her wrists and ankles bound to a chain around her waist. She had a pile of paperwork in her hands and waited as the court worked through its docket. Eventually, her court-appointed attorney, a young woman in a red dress and stiletto heels, came to talk with her. Jess shared her "fast and speedy trial" paperwork with the lawyer and asked if it might have any impact on her case.

The attorney glanced through the paperwork and said, "Well, this changes things." She asked for permission to approach the bench with the prosecutor. Jess waited nervously, twisting her hands around in her handcuffs. For many people in the room— judges, bailiffs, lawyers, security guards, journalists, and legal recorders—it was just another day at work, shuffling through papers and cases. For Jess, it felt like her life hung in the balance. Her mom was sitting in the courtroom.

Jess's attorney handed the paperwork to the judge, who looked wearily through it. They exchanged a few sentences, and then the judge called a recess. When the judge and the lawyers returned, the judge was succinct: "The charges are dismissed."

Jess abruptly slid off the wooden bench to her knees and her hands went up in a posture of prayer. She was confused, feeling like her body had acted without her control. *What made my body move?* she wondered.

When Jess returned to prison, she described the incident to her bunkmate, who advised her to "talk to the sergeant" about it.

"Who?" Jess asked. Her bunkmate described Sergeant Harris, a guard who was very open with the inmates about his Christian faith. An older white man, Harris was nicer than other guards. He enforced the rules, but did so as kindly as possible.

Jess sought him out the next day and described what happened in the courtroom.

"Well." He paused. "What if it was Jesus?"

His question took Jess aback. *Did Jesus save me?* Jess asked herself.

As an employee of the state, Sergeant Harris was not supposed to evangelize the women he supervised in prison. He flouted the rule. "I'd rather be accountable to God than to the state," he told Jess. To give Jess a chance to extend her exploration of faith, Sergeant Harris requested that she be given a work detail in an area he supervised. The sergeant's kindness humbled Jess, who was unaccustomed to people sticking their necks out for her.

Jess's gratitude proved easier to win than her faith. At first, she was skeptical when Sergeant Harris asked her questions about God. She thought people who prayed were "stupid." "There is nothing scientific about prayer," she said to Sergeant Harris. "I mean, why do people thank some magical being in the sky for their food? Their food comes from farmworkers and factory workers who grow and manufacture the food with their own hands."

Sergeant Harris knew Jess had rejected the church. He was not asking her to revisit that decision. Instead, he wanted her to evaluate God. Just because the churches Jess knew were frightening and divisive, did it mean God was? Jess wasn't sure.

Through her conversations with Sergeant Harris, Jess started differentiating Christianity as a theology from Christianity as a set of institutional practices she learned as a child. "Who is God? Who is Jesus?" he asked. "What does it mean to be Christian?" Jess discovered that Christianity did not have to be defined by the fire-and-brimstone fear she learned in childhood.

∼

Within Christianity, a core set of four beliefs defines nondenominational Protestant evangelicalism. Often attributed to the theologian John Bebbington and now adopted by the National Association of Evangelicals (NAE), they are: first, "biblicism," or a belief in the infallibility, or ultimate authority, of the Christian Bible; second, "crucicentrism," a belief that salvation comes through acceptance of Jesus Christ as the Savior; third, "conversionism," a commitment to the importance of being converted, or "born again," through belief in Jesus; and fourth, "activism," a commitment to evangelism, or the work of spreading God's word and bringing the Kingdom of God to Earth.

Believers in these four theological "distinctives" were scattered among multiple branches of American Christianity in the early twentieth century. The NAE was formed in 1942, when the community realized they were better off creating their own association instead of fighting one another. Yet even after they coalesced, nondenominational evangelicals remained proudly individualistic relative to more hierarchically bound faith traditions like the Roman

Catholic Church. Each church, each pastor retained considerable latitude to develop his own theological interpretations and liturgical practices (most preachers are men). Two evangelicals could accept Jesus Christ as their Savior and hold very different visions of who Jesus is. Likewise, two people could accept the infallibility of the Bible but have different interpretations of the more than 31,000 Bible verses that exist.

According to Sergeant Harris (and many Christian evangelicals), the core of what it meant to be Christian was to accept Jesus as the Savior.

Why, Jess thought, *would Jesus save me?*

Sergeant Harris urged Jess to make two lists—one about the things she believed about God, and one about the things she did not believe. On the side of things she believed, Jess put hell. On the side of things she did not believe, Jess put heaven.

"How can you believe in hell but not heaven?" Sergeant Harris asked.

"Heaven sounds so fake," Jess said. Peace and harmony for all, and angels flying around playing melodic songs? "C'mon."

To Jess, it seemed very logical that there would be a place where she would be eternally punished. Sergeant Harris tried to encourage her to recast her notions of heaven and hell in a different light. "You think you are such a horrible person, that all you can conceive is eternal torture." He urged Jess to consider whether heaven and hell had to be actual concrete places. "What if instead of thinking of it as a place, you think of heaven as the state of being in union with God and hell as separation from God?"

That personal relationship with God was at the heart of Sergeant Harris's tutelage. At one point he handed Jess the Bible and challenged her to find promises Jesus made to his people. After poring through the Bible, she realized that Jesus promised to be faithful to his people, even people like her.

The unconditional nature of Jesus's love was, for Jess, a profound realization. She thought about how she had stolen money from her grandmother, her mother, and her sister. She put them in jeopardy by forging checks in their names. She recalled stealing irreplaceable jewelry from her boyfriend's mother, taking her deceased husband's high school class ring, selling it for cash, and buying drugs. *And Jesus still loves me after all that?*

After eighteen months of studying with Sergeant Harris, Jess left prison with a clear sense of her relationship to Jesus. For the first time, Jess had accepted Jesus on her own terms.

As she reentered society, her challenge would be to sustain her faith in a complex world.

～

Jess was released in May 2014. A year and a half later, she found Crossroads. One of the first services that Jess attended replaced the traditional sermon with a recap of Crossroads' work in the Cincinnati community during the prior year. They described an annual day of service called Go Local in which thousands of Crossroads volunteers fanned out through the city to plant gardens, spruce up neighborhoods, clean cars donated to people in need, minister to people in prison, and so on. When Crossroads described their work with the Angel Tree program, designed to give Christmas gifts to kids whose parents were incarcerated, Jess felt a spark of recognition: Angel Tree had given her son Christmas gifts while she was in prison.

Jess considered getting more involved with Crossroads. She loved the weekly services and the array of opportunities the church offered. For the first few months, though, she hesitated to broaden her engagement with the community. Prison had left its mark. She felt unworthy.

When Chuck made his call for people to join Undivided, Jess was intrigued. She had never experienced church as a place to learn about antiracism, and she was ready to question the lessons about white supremacy that had been so ingrained into her family life. But she was also scared. She only knew enough to know how much she did not know.

On a muggy August evening in 2016, Jess forced herself to show up for Undivided. *What if I tell them the truth,* she was thinking, *and they don't want me anymore?* Sitting in her car in the Crossroads parking lot, she watched two Black women walk into the building, hugging and laughing as they greeted each other. Their joy made Jess feel small. Jess took a final comforting drag on her cigarette, crushed the stub into the ashtray, and got out of her car. She tried to compress her five-foot nine-inch frame to make herself less obvious as she crossed the parking lot.

Like many others, Jess arrived wondering whether she'd make it through the whole six weeks. As Jess entered the Oakley lobby, she traced her right shoe over the polished concrete floors. For most, polished concrete made the room feel impersonal, reminding them of the industrial size of Crossroads. For Jess, polished concrete made her feel at home—it reminded her of prison. Jess's small group was evenly divided between white and nonwhite people. Among the nonwhite participants, there were three Black people and one Asian woman.

Jess sat down in the circle. "Hi, I'm Jess," she said. Then she was unusually quiet. Jess generally weighed 170 pounds and had the physical presence to command a room. In most settings, she could make people around her feel comfortable. When she spoke, she spoke directly. In this situation, however, she was reluctant to say anything.

"I was terrified," she recalled.

CHAPTER THREE

THE BRAVE JOURNEY

In April 2001, Stephen Roach, a white police officer in Cincinnati, shot and killed Timothy Thomas, a nineteen-year-old unarmed Black man. Chuck had only been attending Crossroads for a few months. The city erupted into a three-day uprising that locals called the "Over-the-Rhine Riots," referring to the historically poor Black neighborhood where Thomas's family lived. German immigrants had originally settled the neighborhood in the mid-nineteenth century, naming the canal, which was part of the Miami and Erie Canal, after the Rhine River in Germany. Many workers lived on one side of the canal and crossed it each day to get to their jobs downtown. The downtown was thriving. Sitting at the confluence of the Ohio and Licking Rivers, Cincinnati was then a bustling industrial city voraciously seeking workers to fuel its success. The immigrants who came to Cincinnati did not leave lives of abundance in Europe. They fled to what must have seemed like the hinterlands of America in search of work, decency, and, perhaps, a bit of dignity.

These German migrants worked alongside Irish-Catholic immigrants and a free Black community. Countless enslaved people crossed the Ohio River from the slave state of Kentucky in search of freedom. Laboring together in ports and factories that lacked modern-day labor laws, these workers could have been organized to form bonds of solidarity with one another. They were all dispensable cogs in someone else's machine, mistreated by their managers and denigrated by the white Protestant ruling class for being poor, Black, or Catholic.

Without alternatives, the allure of whiteness overpowered any inkling of solidarity the European migrants might have felt with their Black coworkers. Noel Ignatiev, a historian who had spent twenty years as a steelworker before starting a PhD program at Harvard, analyzed the complexity of that choice in his provocatively titled 1995 book, *How the Irish Became White*. These migrant workers instinctively recognized that the way to achieve acceptance into American society was by buying into a social hierarchy that oppressed others. Punching down was easier than climbing up. By demonstrating cruelty toward the Black community, they could deflect some discrimination based on faith or country of origin—and reinforce a system that assigned value to people based on skin color.

Over the course of the twentieth century, the fortunes of white workers evolved separately from their Black counterparts. Black laborers moved into Over-the-Rhine when the Germans improved their lot enough to move out. Poverty outlasted demographic turnover, rendering the neighborhood emblematic of the racialized deprivation that now characterizes Cincinnati. The canal acts as a geographic marker literally separating Black Cincinnati from white Cincinnati.

When Thomas was shot, the uprising in the Over-the-Rhine neighborhood caused an estimated $3 to $5 million in damage. As the unrest spread throughout the city, the mayor issued a citywide curfew. The Crossroads leadership called for a prayer gathering on a weekday evening before the curfew went into effect. About a hundred congregants, including Chuck, attended, standing together in a circle and spontaneously calling out prayers.

Still relatively new to the church, Chuck was not sure what to expect. Crossroads preached messages of inclusion, consistent with the hip, more modern vibe that it tried to cultivate. As a Black man, however, Chuck knew that most white Crossroads congregants were oblivious to systems of racial oppression. As people began to speak, Chuck thought to himself, *There's too many white people in this room for somebody not to say something stupid right now.* He felt tense.

Chuck had first started attending Crossroads in 2000 when he was in his late twenties. He had just moved to Cincinnati from his hometown of Philadelphia for a job promotion with Procter & Gamble. He had grown up in a Black church but became frustrated with it when he saw his friends abandoning it as irrelevant in their lives. Before Chuck left Philadelphia, he created a kind of alternative church for those friends. They met weekly at a local coffee shop, where they could converse in an environment that didn't have the formal rituals of church associated with it. "We would talk about life and politics and everything," said Chuck. The group grew to more than twenty regular attendees. When Chuck moved to Cincinnati, he wanted to find a church like the coffee shop.

He searched online. At the turn of the twenty-first century, Crossroads was one of the few churches with a robust online presence, and Chuck decided to give it a try. Crossroads was not yet a megachurch—by definition, a megachurch has at least two thousand members—but it soon would be. The Hartford Institute for Religion Research estimates there are now about 1,750 megachurches in the United States. Church membership has become so skewed toward big churches that in 2020, the largest 9 percent of congregations in America accounted for half of all churchgoers in the United States. A 2020 survey showed that almost three-quarters of megachurches reported growth over the previous five years, averaging 34 percent in that period. By 2020, the average megachurch had about four thousand attendees each weekend and just under six thousand people who were regular participants, often spread across multiple geographic sites. The median annual budget was $5.3 million, and 96 percent of the budget came from membership contributions.

As in many megachurches, most Crossroads congregants were much younger than the average churchgoer in America. Even though they organized small groups for wine drinkers, rock climbers, and introductory Bible studies, Crossroads never thought to create a grief group in its early days. As one congregant explained, "Young people just don't die as much." The youthful feel was part of what captivated Chuck. Crossroads felt like the kind of church that would appeal to his friends.

At the beginning of the prayer circle, Chuck was pleasantly surprised that most of the prayers sounded like heartfelt pleas for inclusive peace and justice. Chuck relaxed. But then he heard someone say, "God, please deal with *those people* who are tearing up our city."

Chuck's anger flared, knowing the speaker was referencing the Black protesters. *Those people?* he thought. *Whose pain do we care about?* He considered speaking out, but the line between prudence and recklessness was still unclear to him, as he was new to the church. He stayed silent.

Driving home that night, Chuck pounded the steering wheel, questioning whether he, as a Black man, could stay in a community as white as Crossroads. That night, as his new hometown literally burned with rage over racism, Chuck thought, *I'm leaving this church.*

~

Crossroads began in 1995 when a group of eleven coworkers from Procter & Gamble came together because they were seeking a church that was neither boring nor frightening. Many of their friends were turning away from churches that seemed irrelevant, remote, or off-putting. They wanted to build a church that would attract people who professed not to like church.

The first step was to pool their money to pay for an advertisement in a Christian magazine seeking a senior pastor. A thirty-year-old white man named Brian Tome turned out to be their guy. At the time, Brian was an associate pastor in a small Presbyterian church in Pittsburgh. He defied stereotypes of typical clergy. Brian was a former high school football player and a motorcyclist who came across as an avuncular "guy's guy." He usually preached in jeans and untucked casual shirts. He had deep-set blue eyes with laugh lines around the edges that radiated both warmth and intensity. He was over six feet tall and could easily command a room, even though he favored a self-deprecating, goofball style of speaking.

For several months, the group worked meticulously to build the church they wanted, one willing to take risks. Too many churches, they thought, were afraid of upending the staid status quo because they feared upsetting longtime donors or congregants. Crossroads wanted to be different.

Around this time, Brian read a book that a pastoral couple named Bill and Lynne Hybels had just published, *Rediscovering Church: The Story and Vision of Willow Creek Community Church.* It described Bill Hybels's philosophy of appealing to the "seekers," or people in search of meaning who had not yet committed to God. Based on this insight, Hybels had built Willow Creek, one of the country's flagship megachurches. (Its stature declined in 2018 in the face of charges of ignoring sexual abuse.) Brian gave prospective congregants copies of the book to help them understand what he was trying to do at Crossroads. When he gave Chuck a copy in 2001, he inscribed inside the front cover: "This will give you a sense of who we are as a church. But, of course we are not a Willow clone."

Although Crossroads wanted to chart its own path, its leaders aligned themselves with this "seeker-sensitive" movement. Hybels may have coined the term "seeker," but the movement had deep roots in a Protestant missionary tradition that had long been pursuing converts all over the world. For most of the nineteenth century and into the twentieth, many Protestant churches adopted a "mission station" approach, establishing small Western enclaves in Africa, Asia, and elsewhere to create an outpost of European Christian culture and faith. Missionaries would recruit indigenous people to come into the mission station, often enticing them with health care, education, and other services. The underlying impulse at the time was clearly colonial; these missions assumed that acceptance of Christian theology was inevitably intertwined with acceptance of white Western Christian culture. (Later, some twentieth-century missionaries began to resist the colonial legacy.) Converts often became isolated from their indigenous communities, indoctrinated into a way of life that was very foreign to their friends and families.

For centuries, the mission station approach went unquestioned in many parts of Protestantism. In 1955, however, Donald McGavran challenged the iconic mission stations in a book called *The Bridges of God*. McGavran was a third-generation missionary who brought a data-based approach to asking why some missions were so much better than others at gaining adherents. After analyzing data on many missions, McGavran concluded that the traditional mission station approach was the wrong way to promote evangelicalism. Instead of isolating potential converts from their communities, McGavran argued, missions should integrate into the communities they sought to convert, drawing on preexisting social networks. Missions that adapted to the local cultures of the social groups (what he called "homogenous units") grew by scaffolding many groups together, resulting in exponential growth.

Around the same time as McGavran, the pastor Robert Schuller extended a long-standing missionary tradition of applying business principles to the question of church growth. Schuller's strategy entailed identifying the most effective ways to market his product, salvation through Jesus Christ. In 1955, Schuller opened his first church at a drive-in movie theater in Garden Grove, California. At the first meeting of his new church, Schuller stood on the counter of the snack bar to preach and kept his message short to avoid turning people off. He wanted to alter the image of church being too staid and boring. He called his church a "community church," dropping the obscure denominational labels most people didn't understand.

Like Schuller's, the language Crossroads used to build and describe the church had a strong corporate flavor. They thought of themselves as "disruptors" and often used the language of "products" and "marketing" to describe the theological lessons and sense of community they wanted to bring to the public. Even some of the staunchest capitalists cringed at the naked commodification and middlebrow appeals to religion in the name of growth. Others questioned whether it was actually generating more people of faith—the number of attendees might be growing because they enjoyed the "product," but were they actually building and deepening their relationships with God? Advocates for racial justice pointed out that justice cannot be treated like a consumer product. Church growth leaders, many of whom had dubious personal views on racial justice, mostly shrugged in response. They argued that if the church was bringing more people to God, it must be doing something right. Growth was king.

On March 24, 1996, Crossroads had their first public services in the auditorium of the Peoples Middle School in the affluent Hyde Park neighborhood of Cincinnati. They opened as the Crossroads Community Church and advertised the service as an opportunity for "great music, free coffee, and real topics." They wanted to attract congregants who hated institutionalized religion but still desired a relationship with God. As they cheekily put it, they wanted people to say "yes to God" even as they said "no to religion." To their surprise, 450 people showed up, causing an unexpected traffic jam in the neighborhood. Given that the median church in America had only one hundred congregants and was shrinking, the turnout was remarkable. And the number kept growing. Crossroads eventually had to enter into negotiations with the neighbors in Hyde Park to create alternate solutions for traffic flow and parking on Sunday mornings.

～

Chuck had previously left Crossroads because he wanted to join a more traditional Black church. One of his coworkers from Procter & Gamble recommended the Lincoln Heights Missionary Baptist Church, located on the edge of two neighborhoods, Lincoln Heights and Woodlawn, both majority Black middle-class suburbs of Cincinnati. The church had been in the community since the 1920s. Its preacher, Reverend Freddie T. Piphus Jr., was a Lincoln Heights native and had been leading the church since 1984. Still relatively new to Cincinnati, Chuck appreciated that the church could help integrate him more into the local Black community. Chuck started attending every Sunday.

Returning to a Black church was, in many ways, natural for Chuck. When he was growing up, his father repeatedly told him not to trust white people. Chuck's father, born in Missouri, was a product of the Jim Crow South. Chuck's mother had always lived in the Philadelphia area, drawing on her faith as a source of sustenance and strength in a segregated life. Chuck grew up attending a small Black-led storefront Pentecostal Holiness church with both charismatic and fundamentalist roots. Charismatics focused on the spiritual gifts of the Holy Spirit, often seeking visible signs of it in their lives, such as the ability to speak in tongues, handle snakes, or heal from physical ailments. The church proclaimed that women should not wear makeup or pants. His family joked that it was a miracle Chuck hadn't been born in the church because his mother spent so much time there.

The Black churches of Chuck's youth were necessarily distinct from the white churches that dominated the seeker-sensitive movement in the United States. The historically intertwined relationship many white Protestant denominations had with white supremacy meant that Black Protestant faith traditions had always carved their own path. The Black church in the South was born out of resistance to slavery. It originated as covert gatherings among enslaved people, who found fellowship, solace, spaces for self-determination, and hope for redemption within these faith communities. During the Jim Crow era, as many white Protestants opted to uphold beliefs of racial superiority, free Blacks built their own churches. Over time, Black churches became some of the only Black-led social institutions in America. They persisted as crucibles of fellowship, leadership development, and sustenance for Black communities. In contrast, many (but not all) white churches became cauldrons of whiteness, sustaining structures of segregation and oppression.

When white evangelical leaders initially created the National Association of Evangelicals (NAE) in 1942, they preached unity. In his opening speech to the NAE, the newly elected president warned of potential "annihilation" unless they decided not to be "lone wolves" but instead to "run in a pack." The NAE was a self-conscious attempt to diminish sectarianism among conservative white Protestants and advance fundamentalist interpretations of the Bible in the face of threat from white modernists. Unity was necessary for power.

But unity did not cross boundaries of race. In their founding documents, the NAE declared that they were "determined to shun all forms of bigotry, intolerance, misrepresentation, hate, jealousy, false judgment, and hypocrisy." Yet only white people attended their inaugural meeting.

In 1963, Black evangelicals formed their own association, the National Negro Evangelical Association (later renamed the National Black Evangelical Association, or NBEA). Founded by Black clergy who shared evangelicalism's commitment to the infallibility of the Bible, the NBEA made a biblical argument for Christian unity across racial lines. Howard Jones, one of the most prominent Black evangelicals of the time, wrote, "The Apostle Paul tells us how God took the Gentiles and Jews and blended them together into one new man, one body through Christ and His Gospel."

Prominent white evangelical leaders like Billy Graham embraced Jones's vision. With some exceptions, color-blind racial unity became the dominant framework for white evangelicalism's approach to race for the latter half of the twentieth century. They conceptualized racism as a problem of individual sin and prejudice and ignored the way it was tied to questions of power. Graham famously walked down the aisles of a revival meeting tearing down the rope that separated Black and white adherents. But when Martin Luther King Jr. asked Graham to participate in the March on Washington, Graham declined. NBEA leaders quickly came to see the limits of the color-blind approach.

The NBEA became increasingly vocal in their critique, working within evangelical institutions to advance claims of justice for several decades. In January 1990, the NBEA issued a statement calling for white evangelicalism to examine the way "its doctrine, policies, institutions, boards, agencies, and para-church entities" perpetuated structural racism. They called on white evangelicals to "exert pressure for economic justice," to "remove the institutional barriers which hinder progress for Blacks and other people of color," and "to make restitution and repair." In 1993, the prominent evangelical publication *Christianity Today* put a story about

"The Myth of Racial Progress" on its cover, giving voice to a number of Black leaders who argued that white evangelicals had done little to advance racial harmony.

These charges sparked a conversation about race among white evangelical leaders, but little more than that. Throughout the 1990s, they focused on an anodyne version of racial reconciliation, arguing that racial change depended on building interpersonal, cross-racial relationships. A wave of racial reconciliation programs followed. In 1991, Bill McCartney, the former championship-winning football coach of the University of Colorado Boulder, launched an organization called Promise Keepers, which grew virally, developing the tenor and scale of a national movement. Promise Keepers' mission was to redefine Christian masculinity, but McCartney also put racial reconciliation at the center of the organization's agenda. As white people often do, however, he followed in the tradition of a white leader (Billy Graham) instead of listening to the calls from Black leaders (the NBEA).

Racial reconciliation in the Promise Keepers looked like corporate DEI programs layered with the emotional fervor of a religious revival. Its efforts to facilitate reconciliation sometimes created awkward moments for the Black men involved. A reporter at a large Promise Keepers stadium rally wryly recounted watching crowds of white men swarm the three Black men in their section, begging for forgiveness. "I wonder what is running through the Black men's minds," the reporter wrote. These well-meaning rallies ignored the fact that interpersonal atonement did nothing to change centuries of racial subjugation.

The meteoric rise and revival-style popularity of Promise Keepers in the 1990s nonetheless prompted many other Christian entities to adopt its framework of racial reconciliation. The focus was explicitly on interpersonal reconciliation, imagining voluntary, spiritually grounded reconciliation as the pathway to lasting racial change. If people could eradicate the racism in their hearts by building relationships across difference, then racial change would emerge, bit by bit. A *Chicago Tribune* headline on racial reconciliation efforts in Mississippi encapsulated the philosophy of the movement: "Beating Racism, One Friendship at a Time."

Racism, however, cannot be treated as simply the aggregate sum of individual biases. Culture was an archer whose arm moved with the force of history. When it let go, it was not the callow optimism of the Promise Keepers but the arrow of accumulated injustice that pierced its target. Many of these churches integrated more nonwhite faces into their congregations, on their stages, and, in some cases, into their leadership. But culturally, they remained dominated by whites.

In examining churches that worked explicitly toward building interracial communities, sociologist Korie Edwards argued that the persistence of what she called "white structural advantage" and "white normativity" precluded true integration. Edwards's own church in Columbus, Ohio, had a multiracial but majority-white congregation led by a Black pastor. Edwards reports that once, during services there, Lydia, a Black woman in her late thirties, raised her hands in praise, shouting, "THANK YOU LAWD, THANK YOU LAWD, THANK YOU LAWD." That would have been common in many Black churches, but it echoed awkwardly in Edwards's church. Congregants and clergy alike avoided eye contact, shifting uncomfortably as Lydia continued. Eventually, isolated in her effusive praise, Lydia walked down the center aisle of the church to the lobby, where her shouts could still be heard in the sanctuary. After a perplexed pause, the clergy continued with the service, as if nothing had happened. The following week, the Black pastor announced that the church leadership had organized a meeting to discuss appropriate worship behavior, implicitly sanctioning Lydia for her behavior.

Even as Chuck became more integrated into Lincoln Heights, he could not let go of the itch to return to Crossroads. He kept thinking back to the coffee shop gatherings he organized in Philadelphia, and the feeling that Crossroads was building something godly.

One weekend, Chuck's oldest half brother came from Pittsburgh to visit him. He was twenty-one years older than Chuck and had long acted as a father figure. Chuck took him to see Crossroads during his visit. His brother approved. Chuck began to seriously consider going back.

When he started attending Crossroads again, Chuck decided to get more involved. At that time, in the late 1990s, before the age of YouTube, churches used cassette tapes to distribute pastors' sermons to a wider audience. Each week, as soon as Brian finished preaching, Chuck and other members of the audiovisual team would literally run a recording of Brian's sermon to a set of tape duplicators in the church. They wanted the tapes to be ready to distribute as congregants filed out.

Chuck was struck by the fact that Crossroads gave the tapes away. Most churches he knew would charge people. That focus on raising money, a reflection on the ubiquity of the prosperity gospel in Chuck's Philadelphia community, was part of what had turned Chuck and many of his coffee shop friends away from the Black church. Combining elements of self-help, capitalism, and evangelicalism, prosperity gospel churches taught some variant of the idea that God rewarded faith with financial success. Despite being controversial within evangelicalism, it drew many young people Chuck knew into the church, only to disillusion them with false hope. Chuck appreciated that Crossroads, more than any church he had ever seen, gave things away instead of trying constantly to raise money from congregants. Chuck loved exploring his relationship with God separately from worldly concerns like money.

Even after the prayer vigil, Chuck felt he somehow belonged at Crossroads, even if he still remained unsure that he could thrive in a white-dominant church. He was drawn to its culture of risk and innovation. It was more like the coffee shop than any other church he had attended. He also received what he interpreted as a sign from God. "I've never heard the audible voice of God," Chuck said, "but this is about the closest I got to it. I felt very called to go back to Crossroads."

For the first decade or so after Chuck returned to Crossroads, he focused on personal growth. He was building his career at Procter & Gamble and nurturing his relationship with Maria, the woman he eventually married. He continued getting more involved in the Crossroads community. When Chuck was a kid, the pastor in his church had frequently invited him to preach onstage. There, Chuck honed his ability to intuit the collective energy of a room and move it with his words. Recognizing Chuck's talent as a public speaker, Crossroads offered him the opportunity to preach. He proved to be so popular that they offered him a job as a pastor.

In the process of being hired, Chuck confessed to the church leadership that he had long struggled with an addiction to pornography. He knew that revealing his addiction would cost him the job, but he had to be honest. Sure enough, the church withdrew their offer. Chuck, who hadn't confessed his addiction to Maria, by then his fiancée, had to reveal everything to her, initiating a process whereby he committed to recovery. Crossroads then invited him to rejoin their staff in 2007. "I became a pastor," he said, "going through the twelve-step process."

For the first eight years of his time as pastor, Chuck did not talk much about race. He was focused on stabilizing his life and building his career. He and Maria married and had three children, which occupied much of his time.

As Crossroads expanded, Chuck developed one of the biggest

platforms of any Black pastor in a white-dominant church, leading services for one of the largest megachurches in America about once a month, preaching to enormous numbers of people on those Sundays. But over time, it became harder to avoid the indifference to racism that originally drove Chuck from the church. He asked the same question Sandra asked about Undivided: Who was the church for, really? The repeated killings of unarmed Black men in America—Trayvon Martin, Michael Brown, Eric Garner; it never seemed to end—and Crossroads' continued silence on the issue hammered away at Chuck's conscience. He felt a responsibility to speak out.

When he finally did in April 2015, scattered applause erupted across the auditorium as he declared his commitment to working on issues of race. "I'm glad you guys are excited about it," he joked. Everyone laughed.

"Because I'm in tension on it, I really am. I absolutely have faith that there's some things here that connect to my story and how God has wired me. And maybe those are some of the reasons I feel I'm in this church and in this city. But there's a lot of ways this could fail."

He paused, stilling his hands.

"A lot of ways this could fail."

CHAPTER FOUR

THE FIRST WEEK

When Chuck took the stage to open the inaugural session of Undivided, twelve hundred expectant pairs of eyes turned toward him. He took a deep breath. Chuck knew a favorable first impression would be vital to Undivided's success. He had prayed with the planning team before the session began that God would be with them. They had rehearsed the session the week before. Now Chuck plunged ahead.

Sitting in the audience, Sandra felt her heartbeat quicken with anxiety for Chuck as he welcomed everyone to Undivided. The sessions each week would follow the same rhythm: there would be an opening prayer to establish the biblical foundations of their work, a reminder of the ground rules, a teaching from the main stage, an activity in the small groups to put the teaching into practice, homework for the coming week focused on putting people into relationship or action, and a closing prayer. There would be no collection plate or plea for donations. Instead, the planning team was asking people to bring their hearts to the work. That week, Chuck called on Paul's second letter to the Corinthians (2 Corinthians 5:18): "All this is from God, who reconciled us to himself through Christ and has given us the ministry of reconciliation." Each week, Chuck would carefully choose a prayer that demonstrated the consistency of antiracism with Jesus's teachings in the Bible. Lest anyone in the room doubt whether Crossroads should be tackling "political" issues like race, Chuck argued that antiracism was fundamental to their calling as Christians.

After Chuck's prayer, an older white woman named Kathy Beechem took the stage. Because this was the first session of the program, Kathy wanted to provide an overview of the coming weeks and establish the norms they would use to work together. Kathy, a member of the Undivided planning team, had formerly been an executive vice president at U.S. Bank (where she oversaw all the bank's local branches), and was on the executive leadership team at Crossroads. She had been named one of the Twenty-Five Most Powerful Women in Banking by *U.S. Banker* magazine in 2004. After she was widowed, she joined the Crossroads staff as director of all local campuses, becoming Chuck's boss when he was the pastor of Oakley.

As in many megachurches, the ultimate governing body of Crossroads was a Spiritual Board. It decided what kinds of stances the church would take on key issues, including defining what Crossroads calls the "seven hills we die on," the church's statement of the values that defined its identity. To set the cultural context for the church, church leaders frequently talked about the seven hills to integrate them as seamlessly as possible into people's experience of Crossroads. In that first session of Undivided, Kathy outlined a set of ground rules that echoed the seven hills:

Expect to be offended.
Give grace.
Take risks.
Listen for God.
Get honest (use "I" statements).

None of these phrases surprised Sandra, or others in the room. They were all common to the Crossroads vernacular. "Listen for God" reinforced one of the board's defining seven hills, "biblical truth," which was the heart of Crossroads' identity. The church welcomed both believers and nonbelievers into their community but were unequivocal about their commitment to the authority of the Bible. "Expect to be offended" was how church leaders reinforced the hill they defined as "authenticity." They wanted the church to be a place where everyone could "just be real," "get honest," and bring their full selves, warts and all, to the community. That meant that sometimes congregants or church leaders would say things that could offend people. "Take risks" echoed the hill of "excellence." Crossroads always stressed the importance of bringing their "A-game" to everything they did, even if it risked failure. "Give grace" stressed the board's emphasis on relationships. They wanted to build a community where people would "do life together," and open themselves to one another so that everyone could "know and be known." The work would be hard, Kathy assured everyone, but necessary. She encouraged participants to lean into the inevitable discomfort they would experience.

Kathy walked through the weekly themes of the five-week curriculum (the planning team would later add a sixth week): Redeem (an introduction to the program, each other, and the history of race in Cincinnati), Relationship (an opportunity to focus on stepping out of silos and echo chambers through storytelling), Reality (an emphasis on the intersections of racialized systems and structures that disparately shape opportunity in America), Repentance (a focus on personal transformation to move forward), and Reconciliation (an emphasis on reengagement in a different way).

Then Kathy introduced Troy Jackson, the pastor turned community organizer who had joined the planning team. Troy, who had a PhD in history, traced the development of "two Cincinnatis,"

one for white people and one for Black people. He described the
city's legacy as a border town, with enslaved people trying to cross
the Ohio River to gain their freedom, and the painful experiences
of Black mothers and fathers seeking to protect their children
from a world of violent persecution. He explained how laws insti-
tuted after the Civil War ensured that even though Black people were not enslaved, they remained systematically oppressed.
He sketched the city's history through the Jim Crow era into the
contemporary period, demonstrating the deep roots of the racial
disparities that were still so evident in the city. He named Black
neighborhoods in Cincinnati that everyone knew—the West End,
Walnut Hills, Avondale—and narrated the forces that had impov-
erished these communities at different points in the city's history.

Sandra was riveted. Having grown up in California, she knew
little of Cincinnati's past. When she first arrived in the city as a
nineteen-year-old, the stark segregation of Black and white communities in Ohio (and the lack of much other racial diversity) had
been a shock. Cincinnati was the first place someone referred to
her using the N-word. The Undivided lesson resonated with her
experiences in the city, and with the stories her parents shared
about how white people tried to keep Black people down.

Sandra's parents had always taught her that institutional racism in America was a given. Disdainful of the idea that solutions
to racial injustice existed, they saw no need to choose their church,
their neighborhood, or their politics based on prospects for racial
justice. "The Democrats and the Republicans both treat Black
people badly," her dad said. Republicans, Sandra's dad thought,
were at least anti-abortion and pro-marriage. So Sandra grew up
listening to Rush Limbaugh with her dad as part of a small but
devoted group of Black Republicans.

Even though Sandra's parents educated her about patterns of
structural oppression, she was unaccustomed to hearing someone
at Crossroads discussing them. Whenever Crossroads leaders had

previously talked about racism, they focused on the prejudice in people's hearts, rather than the way race structured opportunities in American life. This first Undivided lesson seemed to mark a change in that regard. The planning team had deliberately chosen to start with history because they wanted to signal early on that their goal was to move people beyond just a simple recognition of their personal prejudices.

Man, Sandra thought. *This thing might be different.*

≈

In contrast to Sandra, the younger white man in her group, Grant, listened with the dispassionate distance of someone accustomed to living in a world made for him. He was born in 1987 in Waynesville, Ohio, a town of about three thousand people in the southwestern corner of the state. The picturesque buildings lining the central public square of his hometown looked like they came out of a Norman Rockwell painting. Grant moved through the world with the confidence of someone who had always known he was loved. Initially an only child, he used to stand on a large rock underneath the maple tree in his front yard serenading passing cars with his songs and opinions.

When Grant was eleven, his parents received a call from an adoption agency telling them to expect Hunt, a seven-week-old Black baby boy the next Monday. His parents had been trying to adopt for many years. They were overjoyed.

In Waynesville, however, Grant, Hunt, and their parents had very limited exposure in their everyday lives to people who were not white. Although Grant befriended his one Black classmate, almost 97 percent of the rest of the population was white. In most rooms Hunt entered as a child, he was the only nonwhite person.

Grant's family was determined that the color of Hunt's skin would not matter. "We can't treat Hunt differently because he's Black," was like a family mantra. They educated themselves about transracial adoption, reading books on the subject, and talking to experts and other parents in similar circumstances. They worked hard to expose the boys to different kinds of communities, road-tripping around the country every summer. By the time Grant went to college, he had been to forty-four different states. When family members from Kentucky made racist comments around Hunt, Grant's parents would confront them. Their relatives would defensively protest, "But Hunt is different because he's family." Even though people around Grant's family loved Hunt, they did not love other Black people.

Grant's parents nonetheless constructed a loving home for Hunt, full of sports on Saturday afternoons, Methodist church on Sundays, school, music lessons, homework, and sports practices during the week. A talented athlete, Hunt became an avid base-ball player, traveling around the state and region with his team. Hunt was known in his small town, unlike other Black people, who were strangers to them.

Both Grant and Hunt attested to the incredibly close rela-tionship they had as children. Grant thought his experience with a Black sibling equipped him to guide conversations about race. That was one reason why he signed up for Undivided as a facilitator—though he kept that to himself.

Another reason had to do with his politics. He had been devoted to the Republican Party for most of his life. When he attended a Baptist college in Kentucky, he became an active leader in the Col-lege Republicans, serving as both president of his campus chapter and treasurer of the statewide federation. He even interned with Fox News one summer. He didn't remember ever choosing to become Republican. He had always assumed that Christians had to be Republican, even though, in the twenty-first century, some scholars argued that it was not that people's churches shaped their political beliefs, but that people selected their churches to match their political beliefs.

Grant was so dedicated to the Republican Party that he had once considered tattooing the Republican mascot onto his body, but a friend convinced him not to do it. "You don't know what the party could be in twenty years," his friend had said. At the time, Grant couldn't imagine ever questioning his allegiance to the Republican Party. But Grant listened to his friend. In an unwitting tribute to the intertwined relationship between conservative Christianity and the Republican Party, he decided to memorialize his relationship to God instead. He asked the tattooist to write "In God We Trust" in fancy script across the back of his neck.

The relationship of Christianity and Republicanism evolved from the efforts of Christian leaders seeking to expand their influence in American society in the twentieth century. When evangelicals first came together to form the National Association of Evangelicals (NAE) in the mid-twentieth century, they represented only two million of the sixty to seventy million Christians in the United States. They initially worried about their ability to grow—until the vast popularity of Billy Graham put those concerns to rest. Graham provided the celebrity appeal evangelicalism needed in the immediate post–World War II era. He could even unite some of the disparate intellectual strains of conservative theologians through his energetic preaching and his relentless focus on personal salvation as the core of evangelicalism. With the Cold War as a backdrop, Graham articulated a white Christian American alternative to the threat of godless communists from abroad. White evangelicals reveled in Graham's popularity, and their growing success because of it.

The 1960s and the 1970s threw cold water on their bravado. Witnessing the success of the civil rights movement, the women's movement, and the antiwar movements, conservative evangelicals realized the magnitude of the forces they were up against in an increasingly secular, progressive society. Nothing breeds orthodoxy like threat. Some Christians concluded they needed greater societal power to realize their vision of evangelicalism.

By the 1980s, the Christian Right had emerged as an interlocking set of organizations, leaders, and pastors designed to uphold conservative tenets of Christianity and, implicitly, the cultural legacy of white Christianity. With the winds of white supremacy and patriarchy at their backs, these leaders built broad public followings and developed powerful media empires. Many luminaries of the movement became household names during this time— Jim and Tammy Faye Bakker, Pat Robertson and *The 700 Club*, James Dobson and Focus on the Family, Phyllis Schlafly, Jerry Falwell and the Moral Majority, Jimmy Swaggart, and Oral Roberts. Viewership of Christian media quintupled from the 1960s to the 1980s. The Christian Right seized issues like reproductive rights and sex education in schools to build their base, stoking people's fears of an encroaching anti-white, feminist, peace-loving multiculturalism that seemed on the rise after the 1960s.

The televangelists' millions of devotees became a political weapon they could use to exert power in the public sphere. As elected officials and other politicians witnessed the rapid growth of this movement, they began to court the evangelical leaders who helped anchor the Christian Right. These leaders welcomed the attention from both political parties. As Pat Robertson argued, "God isn't a right-winger or a left-winger." Evangelicals were disappointed by the first evangelical president, Jimmy Carter, a Democrat. In contrast, Ronald Reagan, a Republican, actively courted their support in his campaign against Carter in 1980. Robertson adopted the Republican Party by the time he decided to run for president in 1988, trying to use his large media platform to gin up Christian votes.

Grant was a by-product of this history, growing up in environments—a devout Methodist family and a Baptist college—where it was simply assumed that he would become Republican because he was Christian. But he was starting to question his lifelong loyalty as he witnessed Donald Trump's rise within the party he loved. At first, Grant laughed off a lot of Trump's comments. But when evangelical leaders remained unwavering in their support for Trump even after he simultaneously announced his candidacy for president and his belief that Mexicans were "rapists," Grant became unsure.

Grant sat opposite Sandra during Troy's history lesson. When Troy finished, Chuck directed all the members of the small groups to introduce themselves to one another by describing their first experiences with race and reflecting on the feelings evoked by the history they just learned. The planning team's choice to have people focus on their emotions was intentional, hoping it would move people to a place of greater vulnerability by focusing on their feelings.

The Undivided planning team had hotly debated the construction of the small groups. An advisor they brought in from Procter & Gamble argued that the racial balance didn't matter. Many DEI programs operated on the premise that change depended on teaching people the error of their ways. These programs often treated DEI as an informational problem, as if pouring facts about bias and discrimination into people's heads would remove their blinders and change behavior. In this formulation, the structure of the small groups didn't matter as much as the information the instructor would relay.

Chuck and the planning team instinctively knew those underlying assumptions were wrong. In their minds, Undivided would fail if it only imparted information. Participants, Black and white, needed experiences of vulnerability and solidarity across race, however tentative. The racial composition of the small groups mattered because they would be ground zero for making or breaking such experiences. The small groups were the place where participants would create meaning out of what they were learning and formulate choices about if and how they wanted to continue. They would be the place where people would (they hoped) take their first hesitant steps toward antiracism, carefully observing the reactions of those around them. The planning team wanted to ensure everyone would be part of racially balanced groups that enabled engagement across race.

Sandra and Grant's small group started with some nervous chuckling, because the group had four people who had originally signed up to be facilitators. They traded a few jokes about who was really in charge. Grant shared first, describing his relationship with Hunt. As he spoke, he became uncharacteristically nervous, debating with himself about how honest he should be. A natural extrovert, he had never before been apprehensive speaking about his relationship with his brother—but he realized he had never had this kind of conversation with Black people, let alone Black people he didn't know. For Grant, hesitation was an unfamiliar form of vulnerability. He considered telling a story about his hometown, where a customer used the N-word to refer to Hunt in a restaurant where Hunt was a waiter. Grant paused, worried the story exposed his community in ways that made him uncomfortable.

Grant looked at Sandra, whom he had just met, and the other Black woman in the group. *What if they judge me?* he thought. Grant was not accustomed to worrying about being judged, so he hedged. He shared a different story about Hunt. His parents had come to visit him in college, and they drove to Corbin, Kentucky, to see a movie. Corbin was a small town of about seven thousand people in southeastern Kentucky that was 98 percent white. Grant was standing in the lobby of the theater with Hunt, who was six or seven years old at the time. A young white girl approached Hunt to talk with him, only to have her parents guide her away saying, "We don't talk to people like that." Grant did nothing.

He stopped talking and looked around. He ran his thumbs over the jagged edges of his fingernails as he waited for people to respond. He could tell he had been lacerating them with anxiety while he talked.

Sandra thought about all the times she had bowed to social pressure and ignored racist comments people made around her. She could understand why Grant might not have done anything in that moment. She nodded her head gently. Grant couldn't bring himself to look directly at her, but he noticed her nodding.

CHAPTER FIVE

HIS HEAD IS BURNING

A short white woman with spiky brown hair and frosted tips spoke before anyone else in Jess's group during the first week of Undivided. She, along with an older Black woman, was a co-facilitator of the group. Having grown up in a community with barely any nonwhite people, she had only experienced people of color on TV, and had developed stereotypes of Black women as aggressive and powerful. Initially, she thought her views were harmless but described realizing over time the inherent harm in her stereotypes. Jess was taken aback. She thought of her own large frame and the Black women she knew from prison who were self-assured and outspoken—whom she loved. *Why is this woman saying it is a problem?* Jess found herself feeling a little annoyed. When the white facilitator mentioned wanting to be an "ally," Jess didn't know what that meant.

Jess had arrived at Undivided unsure about how to introduce herself and whether to reveal the stark truth about her family. She decided to be up-front. She was not accustomed to dissembling and didn't want to talk in vague abstractions the way the white facilitator had.

Jess described growing up in Volusia County, Florida, and the poverty, swamps, and unpaved sandy roads that marked her childhood. She described her father and the brazen tank tops he wore to make sure that everyone saw his white supremacist tattoos.

Her father died when she was eleven, but his hate did not. When Jess was twelve and her sister was eight, they were living outside Cincinnati in a trailer park with their mother. Her mom was dropping Jess and her sister off at her friend's house when the girls met the woman's Black boyfriend. Jess's sister started screaming racist epithets, refusing to let her mother leave.

"I carry shame for those things now," Jess said. "But I don't know how else to be. I'm here to learn."

Jess let her eyes roam quickly around the circle, landing on the face of a young Black woman sitting across from her. The young woman gazed evenly at her, but Jess had to look away. The group was silent after Jess stopped speaking. They hadn't gotten to know one another yet, and no one was sure how to react to Jess's frank admissions. They could not ignore what Jess had said, but they weren't ready to engage with it, either. The Black facilitator thanked Jess for her candor, and they moved on to the next person.

Just shut up and listen, Jess told herself. It came time for the young Black woman sitting across from Jess to speak. She was in her midtwenties and had curly hair and a soft southern twang when she spoke. She described the first time she realized as a child that some people thought it was a problem that she was Black. She had been invited by a white friend to spend the night at her house. The girls were enjoying themselves until it was time to get ready for bed. As they were changing into their pajamas, the white girl started to scrub her Black friend's arm with a washcloth to remove the color.

Jess was dumbfounded, but the other Black people in the circle were nodding in affirmation. Jess started to cry.

Both Jess and Grant could have walked away from the discomfort they felt during the first week of Undivided, but neither did.

(While Sandra and Grant participated in Undivided's first session in February 2016, Jess participated in the second, beginning in August 2016.) One of the seven hills that Crossroads articulated on its website was personal growth: "We do expect everyone who is around our community for any length of time to be growing . . . This is a safe place for everyone. But safe doesn't mean comfortable." Jess and Grant each came to Undivided with an openness to learning and a willingness to sustain discomfort.

Sandra, on the other hand, was still not sure what to think after the first session ended. She liked Grant, but he seemed to wear his whiteness smugly, making it hard to believe that he had a Black brother. She felt a little scornful when Grant's wife spoke. Kyla, who grew up in northern Kentucky, described how "the Mexicans" used to scare her by catcalling as she and her friends walked home from cheerleading practice. Sandra forced herself not to roll her eyes. *How can your only experience of race be with Mexicans hollering at you? That's what scares you?* she thought.

⁓

The curriculum the second week focused on the neuroscience of empathy, and the ways in which people's neural systems interact with emotions to facilitate both conscious and unconscious decision-making. The lecture challenged participants to consider the way their previous experiences might have encoded biases into the way they unconsciously responded to people of the opposite race. The alternative to gut reactions, they were told, was to act with empathy, which is the process of moving reactions from the gut into the head, to allow for more conscious decision-making about how to respond. Instead of acting instinctively, the lecture urged listeners to act with intention, using a four-step process to engage the appropriate neural systems to elicit empathic choices. First, decide if the person is worth connecting empathically with. Second, identify the emotional experience he or she is having or describing. Third, recall a time when you had a similar emotional experience. Fourth, act the way you wish you had been treated in that moment.

After the lesson, each small group did an exercise to illustrate people's gut reactions. The facilitators in each group had a set of laminated pictures of provocative images of race and racism in America—a racial justice protest, a Black man drinking from a "colored only" fountain, a Muslim woman in front of an American flag, among others. They showed each picture to the entire group, and then asked participants to notice what their gut emotional reaction was. Then, each person in the small group took turns sharing which image evoked the strongest reaction for them, and why. The facilitators asked listeners to consciously recognize their own reactions in order to elicit more empathic responses, even if they disagreed with the speaker.

When Sandra's group went around the circle describing their reactions to the pictures, she was initially unsurprised by the things white people were saying. But the other Black woman disrupted her complacency by pulling out a picture of two children, one Black and one white, boarding a school bus together. The woman said, "I was scared when I looked at that picture. I don't know where those children are going and what's going to happen to that little Black child."

When Sandra had seen the picture, she thought, *That's cute.* The contrast made Sandra pause. Her parents had taught her to accept the reality that Black Americans would always be treated differently by whites. But somehow she had lost her fear of being around white people.

Sandra's parents were Black southerners who first met in California. When they married, they moved to Sacramento in search of economic opportunity. The goal was to get their children into the middle class. They knew that the poverty rate among Black families was about twice that of white families and wanted a different future for their children. Neither of them had gone to college (according to the 1960 Census, about 8 percent of white adults completed college, while only 3 percent of Black adults did), but they were determined that Sandra and her five older siblings would.

By the time Sandra started school, her parents had saved enough money to move into a quiet middle-class suburb that had large Black and Vietnamese populations. Sandra remembered her neighborhood elementary school as being primarily Black, Asian, and Mexican, with a few white kids.

Sandra's three oldest siblings were struggling to stay in school by the time she entered sixth grade, so her parents managed to transfer her to another school. For the first time, Sandra was in an overwhelmingly white school. She sobbed after the first day, wailing to her mother, "It's so white!" Her mother shrugged, unconcerned about the racial dynamic. She was confident that her children had strong enough roots in the Black community, so she could focus on the educational opportunities instead. Sandra's parents were devout Christians who took their kids to a small Black church on holidays and special occasions as well as a larger multiracial, white-dominant megachurch on a weekly basis. Sandra recalled being in at least one church every day of the week. Her parents liked the array of opportunities the megachurch offered but were committed to retaining a Black church experience for their family. Her mother remained resolute about the new school.

Sandra threw herself into the school community to make friends. She learned to move seamlessly between different social groups: the artsy kids (lots of Asians), the stoners (also racially diverse), and a Christian youth group (very white). In her old majority-Black school, Sandra had fit in easily and was popular and well-liked. In this new school, when she expressed a mild crush on one of the white boys, someone said to her, "You can't date him."

"Why not?" Sandra asked.

"Because you're Black!"

As an adult, Sandra defined that as the moment she decided to make herself "good enough" to date white boys—without asking who got to define what was "good" and why it was associated with whiteness. Racism could operate without racists when the unspoken social mores of a community did the work for them. In the hierarchy of Sandra's teenage concerns, social acceptance superseded antiracism. She loved putting together extravagant outfits and trying to outdo the richer kids with her fashion. It got her the attention she wanted; by the time they were graduating, her classmates elected her Best Dressed. Throughout these middle and high school years, Sandra felt like the onus fell on her to suppress her hurt when people made offensive racial comments. She always laughed loudly, in order to seem unperturbed. "It was my job to be likable," she later recalled.

As Sandra contemplated the picture of the two children boarding the school bus during Undivided, she thought about how hard she worked to become popular in a mostly white school, and the comfort she developed operating in white environments. She was no longer scared to think of Black children with other white kids. For the first time, she realized Undivided could help her learn about herself. "I thought I didn't have a problem with race," she said. "White people were the ones who were racist." But during that second week, she realized, "We all have racial wounds."

Trust accrued in the small groups through the slow accumulation of minute reactions: Sandra's almost imperceptible nod when Grant told his story, Jess's tears when the Black woman in her group spoke, people's frank confessions to one another, their willingness to heed Chuck's pleas from the stage. Sandra had no idea that Grant might not have come back to facilitate if it had not been for her modest nod that first week. Each of these reactions created new possibilities.

By carefully constructing the small groups, the Undivided planning team had stumbled onto a truth they enacted before they could fully articulate it. They intuited that their program would succeed not because of the information they imparted, but because of their ability to create a context that motivated attendees to take repeated social risks regarding antiracism. Participants wouldn't take such risks only because someone told them to do so. Instead, as psychologists argue, the motivation to act depends not only on people feeling confident, but also their belief that their social circumstances are conducive to the actions they want to take. For Undivided to succeed, participants had to feel comfortable enough with one another to practice engaging across race, asking tough questions of themselves and the people around them. They had to be open to a range of answers. And, if the practice yielded social rewards, participants eventually had to claim the work of racial justice as their own. Motivation had to shift from being what psychologists call extrinsic motivation to becoming intrinsic—people had to want to do the work. Unlike DEI programs that spoon-fed people a menu of uncontroversial actions or put them in a legalistic vise, Undivided wanted to free participants to choose antiracism, even if offering such freedom meant some people would not comply.

≈

The third week of Undivided, Grant and his wife arrived late to the meeting. Grant apologized to the group, explaining that he had been with his brother getting haircuts, which took longer than he expected.

"Wait a minute," Sandra said when Grant described why they were late. "You guys get your haircuts in the same place?"

"Yeah, of course," Grant replied.

"And your barber is white?" Sandra asked.

Even if Sandra had initially scorned Grant and Kyla's revelations about their experiences with race, she had begun to respect their willingness to expose themselves so honestly. She gently asked more questions about how the barber treated Hunt's hair. Grant said the barber put a chemical straightener in Hunt's hair and then used a razor to cut it the same day.

Sandra and the other Black woman in the group cringed when Grant described it.

"Do you know that his head is probably burning?" Sandra asked Grant.

At first, Grant listened with the breezy dismissiveness that comes with knowing his own good intentions. But the first few weeks of Undivided prompted him to listen more carefully.

Sandra explained that Black women knew that after using a chemical straightener, they had to take special care not to touch their scalps.

Grant had never before considered that his brother might need to go to a Black barber. Slowly, he realized that he might have spent a lifetime being blind to his brother's needs. He marked his conversation with Sandra as the moment he shifted from complacency to humility.

The teaching that week, on Reality, was an exercise about racial disparities in America, replete with statistics about various forms of inequality. Each small group got a ball of string and a set of Life Area Cards, which represented things like housing, education, health, social norms, transportation, and other domains of people's lives. Each person in the group wore one of the Life Area Cards around their neck, and everyone stood in a circle facing one another. As a facilitator, Grant led his small group through an interactive storytelling exercise. Each person was to tell a story about an experience with one of the life areas. Whenever it touched on one of the other life areas, the speaker would toss the ball of string to the person holding the relevant card.

By the end, their group, like everyone else's, had a complex, interconnected web of string, demonstrating the way disparity in one area was inextricably connected to disparity in another area. "That was what they were trying to teach us about intersectionality," Grant later recalled. But he struggled to pay attention, instead replaying thousands of quotidian interactions with Hunt in his head to discover what he had missed.

Sandra could tell that Grant was distracted during their session. For her part, she was pondering how Grant's family could have raised a Black child without interacting much with other Black people. *God, why do white people adopt Black children?* she asked herself. She wondered what it must have been like for Hunt and thought about saying something more to Grant. But they were still getting to know each other, and she didn't want him to feel like she was intruding.

Grant called Hunt as soon as he got home that night. He realized he had to take apart what he thought he knew about their relationship and relearn a new story.

"Why didn't you ever say that your head hurt?" Grant asked.

"No one ever asked," Hunt replied.

Grant wondered what else had they failed to ask.

As Grant faced the prospect of returning to Undivided the next week, he thought, *I have no business leading this group.* He considered dropping out of the program. But he had never quit anything before in his life, and it didn't feel right to him. *I have to keep trying,* he thought.

When Sandra returned to Undivided the fourth week, she noticed that Grant seemed to be focused on the group with a new intensity. He was diligently studying the materials for the session when she arrived.

Grant looked up when Sandra arrived and smiled nervously. He wondered what she had been thinking about him. Sandra smiled back.

CHAPTER SIX

BELONGING

Each week, Jess was a little surprised to see the one Black man in her group return to sit voluntarily in a circle with her. The man was older than she was, probably in his midforties. He wore jeans and button-down shirts, looking like he could be a dad. Despite being the only man in the group, he had an easy rapport with everyone, often ready with a joke to cut tension in their conversations. Jess had not been able to look at him when she told the story about her dad teaching her that all Black men were rapists. She later tried to sneak sideways glances at him, but when he caught her looking, she immediately looked away, unwilling to hold his gaze. As soon as the facilitators released the group for a break, Jess quickly escaped to find a second cup of coffee before anyone could initiate conversation.

At the beginning of Undivided, organizers projected an image of a heart symbol onto the screen. One word appeared in each of the three corners of the symbol: *Relationships, Identity, Action*. The teaching team wanted participants to know they had to grow in all three directions—reflecting on themselves, getting into relationships across race, and taking action—if they wanted to become part of the solution to systemic injustice. The trick was converting vulnerability into trust, instead of shame. Self-reflection could prompt some participants to become defensive, angry, or unwilling to engage, especially if they felt isolated. Relationships were the antidote. But the challenge, Chuck and the planning team knew, was that they could not force people into relationships. Instead, the curriculum had to evoke experiences of vulnerability that would open people to the possibility of trusting each other.

Jess's group already had plenty of cordial, and even revealing, interactions. But they had not yet constructed relationships, which are distinct from interactions because both people expect the interactions to continue. That presumed future gives meaning to the exchanges people have and shapes the way they relate to each other. Jess was not sure if any members of her group expected to stay connected with her after the program ended.

Walking away from uncomfortable interactions with people like the Black man made it harder for Jess and her group to develop the kind of relationships Undivided leaders thought they needed. Some relationships remain forever transactional, in which both parties constantly seek to protect themselves and their own self-interest. Workplace DEI programs that mandate participation often struggle to move beyond such transactions. They turn DEI work into an exercise in checking boxes. Undivided wanted something different. They sought to cultivate what psychologists called "social relationships," in which people give with consideration of the other person's needs and wants, and without knowing what they might get in return. Such relationships, which are characterized by a sense of acceptance, exchange, and growth, create the sense of belonging people need to build trust.

~

Some small groups in Undivided never achieved that community of belonging. Jess's group took four weeks. Until then, it was Jess's commitment to and trust in Crossroads that made her keep coming back to Undivided.

When Jess was first released from prison, she was too busy for church. As part of her parole, she had to participate in outpatient drug treatment several days a week and check in regularly with her probation officer. To regain custody of her six-year-old son, she enrolled in parenting education classes through the Ohio Child Protective Services and navigated what turned out to be a year-long court process. It was all-consuming. Jess almost lost custody because her felony conviction made it challenging to find a home where she could live with her son. To salvage the opportunity, Jess's mom moved out of her trailer so Jess could move in, enabling her to regain custody two weeks before her son's seventh birthday. Jess never took her family's generosity for granted. Initially, she had been unsure whether they would welcome her back, given the fact that she had stolen from them and forged checks in their names. But her mom and sister warmly welcomed Jess into their lives, even as Jess's sister was pregnant with her first child.

So when her sister began battling a severe bout of postpartum depression, Jess was desperate to do something. She was afraid her sister was going to kill herself, and she didn't know how to help her. Jess can't remember who suggested trying Crossroads. But Jess had been wanting to find a church since Sergeant Harris had helped her develop a relationship with God. She convinced her sister to accompany her.

They felt a little sheepish the first time they attended services in late 2015. Jess and her sister hadn't been to a megachurch like Crossroads before. The brightly lit lobby, the crowds of people milling around, the free artisan coffee bar, and the overtly friendly greeters overwhelmed them. They found two seats in the back of the auditorium.

Both were relieved when the house lights went down, spotlighting the band onstage. Like many other megachurches in America, Crossroads dispensed with traditional liturgical services. There was no reason, Crossroads thought, that prim steeples, august altars, and uncomfortable wooden pews had to define people's church experience. The services themselves also lacked the stylistic trappings of traditional Protestant churches. During worship, there were no altars on the stage at Crossroads and the clergy did not wear traditional religious vestments. The services were multimedia, multisensory affairs with full bands and accompanying singers. An older white congregant in Crossroads who grew up in a traditional Presbyterian church once told me he hated Crossroads the first time he went. "It was so loud. So big. So irreverent." But then he got hooked.

Irreverence was actually a source of pride for Crossroads. They wanted to be funny, hip, and modern, to engage people most churches could not reach. It worked for Jess and her sister. The first time they attended Easter services at Crossroads, the production team shot confetti from the stage, released balloons from the ceiling, and rolled out a giant cake with communion wafers nestled into the icing. "Jesus is alive!" they declared. "It's a party!"

Sitting in the back of the dark auditorium in Oakley, listening to the messages about the promise of salvation through Jesus, and witnessing the impact of Crossroads in the community, Jess's sister discovered a relationship with God, and soon after began attending therapy. After the Easter party in 2016, she decided to get baptized. Baptisms in nondenominational evangelical communities were often literally immersive affairs—the baptismal candidate was fully dunked in any available body of water. For Jess's sister, it was a water tank Crossroads set up on the main stage in Oakley after weekly services. People lined up to get baptized under the spotlight while onlookers cheered. When Jess's sister was pulled out of the water, dripping wet and committed to Jesus, Jess cried. A volunteer was waiting with a towel for her at the end of the baptismal tank, but Jess grabbed it out of the volunteer's hands. "Let me do this part." She wrapped her sister in the towel, the two of them sobbing uncontrollably.

"I'm convinced that Crossroads saved my sister's life," Jess said as she reflected on that moment. It felt like atonement. "If I did nothing else, at least I helped my sister find Jesus."

Jess's loyalty to Crossroads engendered a willingness to stick with Undivided even when she was uncomfortable. Connection cultivated commitment.

She was surprised one week in Undivided to see her college professor participating in one of the other small groups. Jess had gone back to school after regaining custody of her son through a statewide program dedicated to trying to help the formerly incarcerated obtain jobs with the state. As part of her degree, she landed in a sociology class with a Black professor. Near the end of the semester, he lectured on the Black experience in America. Jess remembered him beginning his lecture: "Most people think the last racist killed Martin Luther King and then racism was over." Jess cocked her head, pausing while taking notes. *That's not true?* she thought. Implausible as it was, Jess had never questioned the narrative that America's race problem had been solved.

His lecture opened Jess's eyes to things she had never known before—persistent racial disparities in income, wealth, and education, disproportionate incarceration rates of Black men, the history of the Black Panther Party, and so on. He introduced her to words that she had never heard, like *blackface*. During the lecture, she thought about the murders of Michael Brown in Missouri, Eric Garner in New York, and Samuel DuBose in Cincinnati, and the ensuing controversies about policing in America. Until then, Jess had never known what to make of the news, always unsure about the trustworthiness of the media. But by this point in the semester, she trusted her professor. People's ability to enact change was often most potent within trusted social networks.

Jess called her sister as soon as the lecture was over. "You are not going to believe all this stuff," she had said, flabbergasted by how different it was from what they had learned as kids. Each week after Undivided, she did the same, joking on the phone with her sister about her ignorance.

Bonds of community began to emerge in Jess's group during the fourth week. That session was dedicated to helping people excavate their racial identities and break down their assumptions about race. After taking an implicit association test, people stood in a circle and the facilitator read out a list of statements. Those for whom the statement was true walked into the middle of the circle.

For Jess, the exercise started simply enough.

"I grew up with two parents at home."

"I have a college degree."

"I have been incarcerated."

Jess froze.

By then, she had been pretty open with her group about her father and his past. But she had never considered admitting to others in Undivided that she was a convicted felon. She felt unprepared for this moment. The facilitator paused. Jess's mind raced. *I'm in church. Aren't I supposed to be good?* She considered staying where she was. No one else was walking to the middle of the circle. Jess looked down at her hands—she had just gotten a small lotus flower tattooed onto the inside of her left wrist. She described it to her friends as a symbol of "the journey of the spiritual self through life, love, death, and recovery." The petals of the flower were colored in different shades of blue, and the stem was slightly twisted. Jess walked into the middle of the circle and stood there alone.

She locked eyes with Patricia, the older Black woman who was one of the cofacilitators in her group. Patricia blinked and her eyebrows lifted slightly. Cutting the tension of people's gaze with her laughter, Jess said, "I guess no one looks at this white girl and thinks, 'Oh, she's a felon.'"

Everyone laughed. Jess walked back to the edge of the circle.

Later, the facilitator read another statement: "I have been addicted to drugs." Jess walked into the middle of the circle and stood alone, again. This time, her group didn't seem surprised. Jess looked directly at the Black man in the group, whose eyes she had been avoiding. He nodded. Jess smiled with relief and flicked her eyes to Patricia.

"My [child] is in recovery right now," Patricia said.

"I'm still in long-term recovery," Jess replied.

The exercise continued, asking people about their experiences with money, race, and poverty.

"I have gone to bed hungry."

"I haven't had enough money to pay my rent or mortgage."

"I have been discriminated against because of my race."

Jess was surprised to learn that the white, rather than the Black, participants in her group were more likely to have experienced poverty. She thought about all the things her dad and other relatives had told her about Black Americans being poor and lazy. The relief of acceptance loosened Jess's guard. She blurted out, "Huh, I always thought Black people were poor."

As soon as the words were out of her mouth, Jess regretted them. *Oh my God,* she thought. *I just said it out loud.* But others in her group laughed instead of getting angry. They were willing to give her latitude.

As that night's session was ending, one of the women asked if anyone wanted to continue the conversation over dinner. All eight people did. They found a Steak 'n Shake about a quarter mile from the Oakley campus that was open on a Monday night and decided to meet there. The restaurant looked like a classic 1950s diner with black and white tiles on the floor and red pleather seats arranged around Formica tables. There were not many other customers there, and it was easy for the group to rearrange the tables to seat everyone in their group together. Most people ordered burgers.

This impromptu dinner turned out to be a pivotal turning point for Jess and her group. There were two Black women, one Black man, one Asian woman, Jess, and three other white people. The Asian woman, an immigrant from China, described the legal challenges she had to go through to maintain her visa. Jess spoke about her experience in prison and finding Jesus. Patricia, the Black woman whose child was fighting addiction, traded stories about recovery and relapse with Jess. The Black man teased Jess gently about the stereotypes she had confessed to the group that night. His gentle jokes made Jess's shoulders relax. She laughed with him about her ignorance. Generally cautious about the things she shared with others, Jess described herself as a private person, somewhat wary in social situations. But when she was feeling comfortable, she laughed deeply and heartily. "Those are just the things my dad told me," she said.

"It's not just your dad," he said. "Everyone says those things." The group discussed the way local news stations offered imbalanced portrayals of Black and white communities in the city. The white facilitator whom Jess had not liked the first week talked about how she had to work to dismantle media stereotypes of Black people she had internalized in her own mind. Jess felt like she was beginning to understand where the woman was coming from.

The waitstaff had to ask the group to leave at ten thirty because the restaurant was closing. They all got up to go, but they couldn't stop talking among themselves. While the workers wiped down the chairs around them and swept stray fries and spilled sugar packets up from the floor, the group kept talking. It was a Monday night, and most people probably had to go to work the next day, but no one could bring themselves to leave until they were forced to.

Jess finally got into her blue 2007 Scion to drive home to Batavia. She thought about her dad, her struggle with heroin and other opioids, and then her time in prison. She thought about the hours of conversation with Sergeant Harris and felt, that night, that maybe he would be proud.

CHAPTER SEVEN

SURVEY WEEK

Sandra and Grant closed their eyes as they sat next to each other in their Undivided circle. It was their fourth week of Undivided, and Chuck was praying from the stage that people would be open to an exploration of their own identities. They were each on distinct but parallel journeys. Grant was mulling the conversations he had with Hunt. Sandra kept thinking about how differently she reacted to the picture of children boarding the school bus compared to the other Black woman. Who had she become? she wondered. After the prayer, Chuck and Lynn warned people that this lesson could be hard. "This is survey week," they said. "People identify hard truths about themselves."

The session began with a survey designed to measure each person's progression along a journey of racial identity development (the exercise Jess did walking into the middle of a circle came after the survey). Chuck told everyone, "Now this is just one type of identity survey, not the only one out there. No one should feel guilty at all about where they fall on the spectrum. The objective is to show that a positive racial identity, not based on assumed superiority or inferiority, is healthy for all." Facilitators handed out separate surveys for white and nonwhite attendees.

The survey was one of many ways that Undivided sought to

be sensitive to the distinct experiences of white and nonwhite participants—or, to use Undivided lingo, those from the "dominant culture" versus the "nondominant culture." Undivided leaders knew the weight of the status quo tipped any scale of purported racial balance toward white people. But even with years of experience, Lynn and other members of the planning team weren't sure how to handle the inevitably disproportionate burden that nonwhite people bore in exposing injustice. One commonly used strategy in similar contexts entailed creating exclusive space for those from nondominant groups to forge community with one another. This practice evolved from Black workers who gained access to formerly white-only unions and realized they needed to create their own caucuses to articulate their collective interests within the union. In Undivided, the planning team wanted to ensure that everyone had time to reflect on the survey with others who shared their racial identity.

Sandra and other nonwhite participants took a survey that asked them to indicate how much they agreed or disagreed with statements such as "To be a minority is unfortunate." "The problem of interracial disparity is an individual one. You can improve your position if you put in the effort; many minorities just don't want to improve themselves." "I feel compassion toward whites because racism from many of their members and institutions hurts all of them, too." These were the kinds of questions that some DEI programs, scared of sparking backlash, avoided. To circumvent white people's defensiveness regarding racism, some DEI programs did not even use the words race or racism. Instead, they substituted seemingly neutral symbols like circles, squares, and triangles for different racial groups. Undivided waded directly in.

Grant and other white participants took a similar survey with slightly different prompts. They included statements like "Everyone has equal opportunity to succeed in America." "Because I have minority-group friends, I can truthfully claim that I am not racist." "Oppression of any minority group (e.g., ethnic group, gender, sexual orientation, religion, etc.) hurts us all."

Sandra quietly took the survey. Chuck and Lynn then directed people to meet in pairs with someone of the opposite race to discuss their reactions to one or more questions on the survey. That was easy for Sandra. But then the moderators invited participants to meet with someone of the same race. Most of the previous exercises in Undivided had encouraged interaction across racial lines, so Sandra was unprepared to talk with another Black person. But she was game to try. She looked around the room and found a Black woman she had not met before. They pulled two chairs together and sat down to go over their surveys.

Although media conversations often treat the Black community as monolithic, attitudes among Black Americans demonstrate more heterogeneity than is commonly recognized. It is often assumed that all Black people will support policies that provide redress for inequality. But Stanford professor Hakeem Jefferson constructed the Respectability Politics Scale to measure the extent to which Black Americans "emphasized reform of individual behavior and attitudes both as a goal in itself" and "as a strategy for reform of the entire structure of American race relations." These definitions of "respectability politics" originated in historian Evelyn Brooks Higginbotham's study of Black women in the Black Baptist Church in the late nineteenth century. These women focused on the idea that if Black people wanted white people to treat them better, they needed to show themselves worthy of equality.

Jefferson and other scholars argued that respectability was not just an attitude, but engendered its own politics, behaviors, and demands for comportment. Black Americans who adhered to notions of respectability were more likely to feel ashamed of public views of Black Americans, endorse negative racial stereotypes, and support punitive policies that targeted their own group members. Jefferson found that attitudes regarding respectability within the Black community were distributed like a bell curve—most Black Americans were somewhere in the middle in their views on the Respectability Politics Scale. Approximately 12 percent of Black Americans were very resistant to the notion of respectability, but 19 percent embraced it.

When Sandra was sitting knee to knee with the Black woman she had paired up with in Oakley, she was unaware of debates about respectability. But even though she didn't have the language to describe it, she began to feel ashamed that night about the way her drive for respectability had made her prioritize assimilation into white communities over expressing her true feelings about racial oppression.

As instructed by Chuck and Lynn, Sandra and the other woman shared their answers with each other. Suddenly, Sandra felt immobilized. She looked at her answer to a survey prompt asking whether it was easier for her to make friends with white people at work. She had strongly agreed. *Oh, no,* she realized, *I have to admit to this woman that I have so many white friends!* Sandra was usually garrulous, able to intuitively sense how to make people feel comfortable. In that moment, as she sat next to this Black woman, she struggled for words. She had grown up in a family that had raised her to be proud of her Black identity. But she had worked so hard to assimilate into white communities that she had become disconnected from her heritage. And now she had to hold herself to account in front of another Black woman. She tried to cover up her survey answers, as if that would cover up her truth.

Sandra stumbled through what felt like an excruciating ten-minute conversation. Once Chuck and Lynn pulled everyone back together into plenary, they described the racial identity development model. "Racial identity is not fixed," Lynn said. "People are not better or worse based on their answers." Everyone is on a journey, they reassured the audience, including those from both "dominant" and "nondominant" cultures. Chuck and Lynn then described the different phases of identity development for each group. "No one should feel condemned by where they are."

For Sandra, it was too late. She felt ashamed.

"I began a research project on myself that night," she later recalled.

For the rest of the week, she excavated her past to understand why it was that she had rejected her Black identity. Sandra thought back to middle school and high school, when she had taught herself to withstand racist comments, when she had learned to make herself "likable" to white people. She called her older brother who had attended the same school and talked to him about it. She filled her journal with questions and memories. "I didn't realize how much of my identity as an adult was based in my rejections of being a Black woman in America," she later recalled. All week long, she scrolled through the contacts in her phone, or her list of Facebook friends. She marveled at how many people on those lists were white.

During the week, Sandra texted her Undivided group: "How are y'all doin'?" That simple question made her feel like she wasn't alone in her research project.

Grant was relieved to hear from Sandra. She had revealed her sense of shame to her small group during their discussion. Although Grant didn't know how to relate to her feelings, he recognized that she was going through her own struggle, and it made *him* feel less alone. Her friendly text lessened his worry that she would judge him for his ignorance. He contemplated sending a lengthy response but decided to send a short jesting text instead. He felt that responding was more important than exactly what he said.

Undivided had to be constantly sensitive to the possibility of overly burdening nonwhite people by making them responsible for educating white people about race. Grant was grateful to have Sandra in his group—instead of being scornful as she taught him about Black barbers, she was kind, exposing him to questions he had never considered. Anticipating these kinds of interactions, the Undivided planning team considered how to ensure that Sandra, as a Black person, did not feel like she had to take responsibility for Grant's development. Describing the work employees had to do to manage emotions around their bosses, sociologist Arlie Russell Hochschild coined the term "emotional labor" to describe similar work that those with less power often undertook. Balancing the emotional labor for Black and white people in Undivided, and recognizing that the consequences of failure were very different for each group, was a continual struggle for the planning team.

In this case, Sandra was happy to hear back from Grant and another young white woman in their group, Carolyn. Like Sandra, Carolyn had young children at home, and she and Sandra had bonded over their shared parenting responsibilities. Carolyn and her husband were also going through a process of transracial adoption, and she had shared openly with the group her insecurities about parenting a Black child as a white woman. She later confessed to Sandra her fears that others in their small group were judging her. Sandra was relieved to know that she wasn't alone in feeling so exposed.

She and Carolyn decided to get together for a playdate with their children. They met at a small playground near the Oakley campus. As they stood next to each other watching their children play, a white child came up to Carolyn and asked, "Are you in my mom's wine group at Crossroads?" Carolyn laughed. "I'm not, but it sounds fun!" she said. Sandra watched the interaction and realized that in most of the playgrounds she went to, other children and moms hardly came to talk to her. She told Carolyn, who didn't know what to say. But the incident created an opportunity for the two women to share more openly with each other the way Undivided was prompting them to question choices they each had made in the past.

For Grant, Sandra, and Carolyn, it was not only reassuring to find others so deeply engaged in Undivided, but it was also a relief to find others in their church with whom they could have these conversations. Being able to go to a playground with another mom and talk about her own struggles around race was a welcome balm for Sandra.

The curriculum in the fifth week of Undivided asked participants to repent publicly for their sins around racial justice. Chuck and Lynn described the process from the stage. To model the exercise they asked a white woman to speak first. She stood up and said, "I make excuses for my grandfather who says racist things." She offered a little background on her family and then said, "I need to call it what it is," and reckon with the fact that it is "part of the past of my family." After she spoke, a Black woman looked her directly in the eye and said, "You are forgiven. May God bless you to follow through on this change." Chuck and Lynn then asked everyone to engage in the same exercise with their small group.

"It was," Carolyn said later, "one of the holiest experiences of my entire life." (Undivided leaders dropped this exercise from subsequent iterations of the program because they worried it created a sense of false absolution for white people.)

Members of Grant and Sandra's small group turned toward one another. Usually, Grant would have jumped into the silence. But this time, he nudged the young Black woman who was facilitating the group with him to take the lead. Born-again evangelicalism's emphasis on forgiveness meant that participants in Undivided would be accustomed to working on forgiveness. But justice also demands accountability. Grant couldn't articulate why, but he did not feel like he was ready yet for forgiveness, because he was just discovering accountability in his relationship with Hunt.

Grant's co-lead invited group members to share their repentances. When they had met the first week, they all sat back in their folding chairs, subtly arranged to make sure that each member was not too close to anyone else. Silences didn't last too long because the group was not comfortable with them yet. But in this fifth week, they were all sitting closer to one another, some people almost knee to knee, and they were all comfortable with the silence. They could each contemplate their emotions without worrying about what others around them were thinking.

Sandra finally broke the silence. "I have to get this off my chest," she said.

Sandra told her group about all the things that had been on her heart that week. "I have rejected my identity as a Black woman," she concluded. "I have to reclaim my Black tradition." The Black woman cofacilitating the group with Grant looked Sandra directly in the eye and spoke evenly to her. "You are forgiven. May God bless you to follow through on this change." Sandra felt hot tears spring to her eyes.

After reviewing survey data they had gathered the first week, Chuck and the other Undivided organizers realized that almost half the people in the program had never had a person of a different race in their home. So they added a sixth week to the program, in which each small group would gather at one another's houses to share a potluck dinner. They called this sixth week Reignite, hoping that the dinner would become a call to action. (In subsequent years, they renamed the weekly themes. Instead of Redeem, Relationship, Reality, Repentance, Reconciliation, and Reignite, the thematic names all became verbs: Root, Realize, Respond, Reckon, Restore, and Resolve.)

Grant and Sandra's group met for their dinner in the apartment of Grant's cofacilitator. People brought sodas and salads, a slow cooker pot of chili, and a pan of lasagna to share. They spread the potluck out on the dining room table and ate on chairs and couches in the living room. Sandra brought her husband and two boys. Grant played with the kids, holding their youngest son upside down until he squealed with laughter. Carolyn, a preschool teacher, played games with the boys so that Sandra and her husband could eat without being bothered. In a group picture they took after dinner, Sandra's youngest son was snuggled into Grant's lap, and her oldest son made silly faces at the camera. The adults were standing in the living room with their arms around one another. Most of them had kicked off their shoes and were standing on the plush rug in bare feet or socks. Other than Sandra's husband, who was out of view behind the camera, all the adults were beaming.

Sandra posted the picture on Facebook and wrote, "Wrapped up our Undivided groups tonight with potluck in each others houses. We have learned so much about becoming a racially reconciled Cincinnati and I'm looking forward to how we will walk this out in our journeys! The first step of more to come."

CHAPTER EIGHT

MY LITTLE REBELLION

Jess's group met at Patricia's one-and-a-half-story brick home for the final week of Undivided. Jess contributed her favorite homemade spinach dip with bacon and onions to the potluck. Someone else brought a roasted chicken. By then, the group had grown comfortable with one another. They scattered casually around the couches and chairs in the living room when they couldn't fit around the dining room table. Subsets of the group had been gathering each week at Steak 'n Shake after Undivided ended, where they never wanted their conversations to end. Jess sat next to Patricia that night as they shared stories about the struggle of being in long-term recovery. Hearing Patricia bemoan her child's situation made Jess wonder if her mother felt the same way Patricia did.

The next night, Jess was working at an Applebee's in Eastgate, just as she would most nights that fall. She liked the job and felt comfortable with the customers there. She waited tables during the week but bartended on high-volume nights, such as weekends and major holidays, working behind a large, horseshoe-shaped bar made of honey-colored wood. The lacquered counters separated her from her regulars, who were all "male, white, middle-class boomers." They would come in to drink, eat, and expound their opinions to anyone who would listen. Jess was frequently a closer, which meant she'd be left at the bar with regulars until two a.m. As the number of customers waned each night, the regulars would become more vocal with their thoughts.

She was at Applebee's on November 8, 2016, the culmination of the contentious 2016 presidential election. Eight TVs hung from the walls and ceiling around the bar, and every single one was tuned to the election returns. Jess had driven to her local polling place to vote earlier in the day. After voting, she posted a picture of herself in her car on Facebook, wearing a gray T-shirt with a blue cardigan and an "I Voted" sticker prominently pasted onto her lapel. A necklace with a silver cross pendant hung from her neck a few inches from her sticker. "Voting and praying for my country today," she wrote.

She knew it would be a rough night at Applebee's. All fall, her regulars had not been shy about their disdain for Hillary Clinton. They emboldened one another with their sexism and seemed impervious to the idea that Jess might object to their comments. Before starting her shift that night, she changed into her black Applebee's uniform. She momentarily thought about transferring her "I Voted" sticker to her shift shirt but decided against it. She kept her necklace on, though, because it felt like a touchstone as she weathered the relentless commentary. She knew many of her regulars thought Clinton's use of an inappropriate email server disqualified her from being able to be president. Jess could understand that. But the comments that still rankled years later revealed their unvarnished derision for women.

"A woman cannot run this country."

"Women are way too emotional to be president."

"What happens when she has her period?"

Jess's emotions frayed as the evening wore on. She was watching the election returns as she juggled orders and mixed drinks for her patrons. A famous Bible passage tells the story of Saul, who had been sent from Jerusalem to Damascus to arrest the followers of Jesus. On the way, he is knocked from his mule by a blinding light and receives a message from God. Saul is unable to see until several days later, when he receives the Holy Spirit and "something like scales fell from his eyes" (Acts 9:18). All fall, Jess had been incredulous at the excuses people were making for Trump. She couldn't believe the Christians who supported Trump loved the same God she loved. On election night at Applebee's, as she realized that Trump was winning, she felt like the final scales fell from her eyes. "Even coming through Undivided and learning what I learned, I was not seeing our politics through that racially motivated lens," she said. Until that night.

Jess mostly demurred or ignored her regulars when they made sexist or inappropriate comments. She knew it was hard for people with criminal records to find or keep a job, and she was grateful for her work at Applebee's. She didn't want to do anything to threaten it. It had been a rough year for her family. Her son's father had died of an overdose the previous year, and she desperately wanted to provide her son with some stability. She knew she needed employment to make that possible.

But that night was eroding the barricade of Jess's caution. Men were cheering as the news called state after state for Trump. Jess watched the numbers tick closer toward the 270 Electoral College votes Trump needed. She felt helpless. When she couldn't stand it any longer, she switched the TV behind the bar from Fox News to MSNBC. It was the only TV she controlled. "That was my little rebellion."

People groaned but Jess ignored them. She kept her eyes down and continued making drinks, hoping the complaints would dissipate before her manager said anything.

Changing the channel did nothing to change the election outcome. As the restaurant quieted after the dinner rush, the bar became noisier. Past midnight, when most of the tables in the restaurant were empty and the other servers were cleaning up, Jess was still mixing drinks for the patrons who stayed.

"That woman is not fit to be in charge," she remembers one of her regulars saying. Jess felt like he was baiting her. He had been picking fights with other customers all fall, and she knew he had a hard edge to his opinions. She had always ignored him, but now something stopped her from doing so. She thought of walking into the middle of the circle in Undivided when she heard the statement "I have stayed quiet when people made inappropriate comments about nondominant groups." Jess was hardly alone in the circle for that prompt, but she still didn't like being there. She spoke up.

"Oh, so we're only fit to serve you drinks, right?"

He laughed. "Yeah, you're good for that."

Her sarcasm contradicted his glee. She knew he expected her to laugh with him. She didn't. "Do you even know how to make the drink that I served to you?" she asked without a smile.

His eyes narrowed slightly as surprise flashed briefly across his face. Jess wondered if she had made a mistake. "No, no, I don't," he said, turning away from Jess to the person next to him. Jess touched her necklace and kept cleaning the dirty glasses.

～

Change depends on moving people beyond mere recognition of the problem to action. A perennial shortcoming of diversity programs is their general inability to change actual behavior. The gap between what people believe and what they do is so large that scholars have multiple names for it—the "opinion-action gap" or the "principle-implementation gap." Cynics like to decry such hypocrisy—expounding opinions is easier than standing up to fight. But action can also be stymied by a lack of strategic imagination. What kind of action could any one person take that would meaningfully help tackle problems as ingrained in society as racial injustice?

Lacking better answers, many reformers seek to fix social problems by fixing people—but doing so often avoids the structural roots of public problems. In 2002, Yale professor Michael Maniates coined the term "individualization of responsibility" to refer to the environmental movement's seeming unwillingness to pursue political solutions to environmentalism—despite overwhelming evidence that environmental degradation is deeply intertwined with structures of capitalism, lax government regulation, and ineffective policy. The trend toward individualization limited not just how people understood the problem but also the solutions they could imagine. Maniates described asking a group of forty-five Yale students at the end of a semester-long course on environmental problems to rank different solutions. He was disheartened to find that the students' most favored solutions focused on consumer choices—choosing to ride a bike instead of a car, recycling, and planting trees. When he asked why they did not consider policy and political solutions, they shrugged. Those solutions seemed so "fuzzy, mysterious, messy, and idealistic."

Individual and interpersonal solutions had the advantage of seeming clearer and more tractable than systemic solutions. That's why former vice president Al Gore told everyone to change their light bulbs at the end of a two-hour seminar on the global collapse of the Earth's climate in *An Inconvenient Truth*. President George W. Bush similarly told the American public to go to Disney World and not be afraid to go shopping after the 9/11 tragedy. Even if the actions felt performative, they were appealing because they engendered a sense of moral license. Just as confession absolved Christians of their sin, people who changed their light bulbs, bought American, or participated in a DEI training could feel absolved of their complicity in upholding discriminatory systems. Even if their actions made no dent in the fight against injustice, they could feel license to do no more.

The Undivided planning team wanted to move people beyond performative action. People who had felt powerless had to become authors of their own futures instead of consumers of someone else's vision. That was the challenge. By reverting to legalistic exhortations about what to do or reducing the complexity of racism to symbolic actions like buying tote bags, most DEI programs robbed people of the ability to wade into the complexity and identify their own solutions. Justice cannot spring from an abstract system that people do not feel they understand or control.

"We can't just take people through this journey and then drop them off after six weeks," Troy said. "They need an invitation to do something with it." As the sixth week of Undivided came to a close, Chuck, Lynn, Troy, and the other members of the planning team witnessed the small openings, the elusive glimmers of a different tomorrow created in people like Jess, Sandra, and Grant. But they knew they needed more. People needed somewhere to channel their efforts and a scaffolding to continue building their relationships.

The planning team decided to create a set of five "on-ramps" for people. These would present participants with five different opportunities to stay involved in the work of building racial solidarity beyond the six-week program. In 2016, the on-ramps included opportunities to get involved in a municipal campaign to pass a ballot initiative bringing universal preschool to the city's poorest Black children in Cincinnati; to get involved with prison ministries; to volunteer with CityLink Center, a local provider of wraparound services for the poor; and so on. Each of these opportunities varied in the extent to which they would connect participants with structural attempts to correct racial injustice. The Undivided planning team, however, felt that offering an array of options was more effective than trying to funnel everyone into one program. Most of all, they hoped the on-ramps would give people a place to sustain and nurture their nascent relationships.

Jess knew that the prison ministry program was the one for her. She wanted to work in women's prisons, where she could draw on her own experience to support the women who were still incarcerated. Maybe that would be a way to expand her "little rebellion"?

To participate in the prison ministry, Jess first had to attend a day-long training. That's where she met Grant. Grant had been responsible for building the prison ministry program within Crossroads several years earlier. As a child, his parents had long volunteered in the state penitentiary just outside Waynesville, Ohio, as missionaries for their faith. When Grant turned eighteen and was allowed into the prison, he joined them in the work. Eventually he and his wife cofounded their own program, the Four-Seven. The organization's name came from a Bible verse, Ephesians 4:7: "But each of us was given grace according to the measure of Christ's gift." The Four-Seven offered ministry to people not only when incarcerated, but also after they were released.

In 2015, Grant had successfully approached Crossroads about expanding the Four-Seven's work into the church's programming. The Four-Seven organized groups of Crossroads volunteers to visit local prisons each week, where they re-created some of the Crossroads small group experiences, led missionary groups for those in prison wrestling with faith, and ran life skills classes.

When the planning team chose the Four-Seven as one of its on-ramps, Grant developed a day-long training to incorporate Undivided volunteers into the Four-Seven. Jess attended a Saturday training at the Crossroads Mason campus, which was the closest to her home. A large boxy building off a four-lane suburban street housed the church. The Four-Seven volunteers met in a nondescript conference room, where Grant helped lead the training.

Jess, along with about twenty other people, participated for six hours, learning about background checks, security for volunteers in the prison, and the curricula they would be teaching.

Afterward, she approached Grant to speak privately. She was concerned that her felony record might preclude her from getting clearance as a volunteer. Grant reassured her. Unlike Jess, who was accustomed to being thwarted by bureaucracy, Grant was confident he could push through. He encouraged her to stick with the process, because her experience as an inmate would be more of an asset than a hindrance. Jess received clearance.

She was thrilled about the prospect of going back to prison as a volunteer. She thought ironically about all the guards who mocked her by telling her she would be back. *Ha!* As part of the Four-Seven, she would lead a small, racially mixed group of women through a curriculum like Undivided. She eagerly anticipated the opportunity to work with them.

Her enthusiasm soon turned to claustrophobia. When she entered the prison, Jess found herself feeling confined like an inmate again. She and the other volunteers met the incarcerated women in the prison's gym, sitting on squeaky folding chairs arranged in small circles. The high ceilings and wooden surfaces made noise ricochet loudly across the room. But Jess felt like she was trapped in a closet. She managed to stick through the first couple of weeks of volunteering, forcing herself to sound cheery as she tried to lead the women through an Undivided experience. Then she messaged the Four-Seven coordinator on Facebook: "I'm so sorry but I think I need a break," she wrote.

~

The anchor tenant in the enormous strip mall across the street from Crossroads Oakley was Kroger. A variety of other businesses established themselves around the grocery store, including Wild Eggs, a Midwestern chain serving breakfast and lunch, which was located on the edge of the parking lot. Jess met Patricia there some Sundays after services.

Jess and Patricia had become close after Undivided ended, but it wasn't easy to find ways to get together. Patricia had opted for a different on-ramp from the Four-Seven, and she lived on the opposite side of Cincinnati from Jess. Lacking natural opportunities to see each other, Wild Eggs had become their place. Jess loved the chance to get to know Patricia, who never sugar-coated things with her.

Since completing Undivided, Jess had been searching for more information online. One of the exercises in Undivided asked participants to pull out their phones to count the number of people of an opposite race in their contacts. The exercise forced them to consider their own echo chambers and confront the question of how deeply they engaged, or not, with others across race. Jess had plenty of cross-racial relationships because she had stayed in touch with women from prison. For her, however, the exercise highlighted how narrow the viewpoints on her social media feeds were. She intentionally started seeking out Black voices on social media.

As Jess dove into online groups dedicated to racial justice, she often didn't understand what the members were talking about. "Those spaces can be very unforgiving if you don't understand what's going on," she said. Referencing the tendency of extreme voices to dominate online discourse, Jess described the way online ideologues would "literally tear you apart" for using a politically incorrect term or asking a naive question. Even though Jess was sincere in her effort to learn, fear of being policed or castigated for her ignorance rendered her mute in those communities.

So Jess took her questions to Patricia instead. When Jess later learned about the concept of emotional labor from those she followed on social media, she was chagrined. She had never heard the term or considered the idea that she burdened the nonwhite people in her life by asking questions as she developed her own views on racial injustice in America. She brought it up with Patricia at Wild Eggs and apologized. Patricia told her not to worry. She agreed that it was not her job to educate Jess, but she also felt called by God to be in community with Jess.

Jess confessed to Patricia how uncomfortable she felt volunteering in prison. It would be so easy to quit. Jess was still finishing up her degree and trying to fit the Four-Seven in alongside her schoolwork, her job, and parenting. She knew no one would blame her if she took a break, especially Patricia, who understood the importance of maintaining emotional stability as someone in long-term recovery.

Patricia was older and more soft-spoken than Jess. She was quiet after Jess spoke, which made Jess nervous. Then Patricia asked her why she had brought this up.

Jess took a sip of coffee and considered Patricia's question. She felt like a hypocrite. Jess often posted memes on Facebook about the importance of action, which Patricia must have seen. She had shared a picture of George Washington with the words, "I didn't use my right to free speech to defeat the British. I shot them." She posted a Mary Shelley quote from *Frankenstein:* "I have LOVE in me the likes of which you can SCARCELY IMAGINE and RAGE the likes of which you would not believe. If I cannot satisfy one, I will indulge the other." An Ayn Rand quote, typeset against a spare background, read, "I can accept anything, except what seems to be the easiest for most people: the half-way, the almost, the just-about, the in-between."

That's what Jess felt like she was doing—accepting the almost at Applebee's on election night and contemplating walking away from the Four-Seven.

Patricia crumpled her napkin beside her empty plate. She was direct with Jess. "Are you stuck on stupid, parked on dumb? You can figure this out."

They talked it through. Patricia knew that being in the prisons was not easy for Jess, and she was not asking Jess to continue. She knew that Jess needed her job and that she had to be cautious about pushing back on the customers. But she also knew that Jess was really asking whether these choices made her a coward, or someone who abandoned the commitments they had made to each other in Undivided. Patricia asked Jess to contemplate what she felt God was calling her to do after Undivided.

Jess wasn't sure what the answer was. Undivided had inspired Jess to act but she couldn't find her footing and worried she would fall off the path.

CHAPTER NINE

THE NEW JIM CROW

Throughout most of 2016, Grant drove a silver Toyota Prius about 150 miles each day commuting from Waynesville to Columbus for work. Earlier that year, he had taken a job as the deputy communications chief of the Ohio state prison system. Historically, in his view, the prison system had neglected its purported responsibility to not only imprison people but also rehabilitate them. Because of some inscrutable mix of expedience, political pressure, and moral commitment, the head of the system decided he needed to do more to support rehabilitation. Grant's entrepreneurialism with the Four-Seven put him in the director's sights. This job gave Grant the chance to integrate his work in the correctional system with his communications background. He started the new position just as he was completing Undivided. Not yet thirty years old, he was now in a prominent leadership role in a system that had twelve thousand employees and more than forty thousand imprisoned people. Grant savored the opportunity.

About a week after Undivided ended, a prisoner escaped from a correctional facility in southern Ohio, and the department went into crisis mode. Grant's direct boss, who was the head of communications for the entire system, was unavailable because her father had just died. The circumstances pushed Grant into crisis leadership. He thrived. For twenty-four hours, he was part of the war room, working with senior leadership throughout the system to manage media and communications until the escapee was captured. Grant loved the rapid pace, the need for quick decision-making, and the sense that the stakes were high. When he drove home after the capture, it was pitch-dark. Yet Grant felt confident and free cruising through the empty roads to his home in Waynesville.

Most days, though, the roads were not so empty. He had to time his drive around traffic to minimize what was already a long commute. He usually left at six thirty in the morning, to try to be in his office in Columbus by eight a.m. After Undivided, instead of listening to podcasts or music on the commute, he started listening to books on tape. He loved consuming information but hated reading books, preferring osmosis to concentration ("The only books I've read on paper cover to cover are the three Lord of the Rings books and *The Hobbit*," he once said.) He usually favored news articles and frequently stayed up late scrolling through the news on his phone. But during Undivided, someone recommended Michelle Alexander's book *The New Jim Crow*.

Undivided had left him hungry for insight over information. He was still enmeshed in conversations with Hunt about his experience as a Black person in their family, and he thought Alexander's book might help him make meaning of his new learning. Grant was realizing that the protective cocoon his family had tried to form around Hunt separated him from the centuries of Black struggle and self-determination that preceded them. They had attempted to obscure racial oppression instead of confronting it.

Hunt humbled him. Through their conversations, Grant realized, perhaps for the first time, that *his* truth might not be *the* truth. He knew that Alexander's book was about racial subjugation in the criminal justice system in America. He also knew that, whether through ignorance or willful blindness, he had never before considered the racialized aspects of the correctional facilities where he had long been active. Of course, he knew that many of the inmates were Black, but he rarely considered why. Reality can be a one-way mirror when life is good. He simply assumed that Black people were more likely to commit crimes, and that if poverty drove them to it, poverty was a function of people's own unwillingness to work for what they needed.

Growing up in Waynesville, it had not been hard to ignore the complex history of the Black experience in America. Many white communities enshroud it. Grant was an adult before he realized that his hometown had a series of tunnels beneath the town square that were part of the Underground Railroad. Perched on a hill that gave lookouts a good view of impending threats, the historic Hammel House on Waynesville's Main Street had been an important waystation on the railroad. Grant had visited Hammel House many times as a child and had assumed that its history was only about white people. He never thought to ask about anyone else.

Without any understanding of the way structural racism entangled with American life, Grant had thought that providing personal acts of service and mercy was enough. He committed to prison ministry with his characteristic energy. He got his fourth tattoo, in fact, because he wanted to find better ways to relate to those he served in prison. He thought it would give him something in common to discuss with the prisoners. He went to a tattoo parlor with Hunt and asked the artists to etch a Bible verse, John 3:16, onto his chest. John 3:16 is one of the world's most quoted Bible verses: "For God so loved the world that he gave his one and only Son, so that everyone who believes in him may not perish but may have eternal life." Grant preferred the next verse, which he thought was overlooked: "Indeed, God did not send the Son into the world to condemn the world, but in order that the world might be saved through him." He had a version of the first part of the phrase "For God did not send his Son to condemn the world" tattooed in large calligraphy script across his chest. It stretched from one shoulder to the other in a semicircle just beneath his collarbone. He left the parlor looking forward to showing off his new tattoo to the men in prison.

That day, as Grant and Hunt were about to get into the car, Hunt noticed that Grant's new tattoo had a spelling error. The silent "n" had been left out of *condemn*. Grant had the tattooist squeeze the letter in. Even with the awkward mistake (or perhaps because of it), the tattoo went over so well with the imprisoned men that Grant kept getting more.

~

After Undivided, and after listening to Alexander's book in the car, Grant could no longer walk into the office and ignore what he saw. Alexander's book provided a powerful indictment of the pervasive effects of racism throughout the country's criminal justice system. "I didn't know what an echo chamber was until Undivided," Grant said. "And I had been in a massive freaking echo chamber of people who only want to be reaffirmed in their way of thinking. That was me." After swimming in the waters of his own privilege for many years, Grant had finally flopped onto dry land. And, instead of getting back in the water, he committed to learning to breathe in a new environment. He realized that he had what he would later describe as a "white savior complex." His good deeds had seemed more important than the problem he was ostensibly seeking to address. Grant began to question his work. He needed somewhere to turn.

Since Undivided ended, Sandra and Grant had become friends. During the program, Sandra had pointedly asked Grant how many Black people Hunt knew. Ashamed of his answer, Grant invited Sandra and her family to their home in Waynesville for dinner. Sandra brought her husband and her biracial children to meet

Hunt and the rest of Grant's family. Grant and Kyla, who was pregnant with their first child, lived with his parents in his childhood home. Sandra was simultaneously pregnant with her third child, so she and Kyla began commiserating over their pregnancies. Their families became close. Sandra's husband, who had been reluctant to get to know many of the people she was meeting through Undivided, felt comfortable with Grant. Grant was white, male, and conservative like he was. The friendship worked for both families.

Both Sandra and Grant got to know Michelle through involvement with the Four-Seven. Michelle was a Black woman in her midthirties with walnut-colored skin who had gone through the Undivided program with Sandra and Grant. She had been in a different small group, and hers had not clicked the same way Sandra and Grant's group did. Early in the program, a white woman in Michelle's group told her that Michelle "intimidated" her because she spoke so "strongly." Michelle was incensed. *That is her problem, not mine,* she thought to herself. *I should not have to submit to her insecurities or shrink my confidence because of her.* Michelle continued to be outspoken during Undivided. The white woman withdrew into herself. In a small group, one recalcitrant person can limit the experience for everyone else. It was easier for the group to stay at a level of platitudes instead of digging into the tensions. When it came time for the potluck dinner during the sixth week, Michelle decided to skip it.

Nonetheless, when the opportunity to participate in the on-ramps emerged, Michelle wanted to stay involved. She had grown up in Cincinnati in a predominantly white family. She had a white mother and a Black father, but Michelle's father had never been part of her life. She lived with her mother, who had three older white children from a previous relationship. Two unabashedly racist uncles threatened to shun Michelle's mom for having a child with a Black man. Michelle remembers visiting her grandparents, and watching her mother scan the cars outside their house when they arrived. If she saw that one of her brothers was there, she would tell Michelle, "Stay here while I go inside." Michelle's mother would leave Michelle to play alone in the car. Even a mother's grasping efforts at protection can disguise unspeakable harm.

Michelle nonetheless refused to be ashamed of being Black. She grew up in low-income housing developments in Cincinnati, where the schools she attended and the communities to which she belonged outside of her family were largely Black. Other Black families invited her to attend church with them, or she attended a white Mormon church with her mom.

She first went to Crossroads when a friend invited her, but she continued to attend because of its extensive work in the local community. She hated hearing about the missionary work other churches were doing abroad, ignoring the poverty in Cincinnati's neighborhoods. The first weekend she attended Crossroads, a sermon series called I Love Cincinnati highlighted their extensive service programs and investments in the city, including in neighborhoods where Michelle had lived. *This is my church,* she thought. She got to know Grant and Sandra when they all volunteered in the Four-Seven.

After listening to Michelle Alexander's book in the morning and working in the Department of Rehabilitation and Correction all day, Grant would occasionally call Sandra or Michelle on the way home. Undivided pushed him to reconsider his experiences in the prison system through the lens of racial justice, and as he got deeper into his reflection, he found himself calling them more and more frequently. Michelle, at the time, was between jobs and had more free time than Sandra, so she and Grant spent long hours on the phone. Grant described incidents he witnessed at work so that Michelle, and Sandra when she was available, could help him make sense of them. He asked them what else to read, and they recommended Bryan Stevenson's *Just Mercy* (a memoir documenting Stevenson's work as a lawyer within a discriminatory criminal justice system) and Jemar Tisby's *The Color of Compromise* (a history of the relationship between Christianity and race).

In one conversation that Grant, Michelle, and Sandra had at the Four-Seven offices in Mason, Michelle described her interactions with the white woman in her small group during Undivided, and her unwillingness to "submit to her insecurity."

Grant responded by describing an instance when he felt Michelle "came at" him. "We're good friends, [but] I was intimidated by you in that moment."

Michelle, peeved, couldn't help raising her voice a little. "Were you intimidated by me, or by the truth?" she asked Grant.

"I don't think it was the truth," Grant said. "Because I didn't disagree with what you said."

"How did I intimidate?" Michelle demanded.

They were sitting at a long table, with Michelle and Sandra next to each other on one side, and Grant across from them. Grant felt like he was being interrogated. He started to speak more slowly. He explained that even though they were friends, when he spoke about certain things, "I want to make sure that what I'm saying is what I'm trying to say. . . . There were times when we were having that discussion where I was trying to formulate my thoughts and I couldn't get them out because you responded before I could talk." Further, Grant noted, "You're very visually demonstrative."

Michelle was indignant at Grant's use of the word *demonstrative.* "That's a very strong word," she said. She and Sandra exchanged looks with each other, raising their eyebrows.

Grant tried to defend himself. "Right now, I can see on your face that you don't necessarily agree with me. . . . [It makes me feel like] you [are] giving me a look with every word that's coming out.

I felt like I had to be careful what I said, because like . . . You're looking at me now. Your eyes are getting a little more closed. . . . You don't even realize you're doing it."

"No, I know *exactly* what I'm doing," Michelle said.

Grant tried to back off. "Okay. Never mind. Then I take that back. I apologize."

Michelle sighed, exasperated. She looked at Sandra, and they tried to explain why Grant should not call Black women demonstrative. "White folks who created our democracy created the idea of what civil and non-civil is," Sandra interjected. "I think we're all in agreement here that American culture and Western culture is dominated and created by whiteness, right?"

Grant nodded slowly.

"I can be talking to Michelle and I can be having these same expressions and squints on my face, and we can be talking very loudly to each other," Sandra said. "This is a rousing conversation [to us]. This is fun." But, as Black women, Sandra explained that if she and Michelle had the same conversation with a white person, they were branded as "aggressive" or "angry Black women." People would ask them to tone it down. "What they're really saying is 'Can you whitewash this conversation so that I do not feel intimidated by your Blackness?'"

Grant sat back, realizing he had never thought of that before.

Humility did not come easily to Grant. He was the kid who stood on a rock pontificating to anyone who would listen. He was the adult who loved being in the nerve center of a statewide manhunt. He stayed preternaturally calm under stress because he was so confident in his own abilities. But Sandra, and then Michelle, kept undercutting that confidence, pointing out to him how limited his view was. For Grant, it was unfamiliar. And unnerving.

But his friendships with Sandra and Michelle anchored him in his quest to navigate anxiety. His parents, who had always been very welcoming, loved Sandra and Michelle. He and Kyla were growing attached to Sandra's young children. And he knew that Hunt loved their family, too. "We didn't start with disagreement," Sandra said. "We started with relationship."

Grant also felt increasingly disconnected from his long-standing political commitments. Prominent evangelical pastors who consistently supported Trump, arguing that he was sent by God, alienated Grant. Trump was testing the ability of any evangelical institution to stay neutral in the conversation about racism in America. He deliberately inflamed people's prejudices toward immigrants, Black people, and other racial minorities to generate support for his presidency. Grant did not like his faith being associated with what he thought were Trump's extreme political views. He felt unmoored from the political institutions that had long structured his life.

Uncertainty slithered from one domain of his life to another. Grant questioned his professional choices as well. *What am I doing here? Why am I in this job?* he asked himself. He wrestled with what it meant to be part of a system that oppressed so many people. He thought about quitting. "Going to the prison cannot be like going to a petting zoo," Michelle told Grant about the Four-Seven.

One day, Michelle volunteered at a correctional facility with a group from Crossroads. She was the only nonwhite woman in the group. When the volunteers arrived, they all had to go through the usual security checks to ensure they were not bringing any contraband into the prison or wearing anything the state deemed inappropriate. For most people, the checks were no problem. A white security guard, however, refused to let Michelle enter. Her jeans, she claimed, were too tight, going against prison regulations. When Michelle pointed out that other white women in the group were wearing similarly fitted jeans, the guard shrugged, confident that her little exertion of power would yield no consequences. Michelle seethed. She went to a nearby Walmart and bought another pair of jeans so she'd be allowed to enter the prison.

Afterward, Michelle was determined to obviate such obstruction in the future. She called Grant the next time she knew he would be in his car driving home from work. At first, Grant suggested that Michelle talk to the group leader to ask him to intervene. Michelle refused.

"I have spent my entire life having to tell people why they should do something about it. It's about time someone like you stood in the gap for me."

For the first time, Michelle was challenging Grant to use his power in the prison system to act. He didn't equivocate.

Grant addressed the guards at the correctional facility to ensure that such incidents would not occur in the future. He worked with the team at the Four-Seven to alter the training they provided so that other volunteers could be better equipped in the future to help people like Michelle when they encountered injustice. He advocated for instituting better training for security guards throughout the state correctional system.

He also began to engage in his own introspection. *How many opportunities have I missed to stand in the gap for someone else?* he asked himself.

When he and Michelle debriefed this incident later, Grant wondered if he should leave the prison system altogether. "Hey, God has you there for a reason," Michelle told him.

Grant, in his Prius driving home, wondered what that reason was.

CHAPTER TEN

THE JUSTICE TEAM

In October 2016, Sandra marched around the courthouse in downtown Cincinnati to advocate for justice in the trial of Ray Tensing. Tensing was a twenty-five-year-old white University of Cincinnati police officer who had shot and killed an unarmed Black man, Samuel DuBose, the year before. The murder began with a routine traffic stop, when Tensing pulled DuBose over for driving a car with a missing front license plate. He discovered that DuBose had a suspended license and opened the car door, ordering him to step out. DuBose pulled the door closed and started the engine. Tensing yelled, "Stop! Stop!" to prevent DuBose from driving away. He reached into the car window with his left hand and drew his pistol with his right hand, firing one fatal shot into DuBose's head. As details of the killing emerged, Cincinnati erupted in anger. Tensing had a long record of racist policing and had been wearing a T-shirt emblazoned with a Confederate flag underneath his police uniform. Protesters filled the city's downtown, demanding justice for DuBose. At the end of July 2015, Tensing was indicted on charges of murder and voluntary manslaughter.

Tensing's trial threatened to cleave the city apart. The shooting occurred three months after Chuck first made his public call to take action around race and five miles south of the Oakley campus where Chuck declared his commitment to racial justice. Chuck had just begun to assemble a team within the church to develop what would become Undivided, and people like Sandra had been part of an outpouring of support for this work. The killing of DuBose "brought what had been happening in the world to our city," as Chuck put it. State-sanctioned police brutality and racial injustice no longer felt abstract.

When Tensing's body cam video was released to the public in July 2015, Crossroads organized a prayer vigil that Sandra attended. Five thousand people showed up. The video had inflamed the public outcry for justice because it undermined Tensing's claim that he had been dragged by DuBose's car before he killed him. Sandra was tense when she went to the vigil.

"We should weep at what God weeps at, and God is weeping. God weeps at injustice," Chuck preached at the vigil. Sandra felt relief wash over her. Until that moment, she hadn't realized how nervous she was that her church would try to excuse Tensing's actions.

The trial of Ray Tensing began in late October, 2016, just before the 2016 presidential election. The Amos Project, a faith-based community organizing group, immediately assembled prayer vigils outside the courthouse and invited other justice-oriented groups to join. Troy, the former pastor turned community organizer on the Undivided planning team, was then the executive director of Amos, and he invited Undivided participants to the march. Sandra noticed white onlookers peering out of windows as she marched with DuBose supporters. Walking along the edge of Over-the-Rhine, she saw a cluster of white women and their children playing in a park that never used to have any white people. Through a mix of public and private investments, parts of the neighborhood had gentrified in the early decades of the twenty-first century. As Jess put it, "It went from attracting junkies to attracting foodies." Sandra had never been to New York, but people told her those parts of Over-the-Rhine looked like the hipster parts of Brooklyn. Close by was a donut shop that sold five-dollar donuts. The scrutiny of these white people unnerved Sandra.

Sandra was there with the Justice Team, which had emerged after Undivided as an incubator for ongoing action to fight racial injustice. Troy had proposed the idea after the first session of Undivided ended. He believed in the importance of what community organizers called a "long-term vehicle for change" to nurture the inspiration people felt after Undivided and ensure it was properly channeled. The on-ramps helped, but Troy felt they needed something more. As a trained organizer, he knew that even when moments of widespread activism propel social change efforts into public consciousness, the vast majority falter afterward. Too often, activism fails to translate into anything durable. A 2009 study randomly selected ninety-eight efforts to alter federal policy in Congress for analysis and showed that they failed 70 percent of the time. Status quo prevailed most often because it reflected existing distributions of power in society. Even change efforts that demonstrated broad grassroots support for their goals won only 50 percent of the time, no better than flipping a coin.

To have a chance at challenging entrenched power, grassroots efforts had to build a powerful base. Troy knew that Undivided needed to create a venue for people from the program to continue working with one another, strengthening a latticework of relationships that could establish the required foundation. Undivided might have shaped people's motivations to fight racial injustice, but they needed to deepen their commitments to one another and learn to strategize together about what kind of intentional action they could take. Troy worried that without something like the Justice Team, people's commitments to racial justice after Undivided could become performative.

Troy's views formed in part from his research into the historical development of the Christian Right. He realized that much of that group's strength within politics came not from their standing in the media, but from their ability to mobilize grassroots leaders who took over local Republican Party institutions. Troy learned that the Christian Right's boots-on-the-ground organizing program had been carefully designed in the 1990s by two men, Pat Robertson and Ralph Reed. Robertson was the famous televangelist who ran for president in the 1988 Republican primary. He used his enormous television platform to raise more money than any other candidate, but performed abysmally at the polls. Robertson's striking loss in the primary sidelined him within the Republican Party, dashing his political aspirations. That campaign taught Robertson a lesson that many political advocates take years to learn—namely, that scale and power are not the same thing.

Robertson had spent years building a communications network that was ineffective for shaping politics. In 1989, however, he attended a fateful dinner where he happened to be seated next to a young political operative named Ralph Reed. Reed had entered Republican Party politics through his involvement with College Republicans. He had a born-again experience when he attended an evangelical church on a lark because he had been feeling unfulfilled by his political work. At the end of the service, the pastor called out to people who were at church for the first time. "This is not an invitation," the pastor said. "This is a command." The command was to accept Jesus as their savior. Reed accepted.

Shortly thereafter, Reed was sitting at his desk listening to his coworkers mock people who believed in creationism. To their urbane political ears, it seemed preposterous. They couldn't fathom anyone would really believe it.

Reed hesitated for one moment but then spoke up. "I believe it," he said.

They laughed, assuming he was kidding. When they realized

he was serious, they laughed again—at him. It was the first of many times when Reed, like many evangelicals living in a secular society, would have to defend his beliefs against the dominant norm. These experiences taught Reed an important political lesson: inaction enables the powerful to maintain their standing. Reed felt that if Christians did nothing, secular modernism would dominate the shape of the world around them. Reed devoted himself to learning to build an active political machine.

Reed spent that 1989 dinner offering his critique of Robertson's campaign for the presidential nomination. Robertson was intrigued by what the young but experienced politico had to say. Having built his career through broadcasting, Robertson had thought that projecting himself into people's living rooms each day would be enough to win an election. Reed said the Christian Right might have an effective air game, but they would never be able to win elections or wield any real political clout unless they built a similarly effective ground game. Robertson enlisted Reed to come work for him.

Together, Robertson and Reed sketched an audacious vision for what would become the Christian Coalition, the lynchpin that would firmly institutionalize the relationship between evangelicalism and the Republican Party. Black churches, they observed, had shown in the 1950s and 1960s that faith institutions could develop effective political ground games. Conservative white churches had not yet ventured into this territory, instead focusing on building relationships with media and political insiders. As Reed described it, most white conservative Christians still "had their noses pressed against the glass of the political culture." So Reed and Robertson set out to penetrate this world, developing what they called a "pro-family agenda" focused on instilling Christian values in public life.

The Christian Coalition's strategy was built on taking over the local party organizations that constituted the Republican base.

Reed started by obtaining church directories and recruiting evangelicals to do the work of local politics. Anyone he found who was not registered to vote would receive a call to register. Then he would train them to do their own voter registration drives, build their own precinct organizations, and effectively take over the local Republican Party without violating the tax-exempt status of the church.

When he first began to contact clergy to ask them to share their church directories or reach out to congregants to ask them to vote, he encountered some resistance. Evangelicals were not accustomed to associating church with politics and resisted the idea of political activity in their church.

"If you choose to disengage [from politics]," Reed would reply, "it will show up on your doorstep in public policies that will undermine and assault your beliefs."

The Christian Coalition built an army of Christian foot soldiers who took over the local apparatus of the Republican Party. They were no longer pawns in someone else's electoral game or TV personalities subject to the changing whims of a fickle audience. Instead, they controlled the game itself.

Troy contrasted what Reed had built with what was emerging from Undivided. Sandra, Jess, Grant, and others were moving from a sense of isolation to a sense of community and finding the tools they needed to speak out about injustice in their own lives. But was it adding up to something more?

Troy reached out to Chuck and Lynn to consider that something more. It was like pushing on an open door. All three of them knew that, within Crossroads, the urge to focus only on relationships was like a magnet pulling away from addressing structural injustice—unless they made an explicit effort to create a countervailing pull toward it.

Chuck, Lynn, and Troy worked together to organize an exploratory meeting in downtown Cincinnati in March 2016, after the first session of Undivided ended. They recruited some of the most ardent Undivided supporters to attend, including Carolyn, the soft-spoken, gentle white woman who had become friends with Sandra. Carolyn invited Sandra to attend the brainstorming meeting as well. In total, about fifteen people showed up at CityLink Center, a holistic social services provider in downtown Cincinnati that Crossroads had helped start. The building had the flavor of a slightly upscale government building. Nervous that hosting a meeting about launching justice-oriented work in Crossroads would not be prudent, Chuck thought CityLink Center would be good neutral ground. Sandra arrived with Carolyn, then sat in the back so she could entertain her toddler during the meeting.

Chuck and Lynn opened by describing what they thought the Justice Team could do and how it built on their work at Undivided. People were enthusiastic about the idea of doing something, but cautious about doing this kind of work in Crossroads. The church never overtly focused on social justice. Chuck and Lynn asked attendees whether they thought they could recruit other congregants to their cause. The prospect of resistance from within Crossroads began to crystallize in people's minds as they considered the question.

Sandra thought back to the first vigil she had attended the year before when Tensing's body cam video was first released. She remembered how relieved she had been when Chuck spoke forcefully for justice. But Crossroads was a growing megachurch in a divided city in a divided state in a divided nation in 2016. It sought the middle ground, not justice. It contained within it those who were pro-Trump and anti-Trump, Republican and Democrat, pro–gun rights and pro–gun violence prevention. Like many other megachurches, it tried to sidestep most controversial questions regarding race. Sandra knew that some in the community were more accustomed to the church trying to take both sides than seeking justice.

Troy got worried when the meeting began to flag. People had real doubts, and he wanted to do something to try to renew the session's momentum. Earlier, he had noticed that Carolyn and another woman named Elizabeth had each brought several other people with them to the meeting. Elizabeth was a light-skinned Black woman with curly hair who had participated in the first Undivided cohort with Sandra, Grant, and Carolyn, but in a different small group. Troy knew that the ability to draw others into action is the mark of a good organizer. Impulsively and perhaps too aggressively, he asked Carolyn and Elizabeth in front of the entire room, "Do the two of you want to try leading the work?"

Carolyn and Elizabeth were surprised by Troy's request, but also thrilled. Troy's ploy succeeded. The meeting regained momentum with Carolyn and Elizabeth's commitment to leadership, and the Justice Team became a reality.

~

Carolyn and Elizabeth spent the summer of 2016 working with each other and Troy to lay the groundwork for the team. Troy trained them on the basic practices of faith-based community organizing and encouraged them to set up individual meetings with a wide range of people to recruit them to the Justice Team. He also invited them to attend an annual week-long training at ISAIAH, the Minnesota-based federation of Faith in Action, the nation's largest faith-based community organizing network. ISAIAH's intensive training focused on motivating people and building skills for organizing. Those who had never organized before often experienced the training as jarring. It aggressively prodded them to identify then vanquish the barriers preventing them from taking action to cultivate the world they wanted.

In one exercise, all of the participants had to read and enact a version of Thucydides's Melian Dialogue, the negotiation between leaders of ancient Athens and Melos. The Melian leaders debated how to handle an invasion by Athens. Outmatched by the Athenians and facing sure loss, the Melian leaders could either encourage their citizens to fight and die as free men or survive as enslaved people. Facilitators randomly assigned Carolyn, Elizabeth, and the other participants to be either Melians or Athenians. The exercise excavated people's orientation toward power, authority, and choice.

At one point, Elizabeth and several other participants were banished from the room because they were asking too many questions. Initially disconsolate, Elizabeth soon became defiant. She realized the game's facilitator had arbitrarily exercised power by kicking them out. She convinced the others in the hallway to march back into the room with her.

Noticing their return, the facilitator immediately pounced on Elizabeth. "What are you doing back in here?" he asked.

"You can't kick us out," she responded. She spoke proudly, thinking she had discovered the point of the exercise. She could stand up to authority.

"I can't?" he asked. His question felt derisive to Elizabeth. "But what are you going to do about it? You have no power here." He stared directly at her.

Elizabeth realized she hadn't thought about what to do next. She shrank back into the wall, deflated by his challenge. She stayed silent for the rest of the simulation.

Later, when they were debriefing the exercise, the facilitator asked her why she backed down. "Who told you your ideas were dumb?" he asked. He had been pushing her toward the next step in establishing her leadership, but she had cowered away. Elizabeth cried.

Designed to uproot people from complacency, the training also equipped them to act on the convictions they professed. Instead of being put off by these kinds of challenging interactions, Carolyn and Elizabeth both finished the week feeling inspired. They each began to shed fears they had long harbored about making people uncomfortable and became more willing to step into the urgency they felt to seek racial justice. Few things are more powerful than people grounded in their own interests, connected to each other, committed to putting their hands on the levers of change. They both returned to Cincinnati ready to build the Justice Team. They decided to put together their own training about organizing for new recruits. They scheduled a meeting for a Saturday morning at Crossroads and invited everyone on their list. They had no idea how many would show up.

Around one hundred forty people, including Sandra, came. Sandra did not want to take on a leadership role, but she was inspired by Carolyn's commitment to antiracism. She and Carolyn had been getting to know each other through hours at the playground, talking and watching their toddlers together. The combination of Carolyn's gentle manner and her steely resolve to act buoyed Sandra. Carolyn wasn't like the other white people she knew. Sandra felt that she could fully embrace her Black identity around Carolyn, even more than she could at home with her husband. And, through the Justice Team, Sandra found a pathway to live out commitments to her Black identity that she had long ignored.

When Sandra came home after the vigil around the courthouse, she wrote on Facebook, "Got to spend some time down at the courthouse this morning praying for those involved with the upcoming Tensing trial. I got to walk a couple laps around the courthouse with some powerful women of God, inviting God's presence in and around this trial! . . . What an amazing thing to see people of faith come together from all different backgrounds to support this city in racial reconciliation. Pray for Cincinnati, times they are a changin'."

～

The next few weeks were intense. Working alongside Amos, the community organizing group that Troy led, the Justice Team tried to keep up their vigil at the courthouse, even as they volunteered for the final weeks of the citywide campaign for universal preschool in Cincinnati. The November 2016 ballot initiative, Issue 44, constituted the culmination of a years-long effort in Cincinnati. A "People's Platform" designed by Amos articulated a set of principles that shaped the proposed policy. Included were targeted resources for the city's poorest children to address racial disparities, good wages for the many Black women who ran home-based preschool programs in the Black community, and the ability of parents to have a voice in shaping the program. Because the initiative would raise taxes to fund the policy, Issue 44 was not an easy sell.

The Justice Team had been actively volunteering in the campaign for months. Sandra was uncomfortable with the idea of cold-calling people or knocking on strangers' doors, so Carolyn and Elizabeth crafted a role for her that played to her strengths: she was to find a prayer or reflection to initiate each of their meetings. Eventually, she started developing these prayer guides not only for their monthly meetings, but also for big events (like the marches and vigils around the Tensing trial), the trainings the group conducted, and sometimes even the weekly phone banks. Sandra loved her role. She pored over her Bible and her book of reflections, drawing on her years of experience in the church to develop appropriate prayers for each event, each crisis.

Her prayers added to the meaning of the work. Over the course of the fall, 250 people from Undivided volunteered for the campaign to pass the levy. The campaign manager for Issue 44, a hardened veteran of state and national politics, noted that municipal levies almost never draw volunteerism like that. "This became a *mission* [for the Justice Team] to live out its faith in the real world," he said, "to put their faith in action in the community."

And it worked. Sandra was thrilled when Issue 44 won so overwhelmingly on Election Day.

The heady joy of working for the first time with a team of people from her church to make change in the world was addictive for Sandra—even though some of her white friends kept disparaging the work. The impact they were having felt tangible, real. She remembers talking to another Black volunteer on the Justice Team. "Man, this is pretty cool," he said. "A big church like Crossroads, majority white, diving into social issues—and asking what would Jesus really be doing? I'm feeling like the tide is changing."

But the Justice Team's ebullient joy was short-lived. By the time Election Day rolled around, Sandra, like everyone else on the team, was exhausted. In the final heady push before the election, the desiderata of everyday life had fallen by the wayside. She needed to catch up on sleep, laundry, grocery shopping, and paperwork from her kids' schools. But the week after the election brought more emotional upheaval.

Just a few days after Election Day, the trial for Ray Tensing ended, and the jurors went into deliberation. Some members of the Justice Team were at the Hamilton County Courthouse when the judge called the court back into session to announce the jury's decision. People gathered together on the courthouse steps. (Sandra couldn't attend because of the impending birth of her third child.) Using his phone to stream a video feed from the courtroom, Troy held a bullhorn against the phone to project the audio into the crowd. They quieted and strained to hear.

After three days of deliberation, four of the twelve jurors voted against a voluntary manslaughter conviction, and the judge announced a mistrial. As news of the decision spread through the weary protesters outside the courthouse, the crowd was eerily quiet. The next day, Troy wrote in his journal, "The pace, intensity and pressure of the past three months was intense, the past three weeks insane, and the past three days, unsustainable." Hoping to forestall the city's anger, the prosecution quickly announced it would seek a retrial, creating hope that a different outcome was possible.

Sandra, who had been listening to the news of the verdict at home, gazed at her children's Black faces. She wondered what kind of world they would inherit as she listened to the judge's voice. Her despondency felt palpable.

PART TWO

BACKLASH

CHAPTER ELEVEN

I TOLD THEM I WAS BLACK

Chuck screamed into the hills of Kentucky. It was late June 2017 and he had ventured into the woods for a walk. *It's just me and God*, he thought. He tore branches from the trees and whipped the trunks around him. Heaving sobs wracked his body as he shouted his anger into the natural world.

Chuck was spending a week at the Abbey of Gethsemani, a Roman Catholic Trappist monastery located about an hour south of Louisville, Kentucky. The monastery was set on fifteen hundred acres of undeveloped land marked by trails hikers have carved over decades. Home to monks who live there year-round, the monastery opened itself to members of the public who wanted to participate in silent retreats. The visits were unstructured and self-guided, following Thomas Merton's exhortation to "entertain silence in the heart and listen for the voice of God." Every year, Chuck made a pilgrimage to the abbey to deepen his relationship with God and safeguard his ongoing commitment to recovery from his pornography addiction.

In the summer of 2017, his visit to the abbey coincided with a one-month sabbatical from Crossroads. He had been on staff for a decade, and the church gave people a special gift when they reached the milestone. Chuck asked for four weeks off. It had been an eventful ten years. Chuck had gone into recovery and successfully managed his addiction. He had become the lead pastor of the church's largest and original campus, Oakley. He and Maria had three children and steadily nurtured their relationship. He had founded and launched Undivided during one of the most tumultuous election years in American history and had become part of a campaign that won universal preschool for poor Black children in his city.

As he anticipated his sabbatical, controversy over Tensing's second trial persisted. A new trial date had been set for June, and a series of competing courtroom motions around the trial had dominated local news in the preceding months. Lawyers debated what evidence was admissible in the second trial, resulting in a ruling that prosecutors could not present the Confederate battle flag T-shirt Tensing wore at the time of the shooting. *How,* Chuck wondered, *could Tensing's views of Black men be irrelevant in the eyes of the law?*

The Tensing controversy also forced Chuck to grapple with his own public leadership in trying to advance racial justice. During the 2016 campaign for Issue 44, Troy had asked Chuck to join the board of directors for the Amos Project. As a member of the board, Chuck had cosigned a letter from the Countdown to Conviction, a coalition of organizations across Cincinnati who joined forces to pressure the city to seek justice for Samuel DuBose. Step by step, Chuck was taking increasingly public stances, even controversial ones, on issues of racial justice.

He was simultaneously navigating the pressures of continuing to pastor the Oakley community at Crossroads, where controversies around the Tensing trial had become very pointed. Tensing was related to one of the eleven people who constituted the original founding team of the church. Tensing himself sometimes attended services at Oakley as unobtrusively as possible. The details of the church's relationship to Tensing were not public at the time, and even most people in Undivided and the Justice Team did not know. But as campus pastor, Chuck knew.

Among Christian faith traditions, evangelicalism has always had a particularly strong focus on second chances. The controversy around Tensing and his actions, however, tested the limits of Chuck's forgiveness. In America's fight over who belongs, who deserves dignity, and who gets to decide, even the clergy responsible for shepherding our souls sometimes struggle. *How do I hold the tension in that moment when I'm pastoring to both sides of this experience?* he asked himself. *But at the same time, what does it look like to be a voice for truth?*

The Black church of his youth had always inculcated a strong sense of Black pride in Chuck, which came to fruition through his activities in college. Chuck had been president of the Black Student Union and worked to elevate Black voices on campus. He immersed himself in authors like Michael Eric Dyson, Carter G. Woodson, and a set of Black nationalist poets known as the Last Poets to deepen his understanding of Black intellectual traditions. All of those experiences formed the backdrop to his work with Undivided, and he was proud of the impact he thought they were having. Following Undivided's success in 2016, Chuck didn't want the response to Tensing's second trial to be a moment when the church would "shrink back" from antiracism.

These tensions followed Chuck into his month-long sabbatical. He spent the first week at a Colorado retreat designed to provide respite for pastors experiencing burnout. Chuck wasn't necessarily feeling burned out—he was buoyed by Undivided and the success of Issue 44—but he wanted to be proactive in his self-care. At the retreat center, he spent a couple of hours each morning with a counselor.

"Can you fully be who you are at Crossroads?" Chuck's counselor asked him.

The question stayed with Chuck as he left Colorado and joined his family for two weeks of vacation in Florida. On June 23, 2017, the final day of his vacation, he drove home with Maria and their three kids from Florida to Ohio in the pouring rain. The radio news announced that the second Tensing trial had been declared a mistrial. This outcome came on the heels of a series of acquittals or mistrials of law enforcement officers involved in the fatal shooting of unarmed Black men around the country. Chuck and Maria were in shock.

"How is it possible that not a single one of them is guilty? How is it that in all of these cases—not most, not some, not fifty percent, but in one hundred percent of these cases—no officer ever gets found guilty?" Chuck sputtered with anger. He thought about his older half brother, Smitty, who had been the "enforcer" in their childhood neighborhood, feared and respected for his physical strength and quick temper. He had protected Chuck, who was nicknamed Little Smitty so that everyone knew they were related.

"You could be free," his brother said to Chuck many years later, "because of what I did. You could see the other side of life." Chuck thought about how vulnerable Smitty was to overpolicing. The failure of the second Tensing trial felt personal. Chuck knew he could not remain silent.

After returning to Ohio with his family, Chuck left for the final week of his sabbatical at the Kentucky abbey. He used the time to reflect on the trial, and on everything else that had been unfolding at Crossroads. What was God calling him to do in this moment? In times of indecision, Chuck always tried to lean into his relationship with God to discern insight. Now, he opened himself to the anger and frustration that he sometimes felt like he had to contain, including at Crossroads. He let himself scream and cry in the woods and viscerally experience the pain. Then he wondered what to do.

During the week, Chuck couldn't help but notice what he perceived to be important coincidences. The monks at the abbey, and the guests they tended to draw, were almost all white. In that setting, Chuck was surprised to see a white person reading Michael Eric Dyson's book *Tears We Cannot Stop: A Sermon to White America*. In all the years Chuck had been coming to the abbey, he had never seen anybody read a book like that.

Later that week, again to his surprise, he saw another person from Crossroads, a white woman who was involved in the church's student ministry. They could not talk to each other because of the silent retreat, but they nodded their hellos. As her time at the abbey concluded, this woman was allowed to speak, and she handed Chuck a small bottle of bubbles, like the ones children played with at birthday parties and picnics. She had spent the week reading a book about the concept of flow by theologian Richard Rohr. For her, the bubbles were a way to remember her flow. She told Chuck she thought God was asking her to give him bubbles so he could be in the flow, too. *Interesting*, Chuck thought. *What flow is God asking me to join?*

There was another Black person at the abbey that week, someone from Cincinnati Chuck knew through their involvement in Issue 44. Never having seen a Black person at the abbey before, Chuck was struck by the coincidence. At one point, Chuck went to the one room in the retreat center where people were allowed to talk. When he arrived, he saw that his Black friend and the gentleman who was reading Dyson's book were both there. The three of them entered into a conversation about racial justice and the controversies around police shootings of unarmed Black men in America.

Evangelical Christians often interpret coincidences as signs from God. Chuck was no exception. *God's with me in my reflection on the Tensing trial*, he concluded.

After years of tiptoeing around issues of race within the church, Chuck felt that instead of containing his anger, God was calling him to share it. When Chuck returned from sabbatical, he knew what he had to do. At Crossroads the next week, he was scheduled to deliver a Spark Talk, which were talks given by different members of the community to introduce and ignite new thinking. Crossroads integrated Spark Talks into weekly services during the summer instead of regular homilies, in an effort to stanch flagging summer attendance. By then, it had been two years since Chuck had delivered his first sermon about race, and more than a year since Undivided had begun. Chuck decided to use the Spark Talk as an opportunity to speak more forcefully about his anger over injustice.

"I knew that one of the things that I was not allowing myself to do was to be fully myself, to be at Crossroads and be angry," Chuck recalled. "I was very, very afraid, quite frankly, of showing my anger. But I knew I had to let people into my heart as a Black man."

Over three days, Chuck went through seven different drafts, incorporating feedback from his colleague Lynn, his older brother, and others. He thought carefully about what to say and how to say it.

Megachurches like Crossroads put a premium on the production value of the service, believing that more people would be drawn to Jesus if the services were more enjoyable. Leaders at Bill Hybels's Willow Creek, for example, advised those who were to speak onstage how to cut their hair and where to buy their clothes. Often, speakers at Willow Creek texted pictures of themselves dressed up for services to obtain approval of their outfits before they went onstage. The attention to appearance was part of a broader effort to fit into an image of hipness the entire production sought to cultivate. Although, as Brian was careful to say, Crossroads was not a Willow clone, they maintained a similarly high production value for all their content.

Each Saturday, anyone scheduled to speak or perform onstage at Crossroads services participated in a rehearsal run by a professional production manager with a cue sheet scripted down to the minute. At one rehearsal, the producer opened by noting that they had sixty-seven minutes of content, but were aiming for seventy minutes of production. "Let's get this right," she said. Brian, who was preaching that weekend, was pacing around the auditorium before he had to go onstage. When it was his turn, he bounded onto the stage and began his sermon, preaching into the mostly empty auditorium. He told a story of "taking a whiz" behind a tree while visiting Israel. "I'm standing there thinking, 'I wonder if Jesus peed on this tree?'" He paused for an anticipated chuckle, then worried aloud that he was speaking too long. "Keep going and we'll fix it later," the producer said. By the end of his rehearsal, Brian was about five minutes over. The production team huddled with the teaching team to identify places to cut.

Chuck did a full rehearsal of his Spark Talk. During the debrief, the producers first focused on the run of show. Chuck had originally been slated to speak between two other speakers—a woman who was to talk about her experience donating a kidney and a scientist who would talk about the relationship of faith and science, as well as his interest in model rockets. During the rehearsal, the producers decided to move Chuck to the end, to give the audience more time to sit with his message instead of moving quickly into a lighthearted discussion of model rocketry.

Then, one of the producers spoke up hesitantly. "Are you sure you want to be so . . . um . . . forceful?" she asked.

"How will that message land on Crossroads' ears?" another producer asked.

"I am very thankful for your feedback," Chuck said, "but this is the message I need to deliver. It needs to be said."

On the day of the event, Chuck took the stage about an hour into the service. He wore jeans and a light blue collared knit shirt. He had a small goatee and was holding his notes on a small iPad. During his speech, he checked his notes more often than usual to make sure he stayed on script.

Chuck started the talk with an easy tone, reflecting on his sabbatical and joking. "I realized I had emotions that I had been muting for a long time," he said. "See, I don't know if you have a Black friend in your life, which, by the way, I highly recommend." The audience laughed. Chuck paused and laughed with them. "But if you do, last week was probably a tough week for them," he resumed. For the first time on the Crossroads main stage, Chuck admitted he was angry—angry that not a single conviction had emerged from all the police shootings of Black Americans. "I am angry about that. I am angry about that, and I think you should be disturbed by it, too." The audience applauded.

"Given this, what am I left to conclude about the dignity of my humanity as a Black person in this country? Or the safety of my two sons when they become drivers in the state of Ohio?" He projected a picture of himself standing on a grassy hill with his two young sons. The evening sun lit Cincinnati's skyline in the background, and Chuck stood behind his sons with his hands affectionately on their shoulders. His older son wore a button-down shirt with a bow tie, and his younger son, barely reaching above Chuck's waist, wore a long-sleeved Henley with three buttons on top. Chuck and both boys smiled broadly into the camera, and Chuck's younger son impishly scrunched his nose.

Chuck challenged his audience to consider their own complicity as white Christians. Chuck described a Black friend of his, who attended a megachurch like Crossroads, as someone who is "trusted, highly successful, and a mature follower of Jesus." Then he read a text his friend had sent almost in its entirety. "The American Christian church has no answers for our divided nation. The God of the Bible has been reduced to a well-orchestrated marketing production designed to deliver comfort to itching ears."

Chuck was using the text as a means of confessing his doubts about his ability to stay in a predominantly white church. "I don't know if I can stay in a white evangelical space if my white brothers and sisters are not grieving with me in this moment."

The room was silent.

Chuck grounded his grief in biblical interpretation, then concluded by challenging people to take an honest look at the church, and then an honest look at themselves. "Let's be a church that is known for our love! There is a reason that most megachurches are predominantly one race or another. It is hard. But [at] Crossroads, we do hard things! Let's be a church that is known for our love." Chuck's impassioned plea drew wide applause.

He ended with a prayer based on Psalm 86:11, where David prayed, "Put me together, one heart and mind; then, undivided, I'll worship in joyful fear."

This sermon, which people in Undivided referred to as "Chuck's lament," put the Undivided agenda more centrally on the Crossroads agenda. But it also caused immediate controversy. "Boy did I get blowback on that one," Chuck remembered.

Many congregants approached Chuck after the service. Some Black people thanked him for expressing what was in their hearts. Five or six white people approached him to express their consternation about what he said. Assured in their righteousness, they peppered him with questions, believing they could present countervailing facts and arguments to undercut their pastor. They objected to Chuck showing pictures of his two young Black sons, arguing that it was a threatening image. Anthea Butler, a Black professor of religion at the University of Pennsylvania, has argued that a commitment to racial subjugation has always been the singular factor that united white evangelicals. Chuck viscerally felt that truth when people perceived his young sons as a threat. *How can those little boys seem threatening?* he thought.

Several days later, Chuck received a call from the executive teaching pastor of Crossroads, his boss and, he surmised, the emissary of the Spiritual Board. Chuck was not privy to board discussions, but he guessed they had gotten pushback from influential voices in the church. "It's power, right? I know they heard from wealthy, influential people who give disproportionately to the church." He guessed that his boss was reaching out to him because of the opposition.

"Hey, Chuck, I'm just calling to check in. How are you feeling after the weekend?" his boss asked.

"I stand by what I said," Chuck answered. "This [racism] is a problem. And it's not right." He referred to the Crossroads notion of the "seven hills we die on." Those were the seven core tenets of the church, the first of which was authenticity. "How can I not say something?" Chuck asked. Chuck did not say this out loud, but was thinking, *Look at my track record. My track record is not divisive. In 2016, you trusted me to come up with a message that was right for bridging within the church. That message didn't offend you because it didn't disagree with your worldview. But I don't want to be ostracized now that I spoke a message that does—because, in fact, it does not disagree with Scripture. It's like, if I come through with the "Can we all get along?" message, I'm getting pats on the back, you love me. But when I start to point to discriminatory systems and structures that need to change, then I'm like the prophets in the Old Testament.* Chuck was thinking of biblical stories about prophets who spoke truth about God, only to be shunned by their communities for speaking out.

Habit pushed Chuck to hold those feelings inside, and his boss did not challenge him further.

"I get it," Chuck recalled his boss saying. "I get your anger, I really do." Chuck wondered if he did. "At the board level," his boss continued, "the question is how do we navigate these tricky waters. We're not going to do anything for the sake of not offending people, but we have to ask how we take people on a journey. How do we help people build understanding?"

The church did not ask Chuck to apologize or retract his words, but Chuck felt that the phone call was a sign that powerful leaders in the church would be closely watching what he did moving forward. Surveillance can sometimes constrain more than punishment. *That's how power works, you know?* Chuck thought.

Five years later, Chuck reflected on his lament: "People saw me for who I was. And I survived it. It gave me the chance to say what I wanted to say in a way that made me feel more authentic. But I kept realizing how deeply emotional this was for white people to hear it. It was almost like, Ooh. I told them I was Black and they're realizing I'm Black now. Now I'm not nice Chuck, I'm not your Pastor Chuck. Only, He's Black. He might think like other Black people think."

Chuck kept thinking about people's reaction to the picture of his beloved boys. He realized that he had been avoiding a crucial question: How far was he willing to go to pursue antiracism? What would he give up?

CHAPTER TWELVE

WHO IS IN CHARGE OF YOU?

In so many social change efforts, outrage sparked initial activism but faltered in driving ongoing action. When things got hard for Undivided participants after the program ended—when the Spiritual Board put Chuck on notice that they were watching him, when Jess decided she couldn't go back to volunteer in the prison, when Sandra's family responsibilities filled her free time—they each thought about abandoning the work of antiracism. But their commitments to one another kept them from giving up. As W. E. B. Du Bois wrote, "Organization is sacrifice. . . . You cannot be strongly and fiercely individual if you belong to an organization. For this reason some folk hunt and work alone. It is their nature. But the world's greatest work must be done by team work." People needed others to hold them accountable, to ask hard questions, to be willing to introduce tension into a relationship, and to push one another to act on their commitments with courage.

In many evangelical megachurches, small groups like the Justice Team were the place where congregants pushed one another to be the kind of people they wanted to be but were scared to become. These groups were the building blocks of evangelical megachurches, creating venues within giant congregations for people to get to know one another and pursue a common agenda.

Warren Bird and Scott Thumma, two leading scholars of evangelicalism in America, found that the percentage of megachurches in America that engaged their congregations in small group practice grew from 50 percent in 2000 to 90 percent in 2020. In 2020, the median megachurch reported that 45 percent of its members were involved in some kind of small group. In a church like Crossroads, which boasted about 35,000 members in 2020, that would be about 15,750 people organized into small groups if each person belonged to only one. They generally ranged from six to ten people, meaning that Crossroads could have had anywhere from 1,575 to 2,625 small groups meeting regularly.

Small groups created honeycombs of intimacy, connection, and loyalty in those churches. As French philosopher Alexis de Tocqueville wrote, "In democratic countries knowledge of how to combine is the mother of all other forms of knowledge." Because people do not naturally possess the skills and inclinations for working with one another, they need venues for learning. Small groups taught people through concrete experience how to act together. In a 2005 article in *The New Yorker* about Rick Warren's famed Saddleback Church in California, Malcolm Gladwell popularized them as the basic building block of Saddleback's success. Bird and Thumma's survey data showed that those who belonged to small groups like the Justice Team were more likely to give to the church, both in terms of time and money. Small groups nurtured commitment, acting as the rare social technology that helped an organization simultaneously achieve both its moral and financial objectives.

For sprawling evangelical communities like Crossroads, the centrality of deep relationships through small groups also had the benefit of being biblically grounded. Dave Ferguson, the leader of one of the largest networks of clergy dedicated to church growth in the United States, often points to a Bible verse (John 3:22) when he describes the value of small groups: "After this Jesus and his disciples went into the Judean countryside, and he spent some time there with them and baptized." It is a short verse, and some biblical translations use the word *tarry:* Jesus "tarried" with his disciples. The original Greek exegesis uses the word *diatribo,* translated as "to pass time" or "to linger." Ferguson's point is that building people's relationship to God is not about engaging them for an hour each Sunday. Instead, it is about lingering—or tarrying—with people long enough to create opportunities for them to find God. "The research tells us that Jesus actually spent 73 percent of his total time with the twelve [apostles], and only 27 percent of his time with large crowds," Ferguson argued. That, Ferguson believed, is what churches should do—emphasize the work of building deep relationships.

Sandra did not always agree with everyone on the Justice Team, but she knew she could always bring to it the fullness of her vulnerability, faults, and questions. These small groups became the unit through which churches as large as Crossroads could bend under pressure without breaking. When Sandra (or anyone else) was frustrated with Crossroads, the Justice Team was the place where she could express her frustration. "My group is my church," she said. Those on the team knew her and knew her faith, so she could express her doubts about her church in a way she could not elsewhere. Small groups created spaces where people could hold multiple truths at once.

~

Sandra asked Elizabeth, the Black woman who co-organized the Justice Team, to meet her for coffee. The two women had gotten to know each other through the team meetings, but Sandra had missed several after having her baby. Each month, a mix of eight to ten Black and white men and women who were the most active leaders with the Justice Team attended, often ordering pizza or bringing food they had around the house to share.

The goal was simplicity. They wanted people to focus on being with one another instead of impressing one another. Sometimes they met at someone's home, and other times they met in spaces at Crossroads or around Cincinnati. The meetings always began with opportunities for each person to share what was on their mind or in their heart.

These check-ins poured the foundation of their relationships. When news of another killing of an unarmed Black man at the hands of the police emerged, a Black parent asked, "How am I going to talk about this with my Black [child]?" Questions like that allowed people to expose their fears, vulnerabilities, and problems to one another, weaving bonds of connection even when the questions remained unanswered. They needed solidarity as much as (or more than) solutions. Carolyn, the white woman in Sandra and Grant's group who co-organized the Justice Team with Elizabeth, spoke honestly about her qualms raising a Black child in an otherwise white family. People shared their thoughts about children in prison, miscarriage, and marital troubles, finding solace in the group. As Sandra put it, "Our hearts were breaking together."

The Justice Team also used their meetings to strategize about what actions and campaigns they should undertake. After Issue 44, the events around the Tensing trial had formed the core of their volunteering. When both ended, they wondered if they should get involved in another extended campaign. If so, what would it be? Where could they be most impactful? Their relational bonds held the group together, even as they disagreed, debated, and deliberated about strategy. Each person knew that for everyone on the team, the stakes were high. Injustice was personal.

The Justice Team meetings helped Elizabeth and Sandra become close, so they began their coffee by catching up. Elizabeth, who had two children of her own, asked about Sandra's baby. Sandra confessed to exhaustion and some loneliness despite her love for her newborn. Her husband hardly took any time off work to help after the birth, and Sandra was also trying to manage her older children, who still required a lot of care. Her oldest would soon be a young Black boy attending school, and Sandra knew that she would have to confront the questions she had been avoiding sooner rather than later. As a Black mother, Elizabeth could relate.

When the Justice Team came up, Sandra and Elizabeth's conversation shifted from relationship to strategy. Elizabeth was not yet sure if they were going to take on a new campaign, but they had been continuing to work with Amos (the organization that engaged them in Issue 44 and the Tensing trial) and its statewide parent organization, the Ohio Organizing Collaborative (OOC). Both were working with a coalition of other justice-oriented groups in the state to develop a statewide ballot initiative around criminal justice reform. That would dovetail nicely with the work many members of the Justice Team had been doing with the prison ministry Grant founded, the Four-Seven.

Sandra was intrigued. She missed the monthly meetings and liked the idea of getting more involved again. Elizabeth offered Sandra a menu of opportunities. She knew that Sandra did not like being a boots-on-the-ground door knocker, but she valued Sandra's gift for drawing people toward her and grounding their work in faith. Sandra could become their prayer leader again, Elizabeth suggested. Alternately, Sandra could help the Justice Team get to know some of the other local groups in Cincinnati who were considering involvement in the campaign. Elizabeth also offered Sandra the chance to recruit other people from Crossroads at services each week.

But Sandra demurred, declining the roles Elizabeth offered.

Elizabeth's instincts, honed from two years of community organizing and the culture of the Justice Team, told her not to let Sandra off the hook. She asked Sandra why she was refusing despite stating an interest in becoming more involved.

Sandra responded nervously. She talked about the baby, describing her responsibilities as a mom and all the things she and her husband were managing. Elizabeth sensed there was something unexpressed underneath Sandra's protestations. She probed again, gently.

Over the previous year, as Sandra had gotten more involved with Undivided and the Justice Team, her husband had become more resistant to it. When Sandra went to the courthouse to pray for a conviction in the Tensing trial, he steadfastly maintained his support for Tensing's acquittal. He kept insisting that by focusing on race, she and other people on the Justice Team were creating a problem. Sandra tried to share what she was learning from Undivided and the Justice Team with him, but it wasn't working. Her husband was spending more and more time online searching for information he could use to prove Sandra wrong.

The highly attuned nature of online algorithms meant that his searches for information to refute charges of racism quickly led him to virtual white Christian nationalist communities. Sociologists Andrew Whitehead and Samuel Perry called white Christian nationalism a "cultural framework" that both idealized and advocated for a fusion of Christianity and American public life. Christian nationalism was based on a sense of urgency derived from apocalyptic Christian views about premillennialism, the idea that the world would become increasingly corrupt until the second coming of the Messiah, when Christ would rescue the faithful and begin a millennial reign on Earth. Not all Christian nationalists knew these theological underpinnings, but nonetheless most believed that it was their responsibility to restore the primacy of Christianity in an increasingly secular public sphere, choosing the pursuit of institutional power over benevolence.

White Christian nationalist views could not, Whitehead and Perry argued, be disentangled from white supremacy: Christian nationalists used the term "Christian" to refer to a white, predominantly male identity that was associated with nativist, white

supremacist, authoritarian, militaristic, and patriarchal views.
This was the Christianity that Jess's parents had learned as a child.
In most circles, it had been disguised by a pretense of racial harmony after the civil rights movement, but Trump's ascendance
encouraged nationalists to rear their racist heads with pride.
Christian nationalists felt that America had, from its founding,
been distinctly white and Christian, and that it should remain
that way.

Sandra observed as her husband's inchoate opinions about
whiteness, masculinity, and patriotism began to fuse into a more
coherent worldview as he spent more time online. He was hardly
alone. Whitehead and Perry found that slightly more than half of
Americans subscribed to some form of Christian nationalism,
partly a sign of how widespread Christianity was in the American population. About 20 percent of Americans saw themselves
as active "ambassadors" of Christian nationalism, and another
32 percent were "accommodators," or people who leaned toward
accepting it even if they were somewhat unsure. According to
Whitehead and Perry's framework, like many other white Christian men in the Trump era, Sandra's husband started as an accom-
modator, but was becoming an ambassador. White nationalist
communities burgeoned as racial issues became more politicized. Police shootings elevated race on the public agenda but
also increased resistance to change.

Their relationship to God became the flag tied to the middle of
the rope in a tug-of-war between Sandra and her husband. As she
sensed the pull of white Christian nationalism on her husband,
she moved in the opposite direction. She was working to reclaim
her identity as a Black woman and deepening her relationships
with Black women like Michelle and others she met through the
Justice Team. Sandra struggled to make sense of the pull between
her own relationship with God and her husband's. How could

they worship the same God? What did this mean about her faith? About Crossroads?

Sandra also revealed to Elizabeth tensions she was struggling with around her own sense of self. She described interactions with white friends that were making her realize how much of her own identity as a Black woman she had suppressed. Now that she was speaking out more, she could feel tension in some of her closest relationships. On the one hand, she was proud of herself for making questions of race a "pain point," an opportunity to expose hidden tensions about race. On the other hand, she felt she was losing the archipelago of support she had built around herself. This tension made her hesitant about staying overtly committed to the Justice Team. She told Elizabeth she wasn't sure she had the time the Justice Team needed.

Elizabeth pursed her lips. She thought about how to respond, looking down as she picked at the thermal wrapper around her coffee cup. After a moment, she looked up at Sandra again.

"Well, who is your God?" Elizabeth spoke slowly. "Who is in charge of you?"

Sandra was taken aback, unable to answer the question. She laughed nervously and told Elizabeth she needed more time.

Sandra found herself mulling the question when she was by herself. She thought about it in the mornings when she journaled and at home when she prayed for patience in her relationships with her friends. As the summer approached, she decided she needed to take proactive action to help her figure out what to do. Who, indeed, was in charge of her?

⁓

Sandra decided to organize a prayer trip for herself and the children that summer. Like the forty days Jesus spent in the desert, the trip would give Sandra an opportunity for forty days of refuge, reflection, and prayer. Her day-to-day social world felt chaotic, and she wanted a break from all the tension. She decided to camp with the children in the woods around Ohio and Kentucky. Her oldest was seven years old, and her middle child was three. She also had a nine-month-old baby. To chart their route, she marked a map with all nine campuses of the Crossroads church. Then she identified a series of campgrounds that marked a circle around all the campuses. She had been reading books by a pastor who described a strategy for prayer that involved drawing circles around your deepest dreams and problems to elicit a more powerful conversation with God. Sandra decided to trace literal circles around Crossroads to circumscribe the church in prayer. It would take them forty days.

Sandra did not have much experience camping, but she was undaunted. She made a plan with her husband. He would help them set up, replenish their supplies, and take down camp every few days. But in between, she would spend her days alone with the children.

Once her husband left the first night, Sandra took the kids for a short walk to explore their campsite, then let them play raucously outside while she made dinner. After they ate, she helped them get ready for bed and tried to coax them to sleep. When they finally quieted, Sandra snuggled into her sleeping bag with the baby next to her. She listened happily to the rhythm of her children's sleep while she scrolled through the notes and messages on her phone. She fell asleep looking forward to the adventure they were beginning.

Sandra jolted awake hours later. It was pitch-black. Suddenly, she heard something fall outside the tent, and the sound of scurrying paws. Silences punctuated rapid staccato bursts of scuffling. Sandra's heart started to pound. After a momentary silence, she heard more noises outside, and realized that animals were pawing through their food. Sandra had made the rookie mistake of leaving food out at night. Terrified about what kind of animals might be outside the tent, she wondered if she should call her husband to pick them up.

Sandra tried to fall back asleep, but each time she closed her eyes, her imagination ran wild. "I felt like I was in the kind of mental traps created in an Alfred Hitchcock movie," she recalled. The sense of peace she had earlier quickly eroded. The long night began to feel like a metaphor for her life. *What am I doing stuck in this tent and stuck in these relationships? Why do I keep these people in my life?* She thought about the second trial of Ray Tensing, and all the time she had put into praying on the courthouse steps during both trials. She thought about the work the Justice Team had done over the past year, and the number of people in the Crossroads community who still did not support Undivided or the Justice Team. So many things in her life felt futile. *Why do I keep pursuing racial reconciliation with these white people who don't give a shit?* she thought. The church's muted reaction to the extended agony of the Tensing trials frustrated her. *Why do I keep pursuing racial reconciliation when the system is never gonna change?*

Dawn came as a relief. Feeling more comfortable in the sunlight, Sandra unzipped the tent and peeked at the mess on the picnic table outside. The neat piles of food and gear she had left were scattered around the table, and a plastic bag of trash had been ripped open. She wondered if they should abandon the trip. The baby started to cry. Sandra hauled the children out of their sleeping bags and cleaned up the mess. Reflecting on her choices after the campsite was in order again, Sandra decided to give the trip more time.

As the days went on, Sandra and the kids developed a rhythm of cooking, cleaning, exploring the woods, and praying. Sandra was struck by how quiet their days felt, and how lonely she was when the kids were sleeping. Through all of their adventures, Sandra maintained a steadfast regime of prayer, seeking signs from God.

The weather changed the second week as a set of Midwestern summer thunderstorms rolled into the area. When the weather seemed to clear, Sandra pushed the children outside to play. The boys needed to work off their energy. The tree canopy around their campsite, she thought, would provide some cover from lingering drops of rain. She spread a blanket under the tree for the baby, and the boys ran and played with abandon. But Sandra had miscalculated. A sudden burst of wind caused a tree branch to fall directly onto the baby's blanket. In a stroke of luck, Sandra had moved her daughter to safety when she picked her up moments before the branch broke. Her seven-year-old son, however, was standing by the branch when it fell. He burst into tears, frightened by the unexpected crash and the ensuing burst of rain. The baby's wails joined her brother's. Sandra tried to comfort her son with one arm while she shielded the baby with the other. Rain poured down around them.

She herded the bedraggled children into the car and helped them dry out. She thought back to a night earlier that week when her son had woken up screaming because of the rain, telling her that the whole trip "sucked" and that he wanted to go home. *God, why am I here?* Sandra asked herself. By the time the kids had changed into dry clothes and settled into the tent, Sandra was exhausted. She told the kids to take some quiet time so that she could rest.

She started with prayer: *God, I thought I could do this, but I am too weak for it.* As she often did when she was despairing, Sandra pulled out her Bible. She flipped idly to find something to read, landing on the story of Hosea. Hosea was a prophet who married a sex worker named Gomer. Sandra remembered learning when she was younger that the story was an allegory for God's patient pursuit of Israel, despite their repeated missteps. In the Bible, Gomer kept cheating on Hosea, and Hosea faithfully persisted in his care. Eventually, Gomer realized the power of Hosea's love and committed to him.

Sandra thought it was a sign. *That's what I have to do,* she thought. *In the end, I pursue because God pursues me. I have to pursue what I think is right.* She finished reading and looked at her children. They had been playing quietly, but when they sensed their mother's availability, they clamored for her attention. She knew it would be hard to repair her marriage, but she had to try. Suddenly, she heard a voice. "Nature, the world, is too big for you, Sandra. Why do you want me to change nature for you? Stop asking me to change. Let me make you stronger." Sandra felt this was the revelation she had been awaiting. She had been asking God to change the world to fit her needs, but she realized that God could be a source of strength if she embraced the world around her. She had to find the strength to make this trip work despite the rain.

Sandra told her children to put on whatever they had that would protect them from the rain. Her son was still wary of going back outside, but she forced the children out of the tent. She would figure out how to make it fun. She splashed in the rain with her older boys, making the baby giggle as she danced around. Her play was infectious. The boys joined her in the fun. They all got muddy and soaked, until the sun came back out and dried the speckles of dirt onto their skin. Sandra no longer felt fearful of the trip.

The next evening was one of the nights when her husband was scheduled to join them. It was also the night that the Justice Team was meeting, and Sandra did not want to miss the gathering. Her husband stayed with the children, setting up the new campsite, while Sandra drove back into town. The Justice Team was meeting that night at a modern coworking space near Oakley called the Living Room. Decorated like someone's home, the space felt cozy and intimate in ways the Justice Team appreciated.

The meeting came at a perfect time for Sandra. She was eager to share her revelation with the others, to take what she had found in her heart and present it to the group. The power of her revelation from God, the relief of being briefly away from her kids, and the feeling of being able to share the fullness of her fears and hopes with other people brought her to tears. With her groups of all-white friends, she constantly had to avoid the "pain points" about race that would send their group into a downward spiral of snide bickering. With the children, she had to be strong even when she felt anxious. But here, with the Justice Team, she did not have to censor herself.

She thought back to survey week in Undivided, when she felt ashamed to be talking with another Black woman. That night, as she told her story, she looked directly at two of the Black women in the group who had become her friends over the past year. They cried with her.

After that night, Sandra's prayer trip continued for four and a half more weeks. When she returned home, she felt renewed in her commitment to working both on her marriage and on Undivided and the Justice Team. She wanted to pursue those she knew she had tension with, just as God pursued her. She knew it wouldn't be easy.

CHAPTER THIRTEEN

DON'T TALK TO ME

Jess sat with her mom outside her mom's trailer in a mobile home community near Batavia, Ohio. A large awning shaded an expansive porch with a long, rectangular table. Her mother sat at the head of the table, and Jess sat to her right. It was a hot, sunny summer day, and they each sipped from glasses of water sweating onto the glass table in front of them.

Around the same time that the second trial of Ray Tensing was taking place in Cincinnati, the trial of Jeronimo Yanez was unfolding in a small town in Minnesota. Yanez was the officer who had shot and killed Philando Castile a year before during a traffic stop. Castile, a Black man, had been in the car with his girl-friend, Diamond Reynolds, and her four-year-old daughter. Immediately after Yanez shot Castile, Reynolds began live streaming the incident on Facebook, capturing her frantic back-and-forth with the officers. Widespread outcry erupted after Castile's death. It took almost a year for the trial to occur, and the judge announced Yanez's acquittal in early June 2017, just a few weeks before the second mistrial for Ray Tensing.

A few weeks after the verdict, the county released the videos shared with the jury during the trial, including footage taken from within the squad car that carried Reynolds and her daughter to the police station. The video captured her young daughter's plaintive pleas begging her mother to stay calm, "'Cause I don't want you to get shooted." Fearing more violence from the police, the little girl assured her frantic mother, "I can keep you safe." The child had acted with love and courage in the face of impossible cruelty, hanging on to whatever innocence she had left. Jess could not stop watching the video, enraged each time. News of the second mistrial in the Tensing case turned Jess's rage into despair.

"I hate it. It's such a pattern," she said to her mom. "I mean, it's just like what happened to Philando Castile. With that little girl in the back seat."

Her mom didn't reply at first, waiting for Jess to finish venting. Then, Jess recalled, she spoke up softly, saying, "He should have complied."

Jess felt her neck snapping back in surprise. How could her mom say that? "Comply? What do you even mean? He did comply." Jess couldn't help raising her voice.

Her mom dug in her heels. "C'mon. He shouldn't have reached across the car." Yanez had started shooting when Castile reached over to take his driver's license from the glove compartment.

"*Mom!*" Jess was yelling. "The officer *told* him to get his license. What the fuck else was he supposed to do?"

"Stop yelling, Jess," her mom said evenly.

"*Why should I stop yelling?*" Jess was furious. "What are you saying that any reasonable person should have done?" She paused. Her mom was silent. "*Tell me,*" she demanded.

"Well, he shouldn't have had a gun in the car."

Jess started to cry as she shouted back to her mom. "It was a *legal* gun."

"*Why are you defending him?*" Jess's mom raised her voice, too.

"*Why shouldn't he be allowed to have a gun? Is it because he's Black?*" Jess kept yelling.

"Stop. *Stop yelling at me,*" her mom shouted.

Jess stood up abruptly. "Don't talk to me again until you figure your life out," she said.

Jess stomped away from the table and refused to talk to her mother for several weeks. They still were not speaking when Chuck delivered his lament the following month. Every time Jess thought about reaching out to her mother, she couldn't bring herself to do it. *She's being so racist,* Jess thought. It was the longest time they had gone without speaking to each other since Jess went into recovery.

By confronting her mother, Jess took a risk that could be more dangerous than material risk. She sacrificed a vital part of the support system she had constructed to protect her sobriety. But she could no longer tolerate her mother's views. She knew her mother could not conceive of the idea that the police officer might have acted unjustly. Everything her mother had been taught rested on a vision of a society in which white-led law enforcement controlled Black people. Jess had finally chosen to speak up instead of acquiescing to those assumptions.

Years of watching Jess struggle to stay sober taught her mother a resolute compassion. She knew she had to make the first move. She reached out to Jess a little over a week after Chuck's sermon. By then, Jess was ready to talk. She had been thinking about the exercises they had done in Undivided and realized that she actually did not know much about her mother's early experiences with race. Because of her dad, Jess had mostly avoided such conversations with her parents throughout her childhood. Once she developed that habit, it stuck. This time, she thought, she could ask her mom to talk about her past instead of fighting about their present views. She asked her mother to describe her experiences of race as a child. She recalled her mother opening up, sharing for the first time that her next-door neighbor growing up hosted the local KKK meetings at their home. "Why didn't you ever tell me?" Jess asked.

Jess realized how distinct her image of Jesus was compared to her mother's. "My favorite Jesus is the radical political Jesus," she said. "I know Jesus loves you—whatever." Jess waved her hands, as if dismissing saccharine images of an anodyne Jesus. "I love the 'No, the way we are doing things isn't working. We're going to tear down this system and it's going to be better for everybody.' That's the Jesus I love." Even though Sergeant Harris never focused on racial justice in his teaching, he offered Jess the gift of freedom in her relationship with God. She could get to know a God who demanded justice.

During their brunches at Wild Eggs, Patricia had challenged Jess to ask herself what Undivided was calling her to do. For many months, Jess remained unsure. She applied to become a facilitator with Undivided and went through the training. She spent hours on social media, trying to advance her own learning about injustice. She contemplated ways to get involved in antiracism, but her mind kept coming back to her own family. At first, Jess worried that channeling her activism toward her family was too minimal compared to the scale of the systemic problems of injustice.

People learn habits of racial subjugation and social control in their households, places of worship, workplaces, schools, and other communities. They then carry those habits into the societal institutions and structures they inhabit, create, deconstruct, and re-create. The cycle becomes seemingly unbreakable—unless someone starts to alter the pattern. That disruption requires people to change their own habits but also to try to remake the social structures that govern their lives. In his analysis of what it would take to overcome the social, political, and economic arrangements that engendered the current state of inequality in America, *New Yorker* contributor Nicholas Lemann wrote, "Consequential human activity takes place through institutions. . . . Media and messaging meant to influence public opinion, organizing campaigns conducted only on social media—these are the snack foods of politics, far less effective over the long term than building institutions that have more conventional functions like structured meetings, ongoing rituals, and planned campaigns." If individuals strike out on isolated journeys of antiracism, but allow the families, workplaces, faith institutions, social groups, and neighborhoods they inhabit to sustain the status quo, change always remains fragile.

⁓

Jess loved football and loved watching with her family. A few months after the fight with her mother, she drove with her son to her grandmother's house on a Sunday afternoon to watch a game. Even though the game hadn't started when they arrived, her grandmother, who was losing her hearing, had cranked up the volume on the TV. Jess poured herself a cup of coffee and settled into one of the gray couches across from her uncle, her mother's brother. Her son thumbed the Artemis Fowl and Charlie Bone novels that lined the built-in bookshelves on either side of the TV. Her grandmother favored young adult fantasy novels, and the fancy spines attracted his attention. Jess reached around the curved arm of the couch to find one of her grandmother's heavy marble ashtrays, using two hands to move it to the coffee table in front of her.

Her uncle was wearing a short-sleeved Under Armour shirt. He was a construction worker and landscaper during the week and always wore clothes that could wick the sweat away from his body. His brown hair was tied back into a ponytail, and he had his own marble ashtray in front of him with a lit cigarette in his hand. The smell of multiple generations of cigarette smoking penetrated the couches and carpets in the room.

Jess had not gotten to know her uncle very well as a child because he had been serving fifteen years in prison. The adults never said much about why he was there. She retained only fragmentary memories of visiting her incarcerated uncle when she was in elementary school, going through security with her mom, waiting at a table for her uncle, his blue prison uniform, the plastic screen that separated them from one another, her mom holding the phone receiver to her ear. Jess only caught bits and pieces of the adults' conversation and distracted herself by peering around the room at the other prisoners. She didn't imagine then that she, too, would someday spend time in a correctional facility.

When her mother handed Jess the phone to talk with her uncle, she wasn't sure what to say. She stared shyly at this man she did not know very well. He chuckled and lifted up his blue prison shirt as if revealing a surprise. It was a new tattoo. He was not a very big man, standing about five eight and weighing about two hundred pounds. He showed her a new swastika tattooed across his entire left pectoral muscle. Only eight years old, Jess didn't know what it was. "This isn't racist. This is about the Third Reich. Hitler wrote this really good book," he said, summoning the pride and belonging he thought he was owed. "This is about me having a home and being proud of who I am." He reflexively defended himself against accusations Jess didn't even know to make. Perhaps his conscience nagged him. Jess just shrugged. At the time, she was not familiar with Hitler or the Third Reich. They were words her dad said that had no meaning to her. She nodded and let her uncle talk, then handed the phone back to her mom.

When Jess later learned enough to be shocked by her uncle, time had blunted the effect. For many years, avoidance was easier than confrontation—Jess steered clear from talking about anything political with him. They focused on football instead.

A brief news segment during one of the commercial breaks prompted Jess's uncle to express his admiration for Donald Trump. Jess kept quiet, hoping he'd change the subject. She alternated drinking coffee out of the mug in her left hand and smoking the cigarette in her right hand.

Jess's heart started to pound as her uncle kept talking. She thought about Patricia. *"Are you stuck on stupid, parked on dumb?"* She almost laughed out loud as she thought about saying that to her uncle. But she still didn't say anything.

He started to complain about all the Black people in prison. Jess felt heat crawling up her neck and into the tips of her ears. She couldn't stand it anymore. *"Are you freaking kidding me?"* she burst out, yelling to be heard above the TV. Her uncle stopped for a moment, surprised to see Jess so animated. Jess spewed statistics she had learned in Undivided about racial disparities.

He scoffed, noting that there were more white people than Black people in prison. He would know, he argued, because he had spent so much time there. Jess put her coffee down on the table so she could throw up her arms. His logic didn't make any sense, she countered, because he had to think about the proportion of Blacks in the general population and compare that to the proportion of Blacks in the prison system. The sneaky problem of denominators. Jess knew she was right, but she wasn't sure if she was making headway. Laying out a mathematical argument made her feel she might win the battle but lose the war. But once she got started, she couldn't stop.

Her uncle guffawed. He grabbed his phone out of his pocket and started searching for a YouTube video he had seen of a Black person standing with a white person in front of a Confederate flag, discussing the depravity in the Black population. He tried to thrust the phone into Jess's hands to force her to watch the video. She refused. "I'm not watching the one token video you found." He mocked her unwillingness to watch it.

Jess hated missing football, but she had had enough. She stood up abruptly, stamped out her cigarette butt, and told her son to get his stuff. "We're leaving," she said.

As Jess marched out of her grandmother's house, she was angry, but also proud. She knew she could have handled the situation with her uncle better. She wished she had not yelled. But it felt better than election night at Applebee's. Being in long-term recovery gave Jess a visceral sense of how hard it was to change, and she had been fearful of her own cowardice, wondering if the lessons from Undivided would be fleeting in her life.

She had already experienced cycles of commitment and relapse many times. The first time Jess went to prison in 2010, she was twenty-two years old. Before her arrest, she spent each day on a quest to find the money she needed to feed her heroin addiction. One day, she went to her grandmother's house. Her grandmother was asleep and had left the door unlocked. Jess walked into the house, removed her grandmother's debit card from her purse, and started to sneak away. *You don't have to do this,* she kept telling herself. But her addiction propelled her to the ATM machine. Even after she had withdrawn the money, she kept trying to talk herself out of it. *Nana will forgive you. Just take it back. Give her back her card.* Until the moment that she purchased drugs, Jess tried to convince herself that she still had a chance to do the right thing. *You haven't bought the drugs yet. You can take the money back.*

When her grandmother discovered the missing debit card, she called the police, not knowing what else to do. They arrested and imprisoned Jess for a week while she awaited trial. Her grandmother testified before a grand jury and begged for her granddaughter to get some help. The appeals worked. The court gave Jess an ILC, or an "intervention in lieu of conviction," which was part of a statewide program designed to give eligible offenders the chance to have the charges against them dismissed upon completion of a court-ordered treatment program. From April to August 2011, Jess participated in a four-month outpatient program at the River City Correctional Center outside Cincinnati. She got clean during that time. The day the program ended, she found a four thousand dollar tax refund check from the federal government waiting for her. Jess relapsed that day.

After Undivided ended, she constantly worried about her ability to sustain the courage to act. But that day, as the TV roared, she could feel herself putting at least some of the things she learned to work.

When Jess drove home from her grandmother's house, she thought about Sergeant Harris, her professor, and the sequence of people who had gotten her to this place. If she hadn't taken that class, would she have considered participating in Undivided? Would she have stuck with it? And if she hadn't stuck with Undivided, would she have become friends with Patricia? If Patricia hadn't asked if she was "stuck on stupid, parked on dumb," would she have yelled at her uncle? When they got home, Jess turned on the TV to watch football and her son disappeared into his room. Jess could see him sitting on the floor amid a pile of LEGO bricks next to the four-foot-tall plastic Ninja Turtle by his bed. Watching him play, Jess wondered what messages about race he was inheriting. Jess texted Patricia to check in and see how she was doing.

CHAPTER FOURTEEN

WHO I AM HERE

Undivided forced Grant to grapple with the question of whether he should, or could, stay in his job. He was still working as the deputy communications chief of the Ohio state prison system. Although he relished the opportunity to have a high-profile public job, he puzzled over whether the Department of Rehabilitation and Correction was the right place for him. After listening to the audiobooks of *The New Jim Crow* and *Just Mercy*, he listened to Robin DiAngelo's *White Fragility* and other books on antiracism. Whenever he was agitated by what he was learning, he called Michelle, Sandra, or other friends he had developed from Undivided to process his questions. He had many, many questions.

From the time he was a child, Grant's impulse toward action imbued him with a decisiveness that served him well professionally but, he finally realized, made him blithely ignorant of people's pain. One of Grant's best friends in high school, Derek, was (alongside Hunt) one of the few Black people in Waynesville. Yet, until Undivided, Grant never realized how blind he had been to the way race differentially colored experiences he and Derek had.

In high school, Grant and Derek had dressed up in costumes to see the movie *Batman Begins*. They arrived early at the movie theater, and Derek drove Grant's truck around the parking lot searching for a parking space. A white police officer started following them in his cruiser after observing them meandering slowly through the lot. Grant never gave it any thought until the officer turned on his lights to stop them. Grant sighed, annoyed by the interruption. Derek froze.

When the officer approached the car, he aggressively questioned Derek. "Are you looking for cars to steal?"

Derek was mute with fear.

Grant spoke up from the passenger seat. "No, Officer, we're just early for a movie and looking for a place to park."

The officer looked at Grant, looked back at Derek, and took in their spandex superhero costumes. He let them go.

Derek later told Grant he had been totally petrified. Grant laughed it off. "That guy's a total douche," he said. Grant had forgotten all about the incident. Many years later he realized that Derek, who had died when Grant was in college, probably had not.

Listening to books about antiracism during his long commutes, Grant came to understand how deeply his own whiteness had circumscribed his thinking. Despite the experiences Grant witnessed through his relationships with Derek and Hunt, he had been ignoring the evidence that there was a pattern.

Sustaining the fiction had taken work. At some conscious or subconscious level, Grant's brain had to compartmentalize what he learned from his experiences with Derek and Hunt separately from what he learned from his politics. When Barack Obama ran for president, Grant had ardently and vocally opposed him: "Every time I posted something about him on social media, I made sure to use his middle name, Barack *Hussein* Obama, just to turn more people off." After going through Undivided, Grant apologized on social media for the way he had treated Obama, calling his own actions "disgusting." Some people undertaking racial reconciliation treated such acts of repentance as absolution. But Grant knew that it was just a beginning. Recognition of his systematic complicity in other people's pain precipitated a determination to act. He carefully considered Michelle's exhortation to use his position in an unjust system of criminal justice for good.

Grant decided to leverage his statewide leadership role in the Department of Rehabilitation and Correction to construct alternative narratives about imprisoned men and women. Typically, the department's social media channels focused on sharing mug shots of escapees. As a leader in the communications office, Grant could instead post photos and videos that humanized the images of imprisoned people. Grant thought it would offer a more three-dimensional perspective on the people in prison; critics objected to the irony of using the state's communication channels to do so. He also started a podcast dedicated to sharing long-form interviews with incarcerated men and women. He asked them about their past, their families, their time in prison, and their future aspirations. He hoped these efforts would alter the public's image of the people in prison, as well as demonstrate the impact of the carceral state on their lives.

But Grant had to work alone. He drove to prisons around the state in search of narratives he could showcase. When he brought his recording equipment into the correctional facilities, barely any of the guards offered to help. Grant pretended not to notice the sullen rebuffs from many of the correctional officers. They knew that he was a cofounder of the Four-Seven, and many of them disagreed with the work he was doing on social media. As Grant put it, "We were part of the Ohio Department of Rehabilitation and Correction but most correctional officers hate that we are not only the Department of Correction. Most of them don't believe in rehabilitation." The officers who interacted with Grant often resented his ability to carry his phone and other equipment with him in the facility because they were not allowed to have cell phones or any audio-visual equipment with them when they were on the job.

The guards used whatever means available to make Grant's job a little harder. When they scanned his equipment during security checks, they carefully enumerated each item, asking him if he really needed this or that piece of equipment. Sometimes, when they brought interviewees to meet with Grant, they would put artificial time limits on the interview. Or they would simply move as slowly as possible in checking Grant in, reviewing his equipment, walking him to a room, and bringing the interviewee to him.

The consistency of the officers' passive-aggressive behavior made Grant feel vulnerable, especially because he was operating in a gray area within departmental policy. Moreover, his job lacked the union protections most of the other officers enjoyed. He developed a visceral sense of how deep and consistent the resistance to his work was.

The backlash Grant—as well as Sandra, Jess, and Chuck—was experiencing was not unusual. Both white and nonwhite people advocating for antiracism commonly experienced backlash from the individuals and communities in their lives. Political scientist Ashley Jardina found that white identity—or white people's sense of their own group identity—increased when they felt like their group was losing status. People fighting for antiracism could activate that sense of threat. In these moments, whites became more protective of the spaces and domains they perceived as their own—their families, churches, and workplaces. That defensive reaction often caused advocates for antiracism to back away from the work. The costs of fighting for justice became too high when their jobs and social relationships became endangered. Backlash won by shutting down people's commitment to change.

Grant, however, counterbalanced his vulnerability at work with the social community he was forming through Undivided, the Four-Seven, and, in particular, friends like Sandra and Michelle. They were coming to his house at least once a month and getting to know his entire family because of Second Saturdays. Grant and Kyla had started this tradition in December 2018, when they decided to invite all of the Four-Seven volunteers to their home for a holiday party. At the time, they were still living in Waynesville in Grant's childhood home with their young children and Grant's parents. They weren't sure how many people would make the drive from Cincinnati to Waynesville for the party during the cold Ohio winter. Eighty-nine showed up. The guests filled the four-bedroom home and spilled out onto the porch, where Grant started a fire in the firepit. Someone turned on music, and others cleared space in the living room so everyone could dance. Children ran amok. At the first party, Grant and Kyla had planned a holiday game before Grant realized, "Forced fun is not fun." People were not there for a game; they were there to be with one another.

As Grant ran around tending the fire outside and guests' drinks inside, he realized that this party probably represented the most nonwhite people in Waynesville at one time in modern history. When the party was over, he wanted to do it again. "Do we have to wait until next Christmas to have people over?" he asked Kyla. They decided to develop a tradition of opening their home to their friends on the second Saturday of every month. They would provide the main dish for dinner, and guests could bring side dishes, drinks, and dessert. Over time, the community expanded beyond the Four-Seven to include friends from Undivided, Crossroads, and other parts of their life.

Sandra and her family became regulars at Second Saturdays. Grant's father would waylay her husband at the front door to see if he wanted any bourbon. Sandra's older children would run off, familiarly finding their way to the basement, where the other children were playing. Being with Grant's family was, in many ways, an easy fit for Sandra's family. When her husband was around her friends from the Justice Team, Sandra sometimes felt embarrassed by the things he said and did. It seemed to her that he was becoming more vocal around her new friends, chafing against the idea of curtailing his opinions, even if they were abrasive. Being with Grant's family was different, though. Sandra thought her husband felt refuge with them in a way he never did with her other friends from the Justice Team. When Grant's father invited him to check out the array of bourbons, he happily followed.

Grant often gave Sandra and Michelle his iPhone so they could pick the music for the party. They looked at the songs Grant had on his phone and jestingly mocked him for his choices. "You can't make us listen to white people music!" they exclaimed. Grant laughed and shrugged, indicating they could choose whatever they wanted. Sandra and Michelle discarded most of his choices and found other songs they liked better.

When Grant and Kyla needed to buy a new kitchen table, they decided to invest in a piece of furniture in a way they never had before. The kitchen table in the home they shared with Grant's parents used to be primarily a repository of mail, paperwork, and packages. But Second Saturdays were becoming such a central part of their social community that they wanted a table to support it. They commissioned a farmhouse-style table from a couple at Crossroads who had just started a new woodworking business. The table became one of their most prized possessions and the centerpiece of the Second Saturday potlucks. Instead of spreading the food out on the kitchen counters, they used the table, creating a more open spread for people to enjoy.

When Grant's parents sold their childhood home and moved to Cincinnati, they all decided to continue multigenerational living. Their new home had to be big enough for all four generations, and for Second Saturdays. They wanted a big backyard where people could gather and enough space to have sixty people in the house. And they wanted a dining room large enough to accommodate their table.

The relationships nurtured at Second Saturdays were necessary to keep people like Grant in the work when the costs of antiracism mounted. The prospect of disappointing friends like Sandra, Michelle, and his Second Saturday community encouraged Grant and kept him accountable to their trust even when he faced backlash at work. Sociologist Mark Warren found that such relationships were the key differentiating factor between white people who continued in the work of antiracism and white people who faltered. Too often, however, people sought to make themselves less accountable to others instead of more accountable. They read books about antiracism, donated money to causes, and patted themselves on the back. Or they attended DEI training sessions that fed them pabulum without doing anything to put them into relationship with others.

Despite all the mistakes of his past, Grant was developing a creeping wisdom. He nurtured his relationship with Sandra and Michelle with care.

～

The chapel in the prison where Grant most frequently volunteered looked like a Goodwill for abandoned churches. Wooden pews in assorted colors lined the front of the room. Scattered chairs dotted the vacant space in the back. The mismatched pews contrasted with high stained-glass windows that gave the room a more majestic feel. A simple cross adorned an altar draped with cloth. When Grant and the volunteers arrived for their weekly visit with the Four-Seven, they always arranged folding chairs in the back into circles to create more intimate groups for their work with the men.

Grant always made a point to chat with all the correctional officers the Four-Seven encountered. The Four-Seven often brought food and other materials into the prison. Sandra and a group of volunteers once brought makeup into a prison, for instance, to treat the imprisoned women to personalized facials, emphasizing that they were still daughters of God, despite their offenses. Grant knew he needed the officers' support to continue such work, so he intentionally trained the volunteers to be respectful of the officers' needs. Whenever they brought food, they made sure there was enough to share.

Grant got to know one guard better than the others, an older white career officer. He and Grant usually joked about Ohio sports. As a lifelong fan of the Bengals and the Reds, Grant found it easy to create rapport with him by sharing his despair about both teams. They rarely talked about the men in prison or Grant's job in the system. During the Four-Seven session, the officer sat silently in the back of the chapel while Grant and the other volunteers led the men through the curriculum. One week, as Grant chatted with the officer after the session, the officer ventured beyond their usual banter about sports. He jabbed his finger toward the prison blocks where the men were headed. "You know, who they are when they are with you is not who they are when they are down there," he said.

Grant knew this officer was articulating something that so many of the correctional officers he encountered felt—that Grant was spreading "fake news." They thought Grant's offering of holistic portraits of the men and women in the system was creating a misleading sense of the inmates. Some guards on social media even trashed the photos and videos Grant posted and questioned their accuracy. This officer, whom Grant considered a friendly acquaintance, was joining the others.

Grant looked at the guard, briefly taken aback. "I get that," he responded slowly. "But who I am here is not who I am when I get home."

Grant waited for the officer to respond, taking in the long

cement corridor where they were standing and the acrid smell of the prison cafeteria down the hall. He thought a look of understanding flashed quickly across the officer's face. But the officer changed the subject.

When Grant got home that night, he wondered how far he could push the boundaries of his job without losing it.

CHAPTER FIFTEEN

NO ONE TRUSTS LEADERSHIP

In January 2018, a prominent member of the Crossroads community wrote a post on the church's public blog, awkwardly titled "The Reasons Why I Support Trump Are for What You May Not Think." The post focused on the author's interpretation of Romans 13, a letter the apostle Paul wrote to the Romans about why they should honor and obey secular authorities: "Let every person be subject to the governing authorities" (Romans 13:1). Throughout American history, this passage had been a cudgel people in positions of power used to reinforce notions of submission to traditional authority. Loyalists to the Crown used it during the American Revolution to preach obedience to the British king. Slaveholders used it to justify slavery in America when it was the law of the land. The Crossroads blog post claimed that people should put their reservations about Trump aside and submit to his authority as president.

The post sharpened a knife that had been cleaving the Crossroads community. By insistently refusing to hide his expressions of old-fashioned racism, President Trump was calling a question that Crossroads (and the entire white evangelical community) had been trying to avoid for many decades: How committed were they, really, to dismantling racism? The refusal of prominent white evangelical leaders to denounce Trump exposed a truth that the community had been clumsily trying to hide. Their congregants and their peers had to face the truth that for some, the commitment to upholding a social order that put white men on top was stronger than any vision of God's universal love. Power trumped justice. Headlines about the ensuing crises within evangelicalism proliferated as the broader faith community fought about charges of racism, patriarchy, and abuse.

These controversies reverberated throughout individual churches across the country and crystallized around specific incidents like the blog post. Within Crossroads, Chuck became the fulcrum of disagreement between church leaders and those in the community who were most upset. The Crossroads blog was a decentralized, online site in which a number of staff, congregants, and other members of the community wrote about a range of issues. Not all of the blog posts were thoroughly vetted before they were posted; most of the church leadership had not seen this one before it went up. The immediate outcry prompted church leaders to remove it. Brian wrote a subsequent blog post affirming his commitment to free speech but arguing that words that hurt more people than they helped should be considered more carefully.

Fury persisted. For many, taking down the post was not enough. "Someone let that post get through," they said to Chuck. "What does it say about our church?"

Like so many other Black leaders navigating white-dominant spaces, Chuck had to make choices about how to negotiate power and compromise on both sides. He, along with Lynn, constantly had to switch between their roles as members of the church staff and leaders of Undivided. Acting with the wholeness of an integrated self in Crossroads was a privilege reserved for those who benefited from the social order. The turmoil in the Crossroads community became like a mirror to Chuck's soul.

Carolyn, white, and Elizabeth, Black, organized key leaders in

the Justice Team and other groups within the church represent-
ing the interests of nonwhite communities to ask for a meeting
with church leaders. Darin Yates, the executive pastor of Crossroads, immediately responded. Darin, who was white, was basi-
cally the chief operating officer of the church. If Brian was the
public face of the church, Darin was the person who managed it
behind the scenes. He had grown up in Georgia as the son and
grandson of pastors and had witnessed the way racial injustice
could divide a community. Along with Kathy Beechem, he had
been an early advocate for cultivating work around racial reconciliation within Crossroads, asking Lynn to develop diversity training
for the Crossroads staff in 2014. When Carolyn, Elizabeth, and
other leaders asked for a meeting to discuss the blog post, Darin
quickly said yes.

Darin, Grant, Sandra, Chuck, Lynn, Carolyn, Elizabeth, and
leaders of some of the other justice-oriented programs at Crossroads gathered in the Fireplace Room, a cozy meeting space that
counterbalanced the tension. Carolyn participated in the meeting
as a leader of the Justice Team, Grant attended to represent the
prison ministry, and Sandra attended as a prominent leader with
Undivided. Chuck and Lynn had to act both as leaders of Undivided and members of the staff.

It was an emotional meeting. A Black leader with Undivided
described how he felt when he was an usher and one of his fellow
ushers told him how much he "fucking hates Obama." A Puerto
Rican leader asked why the church had made such a big effort
to support New Orleans after big hurricanes but had done nothing when Puerto Rico was hit by a similar series of devastating
storms. Grant described how certain sermons were so insensitive
to nonwhite people that he felt limited in his ability to share Crossroads content with the men and women in the prison ministry.
People cried as they spoke. Darin sat and listened soberly. He did
not offer immediate answers, recognizing that it was a moment

for him to learn. He asked for time to talk with leadership to figure out what to do.

The conversation came on the heels of a tumultuous period not only for the broader evangelical community but also for the Justice Team, which remained unsure about where to put their energies. Over the course of 2017, the Justice Team had decided to get involved in a statewide campaign for Issue 1, a 2018 ballot initiative seeking to change the state constitution to reduce the number of people in state prisons for low-level, nonviolent crimes. The initiative would have reclassified crimes like drug possession as misdemeanors and dedicated the funds saved by reducing the prison population to rehabilitation for drug offenses. The Justice Team joined a coalition of groups uniting behind what they called the Ohio Safe and Healthy Communities Campaign.

By Ohio state law, an initiative seeking to change the state constitution needed a certain number of signatures from a certain number of counties across the state to qualify for the ballot. Each of those signatures would then be validated by the secretary of state's office to ensure that only eligible voters were signing the petition. To ensure they had enough valid signatures, advocates of ballot initiatives commonly obtained twice as many (or more) signatures than the minimum required.

The Justice Team took responsibility for helping to obtain signatures in Hamilton County, where Cincinnati sits. They had about six months to get them before they were due to the secretary of state's office. Buoyed by their experience with Issue 44, they were confident they could easily meet their targets. They assumed they would have similar levels of support from Crossroads. To help support Issue 44, Crossroads had allowed the Justice Team to make announcements from the main stage about the work. At one point, Chuck had even taped a video endorsing Issue 44 that became part of the campaign's promotional materials.

It was not so easy with Issue 1. When Sandra and other members of the Justice Team began circulating their petition, they immediately encountered resistance they had not anticipated. People who had supported universal preschool with targeted resources for Black children, as well as people who had participated in the prison ministry, balked at signing the new petition. When they asked for time onstage to talk about the petition, the church's teaching team gently rejected them. When the Justice Team set up a table in the lobby where they could recruit people as signatories, Brian sent them an email asking them to stop using the space.

Grant wrote back to Brian immediately—"You will let us go into the prisons to minister to the inmates, but you won't let us advocate for measures to keep them out of prison?"—but did not get a response.

Grant and Sandra were not privy to all of the conversations Chuck was having internally, but the pushback against Issue 1 started to feel like a pattern within the church. They felt that Crossroads was moving in the opposite direction of the Justice Team. Brian had recently videotaped a sermon with a backdrop displaying a timeline of American history that they felt whitewashed the country's past, omitting key aspects of the Black experience. They felt like communications coming from the church—whether it was sermons from the stage, social media posts, or other messages that were posted on the church's website—were subtly undermining or pushing back against their efforts toward racial justice.

So they were all eager to hear from Darin when he asked the group to reconvene a month or so later so that he could report back on his conversations. Darin arrived at the second meeting with a list of commitments the church had made: they would put a Black person on the Spiritual Board for the first time; they would make equity and inclusion their theme for the year and think more intentionally about reaching nonwhite communities;

and they would provide the Justice Team with a different space for their petitions for Issue 1. Darin soberly reported on the impending changes, seeking to communicate what he perceived to be staunch institutional support for the work of the teams around the table. People listened quietly and nodded politely.

After Darin left, Chuck noticed the glum faces around the table and asked what was wrong. "The head of the church just came in and told you all the things he's going to do," he said. An awkward silence followed, as everyone looked nervously at one another.

Finally, Sandra responded, telling Chuck it didn't feel like it was enough, or very authentic. Having had many conversations with people in the room about their frustration with church leaders who were not doing more on racial justice, Sandra felt brave enough to voice her concerns.

Chuck countered that he felt like he constantly had to walk a tightrope, to figure out how he could support the Justice Team without getting their work shut down. Sometimes he urged them to step back if he felt like what they were doing could trigger a backlash from the church leadership that had the potential to dismantle their work entirely.

Sandra wasn't buying it. "Why are we supposed to walk on eggshells when all the other groups in the church can speak out?"

The room became silent. Sandra had said what many of them were too scared to say out loud. They feared confronting a truth about their own church that they were not sure they wanted to admit.

Sandra's question also cut to Chuck's own insecurities about his leadership. He responded with uncharacteristic defensiveness. "Am I the bottleneck in this group? Am I the one holding you all back?"

"Yes, you're the bottleneck," said Sandra.

People began to murmur in halting efforts to smooth over the tension.

But Chuck was angry. "Well, do you trust the leadership?" he asked.

"Of course not. No one trusts leadership," Sandra scoffed.

There was silence, which Chuck broke: "Well, maybe if you can't trust leadership, Sandra, you should not lead."

Sandra burst into tears. Carolyn jumped into the conversation before anyone else could say anything and said, "Okay, this is really overwhelming for everyone right now. Let's just take a break."

Chuck walked out of the room, but immediately felt bad. He looked for Sandra to apologize, but she had already disappeared. Chuck thought back to when he left Crossroads for a Black church but later returned. He had been so clear about his calling to rejoin the Crossroads community, but now he wondered if it had changed him more than he had changed the church. Had he bent so far to accommodate whiteness that he didn't notice he was breaking?

After a few days, Chuck called Grant to ask for advice about how to repair his relationship with Sandra. "You have to reach out to her," Grant told him. Chuck called Sandra and asked her to find a time to talk. Sandra was honest with him when they met. She said she felt that she was expressing what everyone else in the room thought but was not brave enough to say. They were doing the brunt of the work as foot soldiers for Undivided and the Justice Team, but they weren't allowed to speak up. Chuck apologized.

For the first time, Chuck realized how much his own indecision about how far to push the church was hurting other people.

~

As a program, Undivided moved into a period of some stasis in 2018 and 2019. Six-week cohorts of the program continued within the Crossroads community, but it was not innovating. The leadership team that Chuck had originally assembled to help him build the program stopped meeting after the first year or so. Members of the planning team who were not full-time staff at Crossroads retreated, drawn away by the inevitable pull of their own careers. Most of them became less engaged in the day-to-day operations of Undivided. Running the program fell mostly to Lynn, who continued to recruit and train new facilitators and manage additional sessions at campuses throughout the Crossroads community. Troy, the pastor turned community organizer who helped start the Justice Team, was the main person from the planning team who kept volunteering actively with the program.

Even Chuck seemed to withdraw a little, though he remained the public face of Undivided. Held back by his own indecision, Chuck allowed his responsibilities as campus pastor at Oakley to dominate much of his time. Since he had delivered his lament after the second failed trial of Ray Tensing, Chuck had been wrestling with the question of how bold he wanted to be about pushing the church to change—and whether Crossroads was the right place for him. He hadn't answered the question for himself yet.

On the one hand, witnessing the growth of people like Jess, Sandra, and Grant as they worked with one another for antiracism made him feel like he was doing exactly what he should be doing. Being at Crossroads allowed him to reach white people like Grant and Jess whom he would never reach from the kind of Black church where he had grown up. It provided him with a platform from which he could do the work of building the multiracial bridges he felt were needed.

On the other hand, he thought about the members of the Crossroads community who claimed to feel threatened by the image of his sons. He thought about the pain he felt—and concealed—whenever the church seemed to minimize the work of racial justice. The Trump era was forcing choices upon churches like Crossroads that had long tried to avoid what they perceived to be political issues. When Trump explicitly drew connections between white supremacy and evangelicalism, many adherents yearned for their churches to get off the sidelines. Yet many churches, including Crossroads, waffled in their response.

In 2018, Billy Graham died. He had long helped hold together disparate strands of evangelicalism, and his funeral brought together the hodgepodge elements of the faith. It juxtaposed people like Donald Trump and Vice President Mike Pence, symbols of the institutionalized relationship between certain evangelicals and white conservative politics, alongside Rick Warren, a leader in the less politicized mission-oriented church growth movement. Trump's coalition was seeking to step into the void Graham left and create its own center of gravity within the faith.

Another prominent leader at the funeral was Doug Birdsall, the former executive chairman of the Lausanne Movement (the effort to spread global evangelicalism that emerged after the 1974 convention). Birdsall was a fifth-generation pastor who spent decades serving as a missionary in Asia. He had long been dismayed to see the creeping growth of white Christian nationalism within the Trump-loving contingent of his faith. Watching deeply submerged fissures between growth, power, and justice explode into the open, Birdsall decided to organize a meeting after Graham's death to try to revitalize what he perceived to be Graham's original mission of personal salvation and the missionary spread of the church. He asked the Billy Graham Center at Wheaton College, one of the most prominent intellectual homes of conservative evangelicalism (sometimes nicknamed "the evangelical Harvard"), to host the meeting in April 2018. The invitation indicated that "support of 'eighty-one percent of self-identifying white evangelicals' for Donald Trump is a call to self-reflection on the current condition of evangelicalism." Many luminaries of moderate evangelicalism attended, including the president and CEO of the prominent publication *Christianity Today*, white and non-white pastors of some of the largest and most historic evangelical churches in the country, and leaders of the National Association of Evangelicals (NAE).

Birdsall stated that the goal of the April meeting was to issue a collective statement to articulate a view of evangelicalism that would counteract the public image that was emerging from the Trump era. Shortly after Birdsall announced his meeting, however, the Trump administration announced plans for a June convening of over a thousand evangelical leaders that would represent the more conservative side of evangelicalism. The two meetings quickly came to be perceived in opposition to each other. Some leaders who had agreed to attend Birdsall's meeting got calls from donors critical of their attendance. Birdsall tried to play down the conflict, noting that he had issued the call for his meeting without knowing about Trump's June plans. He had limited success. Tensions kept rising.

Birdsall's meeting began with a series of discussions about key issues of the day—immigration, the role of women in the church, racism. All of the discussions implicitly addressed the hardening of conservative white evangelicalism and its embrace of Trump, even though speakers sought to avoid mention of the president. They wanted the meeting to be about their faith, not his politics. Speakers debated how their community could navigate disagreement without splitting the church, what civil disagreement looked like, and how the church should engage with its growing presence in the Global South. Putting a point on the discussion, Charlie Dates, a young Black pastor in Illinois (who became the lead pastor of Chicago's prominent Progressive Baptist megachurch in 2023), declared, "American evangelicalism has not been able to separate itself from the perks of white supremacy." Two attendees left the meeting early because they felt it was too critical of Trump.

At the heart of the debate among the remaining attendees was the familiar question of how the church should address social and political issues of the day. Should it focus on individual transformation, societal transformation, or both? How directly should it address political issues? Many of the older participants, who were disproportionately white, preached a message of civility and unity. Younger nonwhite leaders disagreed, arguing that unity without repentance was impossible. Unity would emerge only when white people repented for their role in sustaining white supremacy. They desired a bolder statement on current issues.

Disagreement bred disengagement. In the end, the statement Birdsall wanted never emerged. By saying nothing, moderate evangelical leaders left a void in the public image of evangelicalism—a void that Trump and his supporters were only too happy to fill.

A broader movement focused on "deconstruction" of the faith gained momentum within the evangelical community. A number of Black evangelicals were leaving the faith, finding it impossible to affirm their identity as Black people *and* as followers of Jesus. This deconstruction focused not only on racial injustice but also the sexism and patriarchy that pervaded the church. Other nonwhite people, queer people, women, and many others who felt that their faith commitments were incompatible with the increasingly political version of evangelicalism in the public domain, were walking away. Hundreds of women were going public with stories of sexual abuse by prominent leaders within evangelicalism. Institutional reluctance to sanction racism or the actions of these leaders caused widespread outcry. How could people claim to follow Jesus and sanction such abuse? Could their faith and their relationship to God be great if their churches were not good?

When asked about his views, Brian insisted that Jesus was apolitical: "Jesus is my model. My goal is that people would never know where I stand on [political] issues." That was his reason for sidestepping politics. "When we are the church, we should be taking our cues from the Bible, from Jesus. And Jesus lived in the midst of an incredibly politically oppressive environment within the nation of Rome. Like Jesus, all Americans feel some

sense of oppression. . . . And what did Jesus say? Did Jesus try to
rally people against the political powers? He didn't do that, never.
Not a single solitary time. Not a single solitary statement against
the policy of Rome. . . . In fact, the only time he actually talked
about the policies of Rome was in relationship to taxes, and he
said, 'Pay your taxes.' "

Chuck sat at the confluence of these competing currents within
his faith. He prayed about whether he could and should belong
to a church that preached a politics of obedience to a state that
actively subjugated Black people. He loved so much of what Crossroads provided—including the space to build Undivided—and he
felt deep personal loyalty to the church for saving him. Would he
have found his calling as a pastor without Crossroads? Would
he have saved his marriage and survived his addiction to pornography without the church? But he also recognized that the
church's willingness to challenge people in their commitment to
racial justice was bounded by their commitment to having people
accept the systems around them.

Jess did not know Chuck very well but had enormous respect
for the work he was doing. She knew how angry she got talking
to her mother about Philando Castile and wondered how Chuck
maintained his composure in front of the entire church community. "Don't you ever want to flip the tables?" she asked him at an
Undivided event.

Chuck laughed off her question, but it cut to the heart of
his inner turmoil. Should he be flipping the tables more?
Chuck respected the fact that what Crossroads was doing was
working—if working meant bringing more people to God. But
he yearned for his childhood church, where the Black experience
was at the center of everything. *What is God calling me to do here?*
he kept asking himself. Uncertainty yielded hesitancy. Crossroads
was undoubtedly far more successful than any other church he

had ever attended in spreading Jesus's Word. But was it the same Word that he wanted to spread?

At one point, Chuck, Lynn, and Troy took a trip to Columbus, Ohio, to meet with another Black leader working to support multiracial churches. They were considering expanding Undivided into the Columbus area and wanted to talk with her to get her advice. She was not supportive.

"You know," she said, "there are a lot of Black churches that have been doing this work for a really long time. What kind of partnerships do you have with them?"

Her pointed challenge lit a light bulb in Lynn's mind. *Oh my goodness,* she realized. They had gotten so caught up in the Crossroads bubble that they had ignored other Black leaders who were doing the work. They had to get out of the bubble.

On the drive home, Lynn urged Chuck to reach out to other Black pastors. "But what if they see me as illegitimate?" Chuck asked. After having been part of a white-dominant church for so long, Chuck worried that he would not have credibility among Black pastors.

"You have no choice," Lynn said.

Lynn began laying the groundwork for building relationships with other racial justice leaders and reaching out to other churches who might be interested in pursuing the work. Chuck, too, realized he had to move Undivided out of the Crossroads bubble. They also opened discussions within Crossroads, to explore what the appropriate relationship of Undivided was to the church. As she undertook these processes, Lynn decided she had to leave Crossroads. She had been on staff for eight years at that point and her job had shifted from being part of the Spiritual Growth Team to leading Undivided. But she realized she could no longer lead the program because it lacked the depth of support it needed from Crossroads leadership, and it overburdened nonwhite people by asking them to teach white people about their own racism. One morning, she thought she heard the voice of God saying, *Go, and don't look back.* Lynn left abruptly, leaving Chuck and Troy as the primary drivers of Undivided.

Crossroads frequently acted as an incubator for other organizations that would begin within the church but then spin off to become their own entities. Chuck, in conversation with the executive leadership team at Crossroads, decided to follow this model for Undivided. The leadership team recognized the impact the program was having in its community and the way Chuck felt compelled to lead the work. They agreed to give Chuck the time he needed to build the program in other faith communities across America. They offered to continue paying his salary but release him from many of his other responsibilities at Crossroads, while also providing seed support to Undivided as it tried to launch itself onto a bigger stage.

Figuring out the details took many months. Undivided entered into what felt like a chrysalis. Even though it did not seem like much was changing from the outside—they continued to run cohorts in Crossroads, and the curriculum mainly stayed the same—inside, the program was transforming itself. Chuck started doing the patient outreach and relationship building necessary to create a bigger platform for Undivided around the country.

CHAPTER SIXTEEN

IS THIS MARTIN'S DREAM FOR ME?

As tensions with Crossroads heightened because of the turmoil over the blog post and other communications, Sandra and some of the women she met through the Justice Team decided they needed a way to invest more deeply in their own spiritual formation. They asked church leaders for advice. The leaders recommended a Huddle, a small-group Bible study that people could self-organize around a prescribed curriculum. For one year, Huddle groups would gather to study the Bible, immerse themselves in the "characteristics and competencies of Jesus," and learn how to better "be like Jesus." Sandra, five other Black women, and two white women formed a group together. The Huddle became an important space of restoration and renewal for Sandra, where she could rebuild relationships with Black women that she had long neglected.

From their first meeting, the conversations in Sandra's Huddle were very raw. The curriculum focused on helping people explore their relationship with Jesus, but their conversations about faith inevitably intersected with conversations about race. When one of the white women admitted to voting for Trump, another Black woman responded plainly. "I do not trust white women," she said. The other women in the group nodded in understanding. "It is not my responsibility to educate them," the woman continued.

"Get your own house in order before you come to me." Sandra loved it. The Huddle reminded her of what it felt like to attend a Black church. Unlike her other experiences at Crossroads, it was a place where she could bring her full self as a Black woman, a mother, a follower of Christ, and an advocate for justice. The women in the group shared meals together, daily texts, and frequent social interactions. For Sandra, these women became an important part of her journey to rediscover her own identity as a Black woman.

Sandra still had to confront the pain points she had been avoiding in her marriage. After her camping trip a year earlier, she committed to trying to make her marriage work—but in a way that allowed her to be fully herself. Instead of walking away from conversations about race, she wanted to dive into them.

But they were struggling. Most days, her husband left the house before the children woke up and came home after they went to bed. Household duties accumulated endlessly: breakfast, dishes, school lunches, drop-off, grocery shopping, laundry, errands, pickup, naps, snack time, dinner, baths, bedtime. She and her husband couldn't venture into the conversations she wanted without time to have them. Despite sometimes despairing, Sandra kept trying, fueling an ember of hope with her faith.

Patterns of patriarchy infusing the choices Sandra and her husband made about the division of household labor were not uncommon in evangelical Christian (and many other) marriages. Women took care of domestic duties; men ruled the roost. It had not always been so. In the nineteenth century, Victorian Christianity had actually emphasized gentility and restraint for both men and women. Internecine wars within white evangelicalism, however, begot aggression as fundamentalists, modernists, and other groups fought for primacy in the faith. As historian Kristin Kobes Du Mez documented in her aptly titled book *Jesus and John Wayne*, aggression became equated with masculinity in ways that shaped assumptions about the appropriate division of household labor. As the twentieth century progressed, white evangelicals realized they could gain more adherents by playing into patriarchal conventions in society, feeding the masses that which felt familiar and safe. Patriarchy became further entrenched. By the twenty-first century, many evangelical women had joined Sandra in resisting that pattern.

Sandra remembered her father's reproach years before, when she had first considered marrying a white man: "I did not raise you to be some white man's housewife." Sandra had scorned her father in that conversation, but his words stayed with her. Now, as she moved through her beleaguered days, she kept thinking about her father's words. *It's like I'm a house slave,* she realized with a shudder. Once she had that image in her head, she couldn't dislodge it.

As her home life deteriorated, Sandra's relationships with the women in the Huddle and on the Justice Team became even more vital. When she was with those groups, she felt an acceptance she lacked at home.

She texted her husband before her weekly Huddle meeting to make sure he would be home in time to watch the children. He had been late the week before, forcing her to scramble at the last minute to find alternate childcare arrangements. He did not respond. Finally, she called him to ask what time he would come home. He sighed and enumerated all the problems she was creating by pulling him away from work. Layers of desire (to attend the Huddle), duty (to be faithful to her husband's needs), and doubt (what was the right thing to do?) collided in Sandra's mind. She knew he was trying to make her feel guilty, but she refused to comply. She had to prioritize her own needs, and she knew she had to see the women from the Huddle.

"Fine," he finally said. "How long will you be gone?"

"We'll only be meeting for an hour. And I need a little time to get there and back," Sandra said. She knew the meetings often ran over time, but she worried her husband would not come home if he thought she would be gone too long.

"I'll come if you can be home in ninety minutes," he said.

She knew that would not be enough time. She considered objecting, but hung up instead.

As soon as her husband arrived home to watch the children, Sandra jumped in the car and raced to her friend's house. When she walked inside, seeing the other women immediately made her shoulders relax. She could feel her lungs expanding as she breathed in air that felt lighter. The other women hugged her and invited her to sit down. One of the white women was in the middle of a story describing how the Black Lives Matter sign on their front door had been vandalized. This woman and her family lived in a largely white neighborhood in Cincinnati. A Black Lives Matter sign on their porch had been stolen nine times during the last year. This time, the thief stole their sign in the middle of the night and replaced it with a Confederate flag.

The women in the Huddle were pained but unsurprised. The callous assertion of white supremacy into their lives no longer astonished them. They shifted into a discussion of the Bible reading for that week. Sandra glanced nervously at her watch. Thirty minutes had already passed. She tried to pay attention to the conversation, but was visibly distracted. Her tension increased with each passing minute, prompting the other women to look curiously at her. Sandra knew they wanted to understand the source of her anxiety.

She had already shared with them the difficulties she and her husband had talking about race. But she wasn't sure how to explain the fights they had about childcare, household chores, and the complex structure of their lives. On the one hand, she felt like it was her responsibility to take care of the house and the children, and she loved being with them. But her husband had been making her feel increasingly guilty about the way she was running the household. His objections made her feel insecure. She was no longer sure who was right.

She kept glancing at her watch. About eighty minutes after she had left home, a break in their conversation emerged. Sandra jumped up to leave, ignoring the quizzical looks from her friends. She abruptly hugged them all goodbye and rushed out of the house. She didn't have time to address their curiosity.

She jumped into her Mazda minivan and started racing home. Her husband called her, but she ignored it. She heard the familiar ping of a text from him coming through. When she hit a red light, she sent a quick response: "Five minutes away."

When she walked in the door, he said, "You're late. I've been calling you." Sandra ignored him. She started picking up toys around the house and putting them in the right places. The familiar motions soothed her. Blocks in one bin. Art supplies in another. Stuffed animals in the corner. But he kept following her around, repeatedly asking why she was late. She put dirty clothes in the hamper, empty cups in the sink.

"You're not listening to me," her husband said. "Tell me why you were late."

Something inside Sandra broke. Sandra had spent most of her life allowing other people to answer the fundamental question *What should I do?* for her. It was a deceptively simple question whose answer required people to make a complex assessment of what they valued and how they were going to go about attaining it. Parents dictated the answers for their children. Schools dictated to students. Employers dictated to employees. But somewhere in the morass of growing, learning, and working, humans had an ineffable need to carve space to answer that question for themselves. Adulthood should have bestowed on Sandra the autonomy to answer the question independently, but it did not. Instead, her church, her husband, her white friends—they all tried to endow her with a statement of what she should value in life and how she could strategize to attain it.

As her husband escalated his attempts to bend her to his will, driving her from the solidarity she craved with her Huddle, Sandra realized that she had a sphere of influence she had never claimed. Different people would always value different things. Sandra and her husband might never want the same things. But despite how different they were from each other, they each possessed the right to search for ways to make the next day better than the one before. Sandra did not have to conform to his values. Instead, she had to carve her own space to act, to find ways for their spheres of influence to exist alongside each other. She had to claim her own autonomy.

Sandra whipped around. She looked directly at her husband, staring into his eyes as she yelled back. He was already on edge. The exchange erupted immediately into a shouting match. This time Sandra refused to back down. They fed off of each other's anger. The shouting got louder, until eventually, he stormed out of the house.

～

After that night, Sandra and her husband avoided being in the house together. During the week he spent most of his time in the office. On weekends, Sandra slept at the home of one of the Black women she had befriended. At first, Sandra felt ashamed. She worried her friends would think she was weak. But she could no longer hide the facts from Carolyn, Michelle, and a few women in her Huddle—all of whom embraced her. The women, Black and white, gave her space to unpack and debrief the months (or years) of tension she had been enduring. They offered her emotional and logistical support as she tried to create some stability for her children. To Sandra, their embrace felt radical.

Sandra convinced her husband to enter into counseling with

her. She had already been divorced once, and she didn't want to get divorced again. Sandra pushed aside her fights with Chuck and the church over Issue 1 and the church's stances on racial injustice. She needed the church's support. It was still, after all, her church. She reached out to Darin and explained what had been happening. He offered church funds to pay for their marriage counseling.

Sandra and her husband saw each other in counseling and in the moments they had to get together for the children. She reestablished a set of routines with the kids and her household that worked for her. An avid journaler since childhood, Sandra began writing in the mornings again before the children awoke. The rare moment of solitary quiet gave her an opportunity to be in regular conversation with God. She read self-help books and threw herself into Bible study with the Huddle. She was not ready to open up to the entire group because she still felt some shame about her situation, but she engaged wholeheartedly with the weekly explorations of her relationship with Jesus. These discussions became a way for Sandra to ask herself what kind of person she wanted to become.

She wrote a poem in her journal, "Is This Martin's Dream for Me?," reflecting on the sacrifice that her ancestors had made to fight for civil rights. Was she living up to the ideals they had imagined for their Black descendants? She thought about her father's sharp admonition about marrying a white man. She had ignored his advice and was now raising biracial children, worried they might lose their Black identity.

In counseling, Sandra finally forced her husband into conversations about their relationship that he had refused to engage in before. She shared her poem with him and described how it felt when he downplayed her Black identity. Their goal was to learn to disagree productively with each other. For the first time, they were able to have a discussion that didn't devolve into a shouting match. After a couple of months, Sandra felt like she could sleep at home again on the weekends. It took several more months to figure out a way they could both feel comfortable. Through counseling, they negotiated a set of guidelines about communication, independence, and household responsibilities. She wasn't sure what his acquiescence to these guidelines meant, but she was certain that she was standing up for herself more than she ever had before. Sandra prayed that all would be well.

CHAPTER SEVENTEEN

SOMEONE CALL CHUCK

At the end of February 2020, three white men in Georgia pursued Ahmaud Arbery, a twenty-five-year-old unarmed Black man jogging through the neighborhood, cornered him with their pickup truck in a cul-de-sac, and then murdered him. The vicious vigilantism of the perpetrators made this killing stand out on an unending list of barbarous murders of Black men in America.

Arbery's murder coincided with the third week of a four-week series Crossroads had been running called Don't Panic. Like many megachurches, Crossroads organized its weekly sermons into thematic arcs that usually lasted between three and six weeks. The teaching team carefully planned and produced these series for months. Anticipating controversy around the 2020 election, the teaching team had planned a series early in the election year designed to provide guidance for the congregation in navigating the polarized political climate.

The Don't Panic series encouraged Crossroads congregants to reject the political scripts given to them by the Republican and Democratic parties and urged their congregants to follow "the Kingdom Way"—an approach to politics grounded in their commitment to God, rather than either political party. The Kingdom Way meant walking the line between liberal and conservative interpretations of politics. While conservatives believe that "intrusive government is the primary barrier to human freedom and flourishing," the church argued, liberals believe that "a protective government is the primary way to ensure freedom and justice for all." People who chose the Kingdom Way would see that "government is a deeply flawed, human system. But it's also a system that God has used in the past, and will use in the future to do his will."

When news of Arbery's murder emerged the final weekend of the Don't Panic series, the initial public reaction was modest. According to *The Washington Post,* from 2015 to January 2020, there were 1,179 fatal police shootings of Black men. The public had become desensitized. Further, in March 2020, the global coronavirus pandemic distracted the world. But when a local TV station in Georgia released the video of Arbery's murder on May 5, it immediately went viral. Public outcry finally caught up to the brutality. Two days later, the state of Georgia arrested two of the alleged perpetrators, charging them with felony murder and other crimes.

As Grant watched the news and subsequent outcry unfold, he knew the church would have to say something. He had recently begun a new job working on the marketing and production team at Crossroads, leaving behind his career with the Department of Rehabilitation and Correction. The contradictions had become too extreme. His conversations with Sandra and Michelle, as well as his own reading, rendered him increasingly unable to silence his own objections to the racialization of the criminal justice system. Yet as a public employee, he was constrained in his ability to advocate for antiracism. And he was getting more and more passive-aggressive resistance from wardens and correctional officers as he traveled around the state to capture videos and images of imprisoned men and women. Those factors, along with the problems created for his young family by his long commute, convinced him to quit.

People like Grant (reasonably) become unable to inhabit institutions that are irreconcilable with their values, leaving behind those all too happy to acquiesce to the prevailing value structure. This tendency exacerbates the challenge of transforming societal institutions—the workplaces, churches, schools, social groups, and neighborhoods that sustain and reproduce inequality become increasingly homogenous as people self-segregate with others who share their values.

Political scientist Albert Hirschman presaged this dilemma in his 1970 book *Exit, Voice, and Loyalty*. Many organizations, like corporations, operated on what he called the logic of "exit": when people disliked the "product" the organization was producing, they would simply leave. Exit worked in free and open markets, where customers could easily choose between companies encouraged to differentiate their products. Not all organizations operated in free markets, however, and not everyone could effortlessly choose among them. Many organizations, Hirschman argued, had to operate on a logic of "voice." When people were upset, they needed avenues for expressing their discontent—or using their voice—so they wouldn't be tempted to leave. The power of such organizations, including most churches, clubs, grassroots groups, and other social and political organizations, came from generating loyalties that broadened their base. Those organizations had to break down their walls, not build them up. Small might be beautiful, but not when it emerged through self-segregation.

Beginning around the 1970s, however, economic, technological, and sociopolitical transformations incentivized organizations in America to become more and more specialized. Our country's social, civic, and political sectors became increasingly fragmented. Harvard scholar Theda Skocpol and her collaborators studied the historical trajectory of voluntary organizations in the United States. They found that most voluntary associations in the nineteenth and early twentieth centuries were part of regional or national federations that connected local work to a larger political scale. They identified forty-six associations founded between 1733 and 1938 that were large enough to count at least 1 percent of all U.S. adults as members—which would be the equivalent of 2,583,000 dues-paying members in 2020. Few twenty-first-century organizations can claim such scale. Race complicated this history, however. Many of those organizations sustained, without question, race, gender, and other hierarchies that were a source of conflict and differentiation for many voluntary associations in the twenty-first century. Fragmentation emerged in part because traditionally marginalized groups needed their own organizations to better articulate their own interests.

Building multiracial organizations that authentically share power across race remains an ongoing struggle. Hirschman's argument is that a perfect end state might not exist; instead, the goal is to develop democratic processes internal to these collective bodies that enable an ongoing negotiation of power and interests among different people. Those processes only work, however, if people stick around long enough to make them work. This was the dilemma Chuck was confronting in his relationship to Crossroads, that Jess and Sandra faced in thinking about their families, and that Grant faced in his job with the prison system.

In the correctional system, Grant lacked the opportunities for voice he needed. Enduring the visible and invisible wounds of working in a system that contradicted his values became too much. Racism blurred the fragile line between loyalty and oppression.

Grant's new job with Crossroads simplified his life and gave him space to figure out what was next for him. He hoped he could use his perch to push the church to be more public about its objections to injustice. Just before news of the killing of Ahmaud Arbery emerged, Grant had been promoted to a leadership position he wanted to leverage to shape the church's communications. He called a face-to-face meeting for his team despite the pandemic.

He stayed up late the night before, scrolling through social media and other news feeds on his phone. He was infuriated by the details of the story that were emerging. Despite everything he had been learning about racialized violence in America, Grant was still in disbelief that a group of white men felt they had the license to engage in such open vigilantism. He was impatient for the opportunity to take advantage of the platform he had through his new role at Crossroads.

Grant arrived first at the office the next day. He dropped his stuff off in his workstation, located in a bullpen of desks lined by the few private offices for top church leaders. He waited for his team—three other white people and one Black man. When they all arrived, they gathered to discuss what they should do in response to the emerging news about the Arbery murder.

"Well, someone call Chuck," one of his team members said right away. "Let's get him on camera." Everyone in the group nodded their agreement, and the conversation quickly switched to strategizing about timing and how best to reach and engage Chuck.

Grant felt his heart dropping as the conversation progressed. He tried urging his colleagues to consider a response they could proactively develop without waiting for him, but none of them wanted to make any decisions without having Chuck involved. "Someone just has to call Chuck," they kept saying.

Like everyone else, Grant wanted Chuck's counsel, and he knew Chuck would want to say something. But Grant was unhappy that his team seemed immobilized, unwilling to say anything about racism until they heard from their Black pastor. Grant ran his palms along the black plastic coating on the armrest of his chair. He thought about the emotional labor antiracism demanded of

Black people. By then, it was several years since Michelle had told him, "It's about time someone like you stood in the gap for me." Her words reverberated in his head.

At Crossroads, Grant had come to believe in his own responsibility as a white person to help develop antiracist attitudes and behaviors among other white people. He had walked away from the Department of Rehabilitation and Correction, but he felt enough loyalty to Crossroads to commit to the work of exercising voice. He knew that the risks, the emotional labor, and the pain were not as high for him as it was for his Black friends. Further, Grant recognized the role Sandra and Michelle had played in helping him come to terms with his own racism. He wanted to figure out what he could do as a white person to alleviate that burden.

Before his promotion, as one person on a white-dominant production and marketing team, Grant had done what he could to influence the church's messages. When people made racist comments on the church's social media feeds, Grant would immediately delete the comment and sometimes block the user. He didn't want the church's communication channels to publicly reflect the racism he knew existed in the community. When stories of police brutality and other acts of racism burst into the news, Grant reached out to Hunt, Sandra, Michelle, and other nonwhite people in the church community to ask them what they needed to hear from the church. Too often, they would tell him, the church tried to think about what white people needed to hear but neglected the question of what Black people needed to hear. Grant used his role to push the church to articulate more aggressive statements about police brutality and the many racialized comments that President Trump would make.

It wasn't easy. Grant was pushing the church to go further faster, and church leaders were advising caution. When he went to Brian with his concerns that the church was not being responsive enough to the needs of the nonwhite people in their community,

Grant recalls Brian saying, "I absolutely want people of color to feel seen and heard, but I also don't want to give up on the people who are racist."

At first, Grant was angry. He felt that the church was always prioritizing protection of white people unwilling to confront their own racism over the needs of Black people. But when he thought more about his conversation with Brian, it hit home in a way he had not expected. *If Hunt or Michelle or Sandra had given up on me*, he realized, *I would never have changed.* He thought about everyone he had blocked on Facebook, and the other ways he had effectively given up on those he thought were racist.

"That conversation with Brian changed my way of thinking," Grant said. "I began to ask myself how we do both. How do we, as Crossroads, be bold about what we believe God says about justice and equality and equity? But also, how do we get somebody who is racist and bring them back toward somewhere closer?"

There was no formula for the path Grant was trying to follow. He wanted to act on what he felt was his responsibility to move white people along a spectrum toward greater antiracism, but he also wanted to sustain the integrity of the relationships he had formed with Sandra, Michelle, Hunt, and others.

Meanwhile, he cherished the new symbiosis he and Hunt were cultivating for themselves. When Hunt asked Grant to try going to a Black barbershop, Grant agreed. Hunt recommended one that was often packed. For four hours, Grant sat in the crowded waiting area chatting, laughing, and bantering with the other men. When it was Grant's turn for a haircut, he worried the barber would disdain him for being white. But by then, the barber had heard Grant's repartee with the other customers. When Grant sat down, the barber said, "I feel like I'm talking to a brother who is a fellow believer."

Even as Grant tried, he knew that he sometimes disappointed Hunt and his friends when he couldn't move the church in the ways they wanted. Grant often reached out directly to Michelle and others to ask for forgiveness. "You're my brother," Michelle said. "But this is your journey. It ain't my journey."

Grant agreed with the team discussing Arbery that they should ask Chuck to say something. But how could they engage other leaders in the church, white leaders, to respond? He wanted those white leaders to "stand in the gap," as Michelle had urged. Grant reminded his team about the many people in their community who would dismiss what Chuck was saying as, *That's what the Black pastor thinks*. White church leaders had to stand up as well.

Grant's team listened carefully to his impassioned plea, and some started nodding as he spoke. Grant suggested approaching one of the key white teaching pastors in the church, Kyle Ranson. In his new role, Grant reported directly to Kyle, and he thought he could have a frank conversation with him. "Let's put together a script that Kyle can use in a video," he said.

The one Black man on the team objected. "Let's not script him. Let him speak from his heart. That will be more powerful," he said. Everyone agreed.

Grant texted Kyle and they sat down together that afternoon. "This isn't going to be the last time something like Ahmaud Arbery happens," Grant said. Then he posed his dilemma honestly to Kyle. "We want the Black community to feel heard in their pain. But we also want the hearts of people who were marching in Charlottesville to change," he said, referencing the 2017 white supremacist marches in Virginia that had turned violent. Kyle and Grant spoke for over an hour. They decided that in addition to whatever Chuck would do, Kyle would make his own video. Kyle was the head pastor of Crossroads' online community and had his own following that Grant knew would listen to him.

In the video, Kyle wore a bright pink T-shirt with a gray fleece on top. He had a baseball cap turned backward on his head and was walking along a wooded path. He started by talking about viruses. "What makes a virus successful?" he asked. "And how do you [as a virus] achieve maximum destruction?" He said that there were two elements needed for a virus to be destructive—deadliness and avoiding detection. For the first few minutes of the video, it seemed like he was just talking about the pandemic.

But then Kyle pivoted. "There are two viruses" in the country, he said. One was coronavirus, but the other one was racism. Racism was particularly destructive, he said, because it can "remain undetected and unseen by the people who carry [it], so that they spread [racism] without knowing it." He pulled his gray fleece open to reveal the logo on his T-shirt, from a 5K he had run in Georgia several years before. When he and his wife ran the race, they had never worried about getting shot. The video began to show a montage of Black people in the Crossroads community. Kyle now spoke directly to them.

"This shooting has hurt you and brought up pain. As the world looks at you and as the world says we don't value you, that's not what God says. You are valued, you are equal, and we see you." Then Kyle spoke to white people. "Don't say the thing that carries the message and spreads the virus. 'Oh, we don't know what happened.' 'We don't have the facts.' There is a virus on the loose and its goal is to infect you and remain unseen and undetected."

Grant thought Kyle's personal story and the slow lead-up to the conversation about race meant that it would reach a broader audience than it might otherwise. He was proud that Kyle had spoken out forthrightly about the injustice of Arbery's murder—it was, Grant believed, the first time that a white person with power at Crossroads used the church's platforms to speak against racism from a biblical perspective. Baby steps.

Over the next few days, other pastors in the church condemned the killing. Chuck made a video expressing his outrage. Grant worked with a white female pastor in the church to post a video as well. He filmed her speaking during a run, sharing the raw footage of her breaking into tears as she discussed her reaction to Arbery's death. A week later, Brian made a video as well.

The experience helped Grant develop more clarity about what he wanted to do in his new role. As head of marketing for the online church, he worked with his team to think about how they could make more explicit their efforts to advance a conversation about racial justice. Building on the reading he had done about antiracism, he printed a giant poster with a five-point scale that he and his team called the Racism Scale. They hung the poster on the wall of their office. In big block letters on the poster, they wrote, "Goal: Help followers move further down the scale." The five points were:

5: Actively and willingly supports suppression. Openly prejudiced.
4: Thinks minorities "bring it upon themselves." Conscious bias.
3: Believes all people have opportunities. Unconscious bias.
2: Sees a problem. Unsure what to do about it. Feels helpless.
1: Actively working to combat racism. An ally or activist.

The national audiences of Crossroads, they thought, were mostly between three and five on their scale. The people who followed Chuck's public pages in particular were somewhere between two and four. The online community of Undivided was between one and two. In developing social media and video content, Grant constantly urged his team to think about how they could push people from where they were to the next step down. He was pleased to see the church organize a series titled What

Color Is God? In a climate of rampant white Christian nationalism, they wanted to challenge assumptions about the relationship between whiteness and Christianity.

Grant was determined to figure out how to move people down the scale without losing them along the way.

CHAPTER EIGHTEEN

FINDING MY POWER

The American Family Survey found that 34 percent of married couples reported increased marital stress during the pandemic. For most of these couples, increased financial stress was the primary culprit. The same survey found that 58 percent of married men and women said the pandemic made them appreciate their partner more despite the stress. Sandra and her husband were the opposite.

Just as the pandemic shut everything down, Sandra was nine months pregnant with her fourth child. With hospitals closing their doors to all non-COVID patients and policies changing day by day, Sandra decided to have a home birth. When she went into labor at the end of March, her best friend and a midwife worked together to safely deliver the new baby at home. Her husband was not there when the baby arrived.

After the birth, Sandra was initially relieved that her husband would be home while she recovered from labor and delivery. When their other children were born, he had only stayed home for two or three days after the birth before going back to work.

Her optimism soon deteriorated. Instead of relishing time with his family, Sandra's husband seemed to resent it. Sandra worried that he felt confined by his responsibilities at home and his inability to go to the office. He complained bitterly about the pandemic restrictions, relentlessly unfurling his discontent into his family's life. Sandra worried the reading he was doing online made him think the pandemic was not real. She witnessed conspiracy theories flourishing in his mind. Research showed that white Christian nationalism created particularly fertile ground for conspiratorial thinking. A 2021 survey conducted by the conservative American Enterprise Institute found that more than 60 percent of evangelical Republicans believed "Deep State" conspiracy theories. In comparison, only 39 percent of non-evangelical Republicans did. The rapid rise and spread of political disinformation made it hard for people like Sandra to penetrate her husband's echo chambers with reason.

Instead of making things easier, Sandra's husband's presence made things harder. Every time she asked him to take care of a chore, she felt he was fuming with a sense of righteous indignation. They constantly snapped at each other.

Halfway through April, after things had been shut down for more than a month, Sandra asked her husband to fix a long-neglected broken sink. She thought giving him projects to do around the house would relieve some of the tension and distract him from spending time online, which was fueling his discontent.

She miscalculated. Her husband's simmering frustration about the pandemic, his family, and the ongoing tension with Sandra boiled over. He started yelling about having to fix the sink. He accused Sandra of letting the house fall apart, of asking too much of him, of neglecting her wifely duties, of disrespecting his role as head of the household.

Sandra stared at his lips curling over the crooked teeth she had noticed when they first met. She thought back to her parents' objections to their marriage. Her husband's efforts to control her at this moment felt like a vise around her soul. Freedom suddenly became a more powerful motivator than fear.

With the baby in her arms, Sandra started shouting, defending herself. The baby began to cry. Their fight escalated. The older children cowered, trying to stay out of the way. Eventually her husband left, slamming the door behind him. Sandra stared at the closed door, with a two-week-old baby, a three-and-a-half-year-old, a five-year-old, and an almost ten-year-old peeking out from the corners of the room.

This time he didn't come back.

⁓

For Sandra, despondency quickly followed relief. *How am I going to take care of all these kids by myself?* she thought. She knew she needed help. Her body was still sore from labor and delivery, the newborn was barely sleeping, and her older children were getting stir-crazy from being housebound. Sandra called her friends from the Justice Team and her Huddle. She admitted her fear of being alone, even as she knew her marriage was not working. She wasn't sure she could make it without him.

"Girl, you cannot live this way," one of her friends said.

The women rallied around Sandra, providing her with both the courage and the logistical help she needed. Slowly, Sandra patched together a support system. She began to rebuild a new life for herself and the children. "If I hadn't built those relationships with the women from the Justice Team and the Huddle, I would still be in that marriage," she later reflected.

One of the many ways that Sandra felt unmoored was her disconnection from her church. When the coronavirus pandemic shut down in-person services, it was just as easy for Sandra to attend online services at a different church. A church in Philadelphia with a Black pastor had invited Chuck to preach at their service and she tuned in to watch him. Intrigued by what she saw, she watched more videos from that pastor. This preacher, she thought, was speaking to her more than Crossroads was.

Sandra's friends from the Justice Team and the Huddle joined her in exploring other churches by gathering at one another's homes and streaming the services. "We became like the New Testament church," she said. When the apostles first started trying to build the church after Jesus had been crucified, they had to meet secretly to avoid persecution. Sandra knew she and her friends did not have to hide their faith like the apostles did, but she was struck by the way these weekly gatherings felt more authentic to her than services at Crossroads had.

By then, many of Sandra's friends from the Justice Team and the Huddle had begun to feel ambivalent about Crossroads. Their experience of Issue 1 and the subsequent waffling by the church on different issues throughout the Trump presidency strained their relationship with the church. Unlike some other megachurches, Crossroads never preached explicitly white Christian nationalist views from the pulpit. At the same time, with the exception of Chuck and some of the online content that Grant helped create, it often remained silent about what it would take to build a racially just Kingdom of God. Sandra and her friends perceived a gap between the boldness Crossroads had online and what they were doing through their in-person services.

"I felt like Black people had to take a back seat in Crossroads. I wasn't feeling comfortable," Sandra said. "These other churches made me run toward things that I didn't understand and to ask questions rather than to run away."

By the end of May, the baby was barely starting to sleep, and Sandra and her husband had established a détente. He agreed to keep providing financial support for the children and they created a schedule of shared custody. And, for the first time in months, Sandra felt fulfilled by the churches she was visiting.

Then the video of the murder of George Floyd by Minneapolis police officer Derek Chauvin was released. Sandra, along with millions of other people around the world, watched with horror as Chauvin pressed his knee into Floyd's neck for nine minutes and twenty-nine seconds. Protests erupted in cities around the world, and cities like Minneapolis seemed to go into crisis, as protesters and counterprotesters sparred against each other in violent conflict.

Brian immediately got on social media to denounce the murder, calling it the most horrible thing he had ever seen. In doing so, he differentiated himself from some of the most conservative white pastors in the country, who refused to condemn Chauvin's actions. "What you will see in that video are four men slowly and willfully overseeing the death of another. Those men . . . represent a percentage of white Americans. We need to take a fresh and sober look at the state of our country," Brian said. The church organized several live-streamed conversations between Brian and other racial justice leaders, including Chuck.

Kyle Ranson did a video that started with him standing in a grassy field, wearing a gray T-shirt, jeans, and brown work boots. He held a shovel in his hand and told the story of Matthew 25. In this parable, a master entrusted his servants with bags of gold when he went on a journey. Some of the servants used the money in the bags to earn more money, but one servant buried his gold in the ground to protect it. As Kyle told the story, he started to dig a hole in the ground and buried a yellow metal cash box inside. In the parable, the master returned home and was angry at the servant who acted out of fear and did nothing with the money in his care. The parable, Kyle said, was about God asking, "What did you do with what I gave you?" He equated the question to the crisis around race. "What did you do when racism and injustice were running rampant? If your response is that I took the relational currency you gave me and I buried it, saving it for later, for some other cause, God will not tell you that was a wise decision. The right decision is that I took everything you gave me and I spent all the relational capital I had to return more justice, more unity." Kyle took the yellow cash box out of the ground and said, "Change only happens when the majority demand it. Let's demand it. Let's spend the relational currencies that God has given each of us."

The church still was not doing in-person services at the time because of COVID, but they organized an event one Sunday in which people gathered around the perimeter of Crossroads' Oakley campus, standing six feet apart to form a human prayer wall for racial healing around the church. Sandra attended with the Justice Team, relieved to have an outlet for her anger.

But many in the church did not attend. Just as the people who turned out for the prayer wall wanted the church to do more, there was a larger group who wondered why the church was not saying more to support police. When Crossroads posted Kyle's video on Instagram, someone commented, "You had me until you tried to throw politics into it." Grant, who ran the church's social media feeds, responded under the handle @crsrdschurch, "Kyle preached the Gospel and the valuing of God's children. That's not politics."

But not everyone agreed with Grant. Sandra was at home nursing her baby and scrolling through her phone with one hand when she saw an email come through from the Justice Team. She tapped unthinkingly on the notification to open up the email, but then had to read it twice. The email apologized for a prior email they had sent a few days earlier that mentioned the words "defund the police."

Alarm bells went off in Sandra's head. Why are they sending this email? She searched through hers to find the original message, which had come from the leaders of the Justice Team in response to George Floyd's murder. In their email, they invited people to come to a virtual meeting where the Justice Team would be discussing the moment, including things like the protests around defunding the police. Nothing in the email said they necessarily supported defunding.

Sandra texted Carolyn, the white woman who was co-leading the Justice Team. "That email does not sound like you."

She immediately got a phone call back. When the Justice Team leaders sent the original email, someone else had forwarded it to the church leadership and asked, "Does Crossroads support defunding the police?" Church leaders reached out to the Justice Team and pressured them to issue an apology for even mentioning the idea in their email.

"It's such a bait and switch!" Sandra exclaimed. She was frustrated by Crossroads' unwillingness to stand up to pressure from people who objected to the move toward racial justice. She started to cry. All the emotions of the past couple of months came flooding out. Sandra was grateful to Crossroads for all the ways the church had supported her and her family over the years. As she witnessed their reaction to the Justice Team's work, however, she realized she could not depend fully on the church.

Somewhere in this chasm between upheaval and stability, Sandra was finding her own voice. For years, Crossroads had been a place of solace, belonging, and salvation. But as the church tacked back and forth between the opposing viewpoints within the community that it was trying to reconcile, Sandra felt left behind. The message the church was preaching increasingly diverged from the truth Sandra experienced. Yet instead of submerging her own views to the church's, she was taking matters into her own hands.

Sandra realized that she could negotiate her relationship with God on her own terms. "I don't have to access my power through Crossroads. I have to find it myself."

CHAPTER NINETEEN

THE BITCH AT THE PROTEST

At first, Jess pretended not to notice when her coworkers' conversations went silent as soon as she arrived in the lunchroom. After graduating from college, Jess had left Applebee's to take a job as a social worker with the Ohio Department of Job and Family Services. Everyone in her office ate in a conference room that had a long wooden table with rolling black office chairs around it. She placed her lunch down on the table and pulled out her fork to eat. She always heated up her lunch in the microwave down the hall so she knew people could hear and anticipate her arrival. It gave them time to decide how they were going to treat her. Cruelty is easier to perpetrate when it's coordinated. Usually, when Jess arrived after warming her lunch, she would join one of the small groups her coworkers created by clustering the rolling chairs into circles. Now, the week after George Floyd's murder, when the room became silent upon her arrival, she knew she would not be welcome. She sat by herself.

The shift to being ostracized had been sudden. On the previous Thursday, Jess had stayed overnight at the office with another coworker, watching over a child in their custody who did not have a place to go. Jess understood what it felt like to lose her dignity;

she didn't want to extend the same experience to another child. They fed and bathed the child and hung out together. When Jess went outside for a smoke, she scrolled through her Facebook feed, coming across a now iconic picture of a police station in Minneapolis on fire, with someone running across the image with an upside-down American flag in his arms. Jess stared at the picture, wondering if witnessing the murder of George Floyd was awakening people to the horrors of racism. "Philando Castile was my George Floyd," she would later say. The next day, Jess had joined the lunchtime conversations, making her coworkers laugh just like she always did.

As the weekend approached and people around the country took to the streets in protest, Jess wanted to be part of the outcry. She hoped that it would prompt the reckoning among white people that she had long been awaiting. She and her son drove to downtown Cincinnati on Sunday morning and met up with friends to join the march. She didn't give it a second thought when a friend took pictures of her with her son and posted them on Facebook, tagging her in the process. She posted a picture of her favorite poster from the march, a sign that said, "I am not free while anyone is unfree, even when their shackles are different from my own."

By Monday, Jess's coworkers were no longer speaking to her. It was no secret that Jess was the "liberal" in the group, but this time she had crossed a Rubicon she hadn't known existed.

For the first four days, Jess endured the silences and the whispered comments behind her back. But it was not easy. One day, she ate by herself in her office to avoid the discomfort. She felt like she was hiding. So the next day, she went back to the lunchroom, only to be ignored again. After finishing her lunch, she decided to go outside to smoke. As she walked out the door, she heard one of her coworkers say in an intentionally loud voice, "And that bitch was at the protest. So you know what she thinks." Jess deliberately did not turn around. She didn't want anyone to see the tears welling in her eyes.

Jess had always known she had to tread carefully because her political views made her an outlier at work. As Jess described it, the southern Ohio county where she worked was a blend of the Midwest, the Rust Belt, and Appalachia—"*Really* rural," she said. She heard that 80 percent of the students in the public schools in the county were part of Future Farmers of America or the 4-H. It was such a large part of students' lives that the school system shut down for an entire week during the September county fair so that students could display their crops and animals. The population was extremely white and relatively conservative. Jess knew an Asian woman who was married to a white man and was the only nonwhite person in their small town. Knowing that categorization preceded social acceptance for many people, this woman feared others would assume her political views based on her race. Probabilistically speaking, they weren't wrong. Social identities had become so aligned with political views in the twenty-first century that knowing how someone shopped, where she lived, or how she looked often predicted what she believed. Worried that she would be associated with Black Lives Matter or other left-leaning causes, this woman deliberately wore a hat with Trump's slogan, Make America Great Again. She did not really support Trump, but she wanted to signal her distance from "the libs."

A conversation Jess had with her coworkers a few months earlier epitomized the extent of her differences from them. Undivided had opened her eyes to the myriad ways racism was embedded into their systems at work. She often wondered when she should speak out and when she should hold back. "Because of Undivided, I couldn't stop asking questions," she said. "I always feel like the bitch." When she overheard her coworkers gossiping about spotting a woman in their system with a Black man at a local gas station, Jess realized the layered assumptions many of her colleagues had about Black men. Without knowing who he was, they had immediately assumed that he was one of the Black men tagged as dangerous in their database. When Jess challenged her coworkers' assumptions, they reacted by pointing to the data as their defense. Jess realized that nonwhite families in the community were, in fact, disproportionately tagged as threats in the data. She brought it up with her supervisor.

"We need to have a discussion about why the Black dads in our system are marked as a hazard, but all these other white men are not," Jess said to her boss.

"What are you talking about?" her boss asked. "I don't think that's true."

"Sure it is," Jess said. "Let's check it out."

They sat together in her boss's office and looked into the computer system. Jess was right. People feeding data into the system had consistently marked the Black and other nonwhite men as hazards, but not the white men—even in instances when the social workers knew that some of the white men in question were, in fact, dangerous. Jess knew that these tags would have reverberating effects. If the Black men were tagged as dangerous in their database, those tags would follow them into the criminal justice and other public systems.

"Oh, shit," her boss said, dumbfounded.

Jess described that as one of many "weird Undivided things I do in my everyday work. Undivided taught me that sometimes the most harmful stuff often is not the malicious things people do, but the things that are part of a system."

Jess knew it was her responsibility to keep asking questions, but she had to do it in a way that would keep people open to hearing and answering them. Navigating that terrain was not easy. She decorated her office with inspirational posters that helped her think things through, including one with a Michelle Obama quote: "Don't ever underestimate the importance you can have because history has shown us that courage can be contagious and hope can take on a life of its own." (The quote was printed in large colorful letters, but Michelle Obama's name appeared in a tiny font at the bottom.) She taped a quote often attributed to C. S. Lewis (author of the Chronicles of Narnia series and an outspoken Christian) alongside it: "Don't shine so that others can see you. Shine, so that through you, others can see HIM." The quote was printed on an image of a black starry sky, and the word *HIM,* referring to God, was printed in extra-large capital letters. She interspersed these posters with apolitical Star Wars figurines and posters about the importance of coffee and cats. Jess felt the decor would not alienate people who came into her office, and it helped keep her motivated. Her screen saver, which only she could see, read, "Sorry for the inconvenience. We are trying to change the world."

Jess and her coworkers spent much of their staff meetings discussing cases they were working on and families they were supporting. Jess often chafed against the judgments her coworkers made about the families. Sometimes, when people were being particularly harsh, Jess would slowly turn her favorite coffee mug outward toward the speaker to make the words printed across it visible: "God loves the people that we hate." She wanted to remind her colleagues that, as she put it, "if you say stuff like that around me, there's going to be pushback."

Despite these subtle and overt ways that Jess agitated her coworkers, she thought she had a pretty good relationship with most of them. Jess was an easy person to be around because she moved with the air of someone who knew who she wanted to be in the world. Her self-confidence had always been a source of inclusion, not disdain. She was able to befriend some coworkers with whom she vehemently disagreed. A coworker once used the N-word around Jess. Jess lost her temper, shouted at her, and asked her to leave her office. Afterward, her coworker was ashamed of what she said, and Jess knew that losing her temper was not an effective way to shift anyone's behavior. They both apologized. Over time, they learned to be collegial, even friendly.

When Jess left the lunchroom, she went out to the smokers' porch behind her office building and lit a cigarette. She stared at the barbed wire edging the fence around the county jail in the next parking lot. Noticing the security cameras on the back of the building, she decided to walk to her car to call a friend who worked as the technical assistant for the county government. She was not sure if the cameras could pick up her voice, and she didn't want to risk her supervisor hearing the conversation. This friend was not someone she knew particularly well, but she knew he generally shared her political views. She wanted to talk to someone who understood what it was like to work in county government, someone who might understand how it felt to be progressive and work in a rural county. When he answered the phone, Jess unloaded her despair. She started to cry again as she described to him what it had felt like to be ostracized all week for her political views.

"Do you want to find another job?" he asked her. "I can send you some resources." He started ticking through a list of possibilities.

Jess had not expected him to offer her a way out. She wanted change, not exit. Despite everything, she actually liked her job. She liked being able to work with families who suffered from addiction and substance abuse. It was a domain in which she was better qualified than most; she could provide better support to some of these families than people who had not had the same personal experiences she had. She also knew that, as someone with a criminal record, finding another job would not be as easy as her friend might think.

As she considered working elsewhere, a troubling possibility dawned on her: Could her boss find a way to fire her?

CHAPTER TWENTY

I KNEW YOU'D BE HERE TODAY

June was not an easy month for Jess. Her coworkers continued to ostracize her, and Jess thought she might have to look for another job. Each morning, she heard the whispered comments behind her back when she arrived at work. Each afternoon, she pretended not to notice the silence when she entered the lunchroom. On the days she had to be in the office, she was struck by the eerie feeling of unusual quiet.

She tried to spend as much time as possible on the road. As a social worker, Jess constantly had to meet people in their homes. The pandemic had initially slowed her ability to do home visits, but she found ways to do them in COVID-safe ways. The visits, however, had their own precarity. Jess and her coworkers were keenly aware that most homes in rural Ohio likely had a gun. More and more often, Jess found, the residents were high on methamphetamines. The potential for violence meant that social workers like Jess often did home visits in the company of law enforcement officers.

Because of these partnerships, Jess had gotten to know many of the officers in the county over the years. She had become friendly with two detectives in particular who often worked on cases with her. Her coworkers' harsh reaction after seeing pictures of her at

a George Floyd protest gave Jess pause when she contemplated the possibility of seeing the detectives—both of whom were white—on a site visit. She had always been vocal about her views, but she knew that the political turmoil over George Floyd might have created new sensitivities.

In the past, Jess had leveraged her friendship with the detectives and other officers of the criminal justice system to agitate for change. "A lot of times, I can just ask them a quick question and say, 'Hey, have you thought about this? Why do we do this this way? Have you ever stepped back and looked at this?'" she said. She had found ways to gently point out the inequities built into the system and was proud of how she had helped people see things in a new light.

Jess decided to reach out proactively to her two detective friends. "That's the thing Undivided taught me," she said. "If you build relationships with people, true relationships, you can have hard conversations. You can help people move their goalposts without moving yours. For me, Undivided was the springboard for that." She thought carefully about what she wanted to say and then texted them: "I just want you to know that I'm going to share some things [online] you might disagree with. I believe in defunding the police. I think we have a policing problem in America, but I want you to know that I really respect you and the work that you do."

Not too long afterward, Jess heard the familiar ding from her phone. She saw a text notification from one of the detectives. He sent back a laughing emoji. "You think we didn't already know that about you?" he wrote. Jess laughed out loud, greatly relieved. It was the first time in several days that she had laughed audibly at work.

Another ping came through. It was the other detective. "We know you. Don't worry."

Jess wrote back. "Well, if you want to unfollow me for a while, it's okay," she texted. She saw the dots on her phone and knew that he was writing back right away.

"It's okay," he wrote. "We know you're a good person."

"Okay," she wrote. "But if there's anything I share that you want to talk about or you think I'm wrong about, come talk to me."

After that text exchange, neither detective approached Jess for a couple of weeks, except for a few jokes here and there. At the end of June, however, the national political turmoil struck close to home for people in Jess's community. A woman who worked as a substitute teacher and craftswoman in Bethel, Ohio, had organized a local protest for racial solidarity. Bethel was a small town of about 2,600, 99 percent white. Protest organizers avoided the words "Black Lives Matter" in advertising the protest because they knew it would be too politically charged for their area. Instead, they tried to plan it as a unity march that would bring different parts of their rural community together.

Despite their best efforts, controversy erupted. The right-wing media somehow fixated on Bethel, Ohio, and began telling their followers that antifa was coming to the protest. Rumors circulated locally that busloads of protesters would be descending on Bethel from out of town. Fearful locals began to coordinate with one another in what they thought was a necessary effort to protect their community. The owner of a gun shop in downtown Bethel urged his customers to prepare for a violent antifa invasion.

On the day of the protest, journalists estimated that eighty to a hundred people showed up to advocate for unity. The counterprotest was much bigger and better armed. Hundreds lined up along Bethel's Main Street hours before the protest carrying Confederate flags, shotguns, and baseball bats. A long line of motorcycles blocked the path marchers had originally designated. After so much fear of outsiders coming into the county with antifa, it was actually the counterprotesters who mostly came from elsewhere. When the marchers arrived, their route was supposed to take them past a church that was located across from the gun shop whose owner had urged his customers to arm themselves. As they approached the church, a menacing line of counterprotesters confronted them. They began jeering and yelling, pushing the marchers to the ground, ripping up their signs, and yelling at them to leave—even though most of the marchers lived in the town. Short video clips of the clashes went viral on social media.

When Jess arrived at work on the Monday morning following the violence, one of the detectives was waiting for her outside her office.

"Somehow I knew you'd be here today," she said to him.

"What happened yesterday?" he asked. Like so many other people in the area, he had been reading about the violent tendencies of Black Lives Matter and the role the left played in fomenting violence. He was confused when he saw the counterprotesters instigate violence against peaceful marchers. "It doesn't fit," he said.

In a society plagued by disinformation and distrust, researchers found that nothing was more effective than personal experience in pushing people to see old things with new eyes. But they often needed others to make meaning of what they saw. Was the violence perpetrated in Bethel an outlier, or was it indicative of a bigger pattern?

Jess smiled. She was frustrated that so many people, including her friends, believed the rumors they heard. But she was also happy that the detective trusted her enough to come talk to her. He spent almost an hour in Jess's office that morning, unpacking what had happened in Bethel. They discussed not only the local protest but also the larger Black Lives Matter phenomenon. Jess shared more of her own story to push her friend to think more about his own biases.

That conversation revealed a truth about Undivided, the onramps, and the Justice Team that Jess had not previously understood. She originally thought the goal of the six-week program was to inspire people's journey toward antiracism. But Jess realized that the true impact of Undivided was not as a prejudice reduction program, but rather as a learning experience that inspired action. The program became impactful when people like Jess spread that learning through their social communities, transforming them in the process. That's why the on-ramps, the Justice Team, and relationships like the one Jess formed with Patricia and the one Sandra formed with Grant were so important. People needed those friendships and groups to cultivate and sustain the courage to act.

The program worked, in other words, not by converting committed white supremacists to antiracism. Instead, it sought to find the "other evangelicals"—like Jess, Sandra, and Grant—who sensed, as organizers would say, a gap between the world as it is and the world as it should be. At the most basic level, Undivided equipped these participants to understand both the interpersonal and systemic dimensions of racial injustice and offered them tools to have difficult conversations around race. If the tinder lit, the program became a means for people to form relationships in which they could admit hard truths, take risks, inspire one another to action, and hold one another accountable for their mistakes. By freeing people to choose, on their own terms, what they wanted to do, Undivided hoped to instigate a larger program of change.

The detective was not the only person confused after Bethel. That morning, Jess noticed that most of her coworkers stopped ignoring her. Many had already reassessed their willful rejection of Jess, and her relationships with them had started to thaw. Going into the lunchroom was no longer as fraught as it had been in the early days of June. The controversy in Bethel accelerated the return to normal. Many of her coworkers had friends or family members who had attended or been somehow involved with the event in Bethel. Some had gotten involved in the counterprotest, thinking that it was part of their responsibility to protect their

community. They were flabbergasted when it was the counterprotesters, not antifa, who had instigated the violence. Jess realized
anew the depth of their misunderstanding.

That afternoon, when Jess went outside for her usual smoke,
she felt freed of her worries about quitting or being fired for the
first time in a few weeks. She knew that she hadn't handled everything perfectly. But she felt like she was doing what she should be
doing. "If I left, then who would be the voice? Who would speak
up?"

~

A week after the Bethel march, Jess decided to get another tattoo. She knew exactly what she wanted. One of her favorite
characters from the Nickelodeon show *Avatar: The Last Airbender*
was Katara, because of a specific episode in the third season titled
"The Painted Lady." In this episode, Katara and her brother are on
a targeted mission but unexpectedly come across a village ravaged
by war and military occupation, full of sick and struggling people
desperate for food and medicine. Katara wants to stop and help,
but her brother refuses, reminding her of the urgency of their
bigger mission. Despite his protestations, Katara uses her powers
to sneak into the village to provide the food and medicine they
need. At one point, Katara says to her brother, "I will never ever
turn my back on people who need me."

Jess had Katara's colorful image inked onto her upper arm,
from her shoulder to her elbow. She often looked at it during her
ongoing conversations with her uncle who had the swastika tattooed on his chest. Jess persisted in her conversations with him,
and she was proud, over time, to witness the evolution of his
views. He began questioning the white supremacist beliefs he had
learned in prison. Eventually, he decided to try to get the swastika
tattoo on his chest removed, in a symbolic effort to leave the hate
behind.

ORDINARY PEOPLE

On August 27, 2020, Chuck logged on to a Zoom session of Undivided with a group of about twenty-five evangelical church pastors, congregants, and staff from around the country. There were leaders from a small multiracial church in New Jersey, a growing white-dominant megachurch in Michigan and another in Texas, and one of the largest white-led established megachurches in Alabama. This session was part of Undivided's effort to spread its program to other churches around the country.

It had been a hard week in America. A white police officer had shot and severely injured Jacob Blake, a Black man in Kenosha, Wisconsin. Days of protest erupted in the streets, during which Kyle Rittenhouse, a white teenager from Illinois, shot three protesters and killed two with an AR-15 style rifle, escalating the tension. NBA players had just announced a strike, refusing to end it until the league took greater action toward racial justice. The events in Kenosha came on the heels of a summer of unrest that started with the murder of George Floyd in Minneapolis. Peace felt precarious.

The Undivided cohort had been meeting for three weeks at this point, and Chuck eased into the session. After an opening prayer, Chuck altered the usual Undivided agenda to give people a

chance to reflect on the current events in America, inviting participants into small breakouts to discuss with one another how they
were feeling. When they reconvened in plenary, several people
spoke, recounting their weariness and pain.

A Black pastor spoke passionately. "I am unapologetically
Black. And as a Black man in America, what I am feeling is this:
This. Has. To. Stop." He paused. "And it won't until America
bends its knees in humility and prepares to do the work. The
work."

Chuck agreed emphatically. He sat in silence, letting people sit
with the pastor's exhortation, then he spoke up: "In this moment,
I pray that God is saying, 'Seriously, Church? Seriously?'" Chuck
referenced the white church's historic inaction on racial justice
and the deep racism embedded in the institutions. The world
is moving, he said, and God is trying to speak to the church. To
Chuck, evangelicalism was coming to a decision point. "Okay,
here it is, Church. Here's the moment—what are we going to do?"

It had been a few months since Undivided had officially
become its own nonprofit organization. Gestation had been slow.
Its emergence as an independent entity happened to coincide with
the summer of protest after the murder of George Floyd. Creating
an organizational distinction between Undivided and Crossroads
enabled Undivided to develop its own response to that summer of
racial reckoning. Chuck and the other Undivided leaders reached
out to their community in the immediate aftermath of Floyd's
murder, creating spaces for congregants to gather and grieve.

As Chuck and Troy considered the next phase of growth for
Undivided, they decided they had to make way for a new generation of leadership. They recruited a Black woman, Brittany Wade,
to become its first executive director and lead the program's transition to a national organization. Brittany worked with another
Black woman, Courtney Walton, to revamp the curriculum.
Chuck, Troy, Brittany, Courtney, and the rest of their team were

working to expand Undivided to other churches and organizations around the country.

Meanwhile, the push to digital content during the coronavirus pandemic grew the audience for Crossroads—and, by extension, Grant's work—by orders of magnitude. Churches all over the country had to move online, but Crossroads was ahead of the curve because they had always been committed to using technology in their work. During the pandemic, they amplified their efforts. By 2021, half a million people tuned in to their online services each week, and almost ten thousand people from that group actively tithed to the church. They also built a following of 1.5 million on social media (up from about 64,000 before the pandemic).

In March 2021, Chuck and Grant led a group from Undivided and Crossroads on a pilgrimage to Alabama to interview civil rights icon Bryan Stevenson. Stevenson was the founder and executive director of the Equal Justice Initiative, a human rights organization in Montgomery dedicated to protecting the rights of the incarcerated and the mentally ill, as well as exonerating innocent death row prisoners. Stevenson had been launched to fame by the runaway success of his book *Just Mercy,* one of the first books Grant listened to on tape. In his new job, Grant had proposed a video series on racial justice for Crossroads, featuring not only Stevenson but also historic sites in Birmingham and Selma, Alabama. The teaching team agreed.

Their visit came three months after the power of white identity politics and its relationship to evangelicalism had been on full display. On January 6, 2021, strains of white Christian nationalism yielded unprecedented violence as Trump supporters stormed the United States Capitol building, some claiming they were doing it in Jesus's name. "Give it up if you believe in Jesus!" one protester chanted. Trump, they believed, was an agent of God. For years, evangelicals had tried to deny the relationship of their faith to racism. As Christian nationalists waved Confederate flags in the name of Jesus, however, the role of racism in fueling parts of white Christian identities had become impossible to deny.

Grant watched in horror. He could not help but realize how much he had changed. "If that had happened seven or ten years ago," he said, "I would have been there."

Now he brought his team to Alabama to create content that would push Crossroads and Undivided's adherents to understand a different vision of God. While they were there, they also shot film at the Equal Justice Initiative's Legacy Museum, the jail in Birmingham where Martin Luther King Jr. had been imprisoned, the Rosa Parks Museum, and the Edmund Pettus Bridge in Selma, where state police officers brutally beat civil rights marchers in 1965 on Bloody Sunday. Chuck and his wife, Maria, brought their children with them. Troy accompanied the production team, drawing on his background in history to offer context to the sites they were visiting.

They spent time with Lynda Blackmon Lowery, who was one of the youngest marchers on the bridge on Bloody Sunday. She was fifteen years old at the time. In an interview she taped with Chuck, she recounted being beaten and kicked by sheriffs as they tried to march across the bridge. It was a gray spring day, and Chuck and Lynda sat in metal folding chairs under an umbrella with the Edmund Pettus Bridge in the background. Lynda told the story that she must have told many, many times before, but tears rolled down her face as she spoke, the pain still raw.

Later that day, the production team shot footage of Chuck and other members of their team walking across the bridge. A young Black man on the Crossroads staff spoke with Chuck on video, reflecting on their experiences in Alabama. The production team allowed themselves extra time for everyone to take in the moment, processing the emotions they all had been feeling the entire trip.

Then Chuck asked for time to experience the bridge with his

family. It felt like holy ground to him. He thought about the nameless people who had voluntarily endured unspeakable violence to stand up for justice. He thought about his grandmother, who had lived through the era of segregation. When his two younger children scampered ahead, Maria hurried to keep up with them. Chuck walked alone with his oldest son across the apex of the slightly arched bridge. The videographers shot Chuck walking with his son. This was one of the sons whose picture was described as threatening when Chuck showed it on the screen a few years earlier as he preached his lament.

So much had happened to bring Chuck to this moment. There were his early years at Crossroads, when he considered leaving the church after the muted reaction to the shooting of Timothy Thomas. There was the sermon he delivered in early 2015, launching Undivided. There was the pushback he had gotten at the time, and since then. It had been six years since that sermon, and now he was in Selma on behalf of the church.

The production team started packing up their equipment when the shoot finished. Grant wound his way to the spot where Chuck was removing his lapel microphone and hugged him. Chuck knew Grant had conceived of the trip, and that he had pushed the church leaders to enable it. "Man," Chuck said to Grant as they embraced. "Can you believe we are here?"

Grant started to cry. "I can't believe we pulled this off," he said. He wasn't the only one crying.

The team packed up and hauled their equipment to their next destination, Brown Chapel, the AME (African Methodist Episcopal) church in Selma where the Southern Christian Leadership Conference often gathered during the civil rights movement. Outside the chapel, they stopped by the Civil Rights Freedom Wall, a memorial to local residents who had participated in and, for some, been martyred in the struggle. "These are the names that might not be in our history books," Troy said. He and Chuck read aloud the names of teachers, high school students, congregants at Brown Chapel, and hospital workers. "This is why the movement happened," Troy said. "Because of these men, women, and children who put their lives on the line."

The next day, they would go to Montgomery, to spend the day with Bryan Stevenson. There, they would visit the Legacy Museum, tracing the history of enslavement, Jim Crow, racial terror lynchings, and the development of the carceral state.

When Chuck finished reading the names, he asked the team to reflect on what they were feeling. The group paused in silence. Then, one person spoke.

"I'm struck . . . by the ordinariness of people who change history."

∼

It had been many months since Sandra had been at Oakley. She had stopped attending Crossroads after the pandemic had created an opportunity for her to explore other churches online. Once she started attending services again in person in late 2020, she no longer felt like Crossroads was the right place for her. Instead, she had been attending a small start-up church in Cincinnati led by a Black couple. In the months after George Floyd died, her divorce, and the 2020 election, this intimate community felt like the salve she needed. She eventually took a job in the church running their social media feeds for about a year.

One day she was at Crossroads with a video team to do some filming. She walked through the double glass doors into the familiar lobby, taking in the high ceilings and the smell of coffee. For a moment, she felt nostalgic. Her father had recently died after a long battle with cancer. Sandra had flown home to California for the funeral. During the flight, she thought about the pancakes her father used to make as he listened to Rush Limbaugh in the morning, and his admonition that he had not raised her to be a white man's housewife. As she navigated life after separating from her second husband, she felt like she was starting to realize her own self as a Black woman, but regretted that her father would not be there to witness it.

When Sandra returned to Cincinnati after the funeral, she got a call from the church where she had been working. They no longer had the funds to pay her. Sandra was mulling her next steps as she accompanied the video team to Crossroads. She texted Grant to see if he was around. "Want to grab lunch?" she asked.

"I can't today," he texted back. "But what's going on? What are you doing here?"

Sandra updated him about her job. "Let's talk later," Grant texted back.

In a phone conversation later that week, Sandra told Grant she was hoping to continue to do work in media and communications, similar to the work he was doing at Crossroads. Grant had been considering whether to tell Sandra about an opening he had on his team at Crossroads. He knew about Sandra's long history with the church, her ambivalence about the community, and the awkwardness that might ensue if they worked together. But he opted to let her know about the job opening and decide whether she wanted to pursue it.

"C'mon, Grant," Sandra said. "I don't fuck with Crossroads anymore."

They both laughed. "Well, my team is different," Grant said. He didn't push the conversation but encouraged her to keep it in the back of her mind as she considered her next steps.

Sandra spent several weeks thinking about what she wanted to do. She and Grant had been friends for years, and she knew he had been trying to use his position at Crossroads to expand their work on racial justice. But she wasn't sure how successful he could really be. He was just one person.

She applied for several jobs and networked to find other

opportunities. But as Christmas came and went and the new year began, she thought more seriously about Grant's offer. The job he had available was a better fit than anything else she could find. But she was hesitant about joining the Crossroads community again. She decided to call an older Black woman friend who worked part-time for Crossroads. This woman had worked at Procter & Gamble for many years and then joined the Crossroads staff almost a decade earlier. She had seen the church grapple with questions of race and diversity for many years. Sandra had gotten to know her through some work they did on Undivided, and she respected her opinion. She knew this woman would be honest with her.

"If you were considering working on another team at Crossroads," her friend said, "I would tell you not to do it. But this is the best place for you at Crossroads. Grant built the team, and you'll have more people who are aligned with you there than anywhere else. They have a different culture on that team than the rest of the church."

In early 2021, Sandra took the job.

Just after the winter holidays, she posted a video of her children on Facebook set to the song "That Day" by Jeff Kaale. Her four children ran down the street bundled in their winter jackets, with the oldest leading the three younger children. The baby ran the slowest, always hanging ten or twenty feet behind his older siblings, his short legs struggling to keep up. In her comment, Sandra started by defining *kujichagulia,* the Swahili word for self-determination and one of the principles of Kwanzaa. "To define ourselves, name ourselves, create for ourselves and speak for ourselves," she wrote. "These last two years have been formative to say the least. One thing I'm carrying with me is the ability to determine my own destiny. For a long time, I watched other people pursue their dreams and believed I never could. Now, in faith, we do the things we're called to do, even if we have to get back up and try over and over again."

RADICAL GRACE

There is no way of knowing what will happen next with Undivided. It is continuing to put down roots in other churches and organizations around the country and partnering with other Black and white leaders pushing to change evangelicalism from inside. People like Brittany are taking on a new mantle of leadership. She has led the team through a period of upheaval and transition during the overlapping crises of the coronavirus pandemic and the outcry over the killing of George Floyd. Even as it spreads, critiques that have always plagued the program continue. Brittany and Courtney revamped the curriculum to take it online, and they used the opportunity to fix what they saw as some ongoing issues. They had to figure out a way to provide a history lesson that was not grounded in Cincinnati. How could they make it feel concrete and personal to people coming from all over the country? They sought to build a curriculum that minimized the burden on nonwhite people to explain racism to white people. And they wanted to make it relevant for those who came from a wide range of churches, not just megachurches like Crossroads.

Even though Crossroads gave them a generous grant to support the first year of their work, they also had to create a business model to make Undivided financially sustainable. Brittany joined

Chuck and Troy in building its public profile, seeking people from throughout the country who would give Undivided a try. When Chuck had first thought about expanding Undivided in 2018, Dave Ferguson, a prominent white evangelical pastor and church planter, had urged him forward. "There is a hunger for this out there," Dave said. But was there, really? Troy, Chuck, and Brittany were going to find out.

They spread into other evangelical megachurches like Community Christian in Naperville, Illinois, and Kensington Church in Troy, Michigan. They also expanded into some non-church environments. In the summer of 2020, Achmed, a Black graduate of Undivided from Crossroads, had reached out to Chief of Police Mike Mills in his hometown of Miami Township, a suburb of Cincinnati. "What are you doing to keep people like me safe?" he asked. Mills invited Achmed to have lunch with him and discuss it. Over burgers and milkshakes, Achmed described his experience with Undivided. "Let's do it here," the chief said. Achmed had never imagined such a possibility. Several months later, the chief had recruited a group of officers from his department, as well as other city leaders, to go through Undivided. Brittany and Courtney scurried to develop a secular version of the curriculum for the township.

In the midst of a moment of racial reckoning across America and throughout evangelicalism, they had to navigate the tricky politics of race within their faith. As white evangelicalism more broadly went into crisis during the Trump era, Undivided became part of a broad and varied landscape of clergy, congregants, and other leaders speaking out about their faith's historic inaction on racial injustice. That landscape includes academic theologians, prominent pastors, Christian influencers, and congregants begging their churches for more. It includes leaders from a diverse range of racial backgrounds and a diverse range of theological traditions within evangelicalism. Undivided undeniably carries the imprint of the white-dominant, seeker-sensitive tradition from which it emerged—yet it exists in the same theological space as people following traditions of liberation theology that shaped those like C. René Padilla, the pastor who spoke out fifty years earlier at the Lausanne Congress. Undivided is not *the* leader in this space, but it's *a* leader in a tapestry of people and groups acting, deliberating, disagreeing, and organizing.

In many ways, the work still feels fragile. Undivided is like a grain of sand in an oyster shell. If the oyster recognizes the sand as an irritant, it turns it into a pearl. If not, then the sand remains just that—a grain of sand. Can Undivided become a pearl? Will the efforts of all the people they are animating into action add up to something more? Will the structures they create to sustain the work they are doing be able to withstand the forces of backlash—which are only likely to grow?

As Undivided spread, so did the resistance to it. Just like Jess, Sandra, Chuck, and Grant, the people in churches like Community Christian and Kensington and organizations like the Miami Township police would have to make choices about how far they were willing to go. For all of them, resistance was not abstract. Sandra experienced it in her marriage and her friendships. Chuck experienced it from people he had pastored for years. Jess fought with her mother and risked her job and social connections she had long held. Grant felt it in his job and had to leave it behind. They even experienced it from their church.

In the summer of 2022, Crossroads ignited a controversy when Brian invited a speaker onto the Crossroads main stage who had a history of making transphobic and homophobic comments. An anonymous group posted a PDF file online entitled "A Peek Behind the Curtain: Stories of Harm from Crossroads Church in Cincinnati, Ohio." The document detailed extraordinary pain that those from the LGBTQIA+ community and beyond experienced in Crossroads. Even though the controversy was not about racism, it kindled a larger one about how willing Crossroads was to act on questions of injustice. The answer remained unclear. Church should be the place where people go to find refuge, where they can open their souls and find healing in a savage world. Yet for so many people, churches represented the opposite.

Resistance in all of these cases was specific, concrete, personal, and painful. People were forced to reexamine who they were, what they believed, what they must do because of what they believed—and what they were willing to risk.

Despite the risk, they all persisted in the work.

～

I started this project because I wanted to understand how people seeking to make change in something as complex as racial justice persisted in the work and thought about what they could and should do. I wanted to observe if and how social change worked within an organization as complex, multifaceted, and unexpected as Crossroads. But as I got further into the research, I realized I was learning about much more.

For the first time in my life, I developed a visceral understanding of the Christian concept of grace, the belief in unmerited favor from God. People in Undivided were willing to risk some of their deepest and most personal relationships to stand up for justice. This courage was not scripted by the how-to manuals on antiracism. Instead, it was rooted in a deeply personal commitment to a vision of the world that Jess, Sandra, Grant, and Chuck were desperate to see realized. And what is justice but unconditional love for and belief in the dignity of all people? In other words, what is justice but the belief that everyone deserves grace? I remember Sister Leigh teaching us about grace during my Roman Catholic Traditions class in high school, but it wasn't until I spent seven years studying Undivided that I really understood how grace can operate in the world. For the people I met in Undivided, their deep, abiding belief in God's grace manifested itself as the courage to fight for one another's dignity.

I also began to understand anew what radical change really means. Most use the word *radical* to refer to change that is extreme. Jess loved a "radical political Jesus" who would upend the system and make it work for everybody. But the word *radical* actually comes from the idea of being *rooted*. Change is radical not when it is extreme, but when it makes change from the roots up. And what I learned from the people I met through Undivided was that making change not only had to alter the roots of an unjust system, but it also had to be rooted in real people. Systems as complex as racism in America do not change when disconnected people without any roots in a community yell a little louder or reshuffle a few priorities. Instead, it changes when people rooted in their own interests and connected to one another organize themselves into just structures that enable them to put their hands on the complex levers of change.

So even as I remain unsure about what direction Undivided as a program or Crossroads as a church might take, I find myself believing that the march toward justice will find its resilience not necessarily in any one DEI program, any one church, or any one leader, but rather in the people who commit to grace, to one another's dignity, and to the work it takes to create a world that recognizes it.

In September 2019, a small group called Evangelicals 4 Justice organized a conference in Chicago called Liberating Evangelicalism: Decentering Whiteness. Their goal, the organizers said, was to build a "Jesus-centered vision for social justice." They recognized that they were bringing together a group of people who were feeling disaffected by evangelical politics, people who disliked that evangelicalism had become so partisan. At the same time, they knew that not all of the dissidents would agree with one another. Some attendees wanted to disavow evangelicalism altogether, while others wanted to reclaim and redefine what it meant. Some attendees came out of white-dominant evangelical traditions; others came out of Black, Latino, Asian, and Native American churches.

The goal of the gathering, however, was not consensus: "By learning to be in conversation with each other in these divisive times, we hope to model the practice of Jesus who associated with all members of society in order to enable the body of Christ to learn from all perspectives, particularly those who are most socially marginalized." The group wanted to build a set of relationships among people willing to critique their faith from within. The outcome they imagined was not a set of agreed-upon orthodoxies, but instead a set of relationships that could become sites of new possibility. They posited that the relationships themselves were an intrinsically valuable end.

A scholar observing the conference argued that they were developing an approach that was "revolution by trial and error." There was no clear path forward for these agitators, but they recognized they would never be able to restore their faith to what they believed to be its true values unless they got into a relationship with one another.

No one from Undivided attended the conference. But as I witnessed the tumultuous experiences of those like Sandra, Grant, Jess, and Chuck seeking to do the work of racial justice, I realized that their revolution was one of trial and error. Undivided was the spark for a journey that could go in many directions. Those directions could be good or bad, forward or backward. They could lead people to safety or to danger. The complexity of embracing people's full humanity across a range of differences meant there was not a clear path forward. The work of Undivided was, instead, to create a space that would enable "revolution by trial and error." Holding on to that space, however, was no easy task.

Years ago, when I lost a loved one in my family, I sat on the couch in our living room contemplating my grief with my friend Bill. I was frustrated that people around me wanted me to move on, to package my pain into a neat bundle I could hide away. Bill understood. He had lost his mother when he was in high school. "A lot of times when I talk about her, my sentences just trail off," he said. "It used to bother me because I couldn't give people the neat answer they wanted, but now I wonder if that's how it should be."

I was often reminded of that conversation when I talked with Jess, Sandra, Grant, Chuck, and all the people in this book. None of them were sure where Undivided was going. They weren't sure where their faith, evangelicalism, was going. They weren't always sure where they themselves, as individuals, were going. But that was okay. Maybe sometimes living at the edge of social change, at the seams between the world that we have and the world we are hoping to create, means that sometimes our sentences just trail off.

ACKNOWLEDGMENTS

Chuck, Grant, Jess, Sandra, their families, and all the people I met through Undivided—including Lynn, Troy, Elizabeth, Carolyn, Michelle, Charla, Beverly, Cameron, Brittany, Courtney, everyone from the Undivided planning team, the women from the Huddle, the men from the Dude Group, and many, many others—granted me the tremendous honor of their trust and the gift of their stories. My deepest gratitude goes to them for their patience, courage, generosity, and friendship. Even those who are not mentioned and stories that are not told in the book remain a source of inspiration, and I offer my sincere thanks to everyone for the great privilege of learning from their experiences.

I am also grateful to many leaders and congregants at the Cross-roads Church for talking with me—including Kathy Beechem, Kyle Ranson, Brian Tome, and Darin Yates—as well as people from other communities who have participated in Undivided, including the Kensington Church in Troy, Michigan; Chicago's Community Christian Church; the Stadia Church Planting Network; Chief Mike Mills; and others. Beyond Undivided, many people in Cincinnati and in myriad evangelical communities across America magnanimously allowed me to learn from them, tolerating my many questions, inviting me into their spaces, and correcting my mistakes with compassion. I am especially grateful to Dave Ferguson for the many conversations, connections, and the invitation to the Exponential Conference.

For many years, I have learned humbly from so many organizers leading the fight for racial justice in America, and I hope those lessons emerge in this book. Many colleagues who are scholars of race, race politics, and racial subjugation in America helped me wrap my head around a rich, complex area of study and make sense of what I was seeing in the field. These are the people that historic leaders like Ella Baker have always lifted up: "You didn't see me on television, you didn't see news stories about me. The kind of role that I tried to play was to pick up pieces or put together pieces out of which I hoped organization might come. My theory is, strong people don't need strong leaders." It is the leadership of these strong people who have taught me how to envision and seek to enact the world that we need.

More people than I can name gave me feedback on specific parts of the manuscript, or helped me noodle through particularly complicated parts. I owe special gratitude to Michael Bader, David Blagg, Jane Booth-Tobin, Luke Bretherton, Curtis Chang, Jennifer Chudy, Matthew Denney, Henry Farrell, Jason Garrett, Daniel Honig, Jae Yeon Kim, Larry Lin, Jamila Michener, Grace Park, Jennifer Parker, Ethan Rome, Scott Shane, Sarah Szanton, Mark Vaselkiv, Francie Weeks, and Audra Wolfe, who all offered crucial bits of feedback and slogged through embarrassingly messy versions of the manuscript with generosity and acumen. When I could no longer critically see the words on the page, Hunter Gehlbach sacrificed an entire weekend so I could read, literally, the entire manuscript aloud to him. I thank Maneesh Arora for being such a terrific partner on the Undivided survey research, Elizabeth McKenna and Michelle Oyakawa for partnering on research around Issue 44, Ester Fang, Selma Khalil, Stella Lee, and David Patterson for able research assistance, and Joshua Houston for help editing.

I am at a loss for how to properly thank my editor, Jon Segal. The book would not exist without him, his vision, and his willingness to take a bet on a nascent project. Working with him has transformed the way I think about writing and given me the rare privilege of learning a new craft. He inspires a commitment to excellence through his love of and respect for books, and I feel enormously lucky to benefit from his careful, compassionate counsel. I am grateful to the entire team at Knopf, especially Vanessa Haughton, Kayla Overbey, Isabel Ribeiro, and Kelly Shi. What a dream to publish with them.

Zoë Pagnamenta has been an agent extraordinaire, offering essential advice and emotional support and patiently helping me navigate the world of trade publishing.

Institutional support from the Ford Foundation, the Hewlett Foundation, and the Sieja Family Foundation was invaluable to the project. The project began when I was on faculty at the University of California in Santa Barbara and came to fruition during my time at Johns Hopkins University. I'm grateful to many at both institutions, especially all the friends who have become like family at the SNF Agora Institute. The dedication (and forbearance!) of the senior staff of the institute—Mary McBride, Catherine Pierre, and Stephen Ruckman—made work on this book (and so much else) possible. I hope this book can be, in some small way, a tribute to the exceptional leadership and contributions Catherine made before her untimely passing. The mysterious and masterful magic of Lydia Gerres somehow makes all the pieces of my life work.

As hackneyed as it is, I have to close by thanking my family. I wish I could do so in a way that appropriately conveys the extent of my gratitude for them. My older brother, Peter, has always been a champion to me and for me, offering advice and encouragement in ways that no one else can. The Gehlbachs, Conklins, and the other Dallas Hans have patiently—and kindly—refrained from asking too many questions over the many years of this project. For this book in particular, the example set by my parents' and grandparents' lives (Han Man Soo, Lee Shin Chan, Choi Gyu Sup, Jeon Soon Ok, Kye Jong Han, and Jung Won Han) formed a beacon of courage and hope far more powerful than any words. Finally, there is no way to properly acknowledge how much Hunter, Kaya, Jaemin, and (in our hearts) Kaeson bring to my life. They each possess an extraordinary humanity that astounds me daily. I can only hope they recognize the ways they are my everything.

SOURCES AND METHODS

This book relies on almost seven years of reporting, beginning in 2016. The project began as an academic study of grassroots organizing campaigns. I stumbled upon Undivided because they were so involved in what would become the 2016 Issue 44 campaign for universal preschool in Cincinnati. As I got to know Undivided and the broader Crossroads community, I realized there was another story to be told. I immersed myself in research with the leaders and participants in Undivided, talking with anyone who would engage with me and working with the Undivided leadership to gather survey data on people going through the program. I also read more deeply into the existing scholarship around the relationship of faith, race, and politics in America.

Whenever I was directly observing the activities of Undivided or talking with people in the program, I took extensive field notes and then sat down at night to formulate the hastily scribbled notes into more coherent reflections on, and a record of, what I had seen and heard. When I was in a conversation with just one other person or a limited number of people, I asked permission to tape whenever I could so that I would have a recording of our interactions and conversations. I transcribed about two-thirds of those recordings over the seven years of reporting. Altogether, this project generated more than 2,858 pages of typewritten notes and transcripts, at least three notebooks full of handwritten notes, and an additional 1,471 hours of audio and video recordings—not to mention myriad conversations that were not formally recorded.

Over the years, I observed and spoke with many people who participated in Undivided through other churches and workplaces in America. I also talked with a number of other faith leaders inside evangelicalism and outside of it to learn more about the historical and contemporary context of the program. And I talked with and observed a number of people leading DEI or racial justice work in faith-based and other organizations in America, as well as organizers trying to engage grassroots communities in the work. Talking with all of those people gave me enormous insight and perspective on both Undivided and the broader context of the people profiled in this book.

To report on anything that happened prior to 2016, I had to rely on people's memories. In addition, there were a number of private interactions that people described to me because I was not there. In all of those cases, I tried to triangulate sources as much as possible by getting multiple accounts of one incident or tracking down primary source evidence that helped me understand it. Such sources were not always available, but I did my best to reconstruct the scenes and the dialogue as reported to me. In addition, because the book traces a deeply personal journey for each character, I had to rely on those characters' descriptions of what they felt even in situations that I observed. To ensure the greatest possible accuracy when reporting on people's reactions or private interactions, I sat with Jess, Grant, Chuck, Sandra, and other key characters to read aloud each scene in which they appeared. They patiently listened and corrected some minor factual details. As explained in my author's note, there were a few details that Sandra felt were too revealing of her identity that she asked me to exclude, which I did.

NOTES

The following notes describe specific sources that were used to substantiate particular points or details in the book. Throughout the book, any Bible verses were quoted from the New Revised Standard Version, except for one verse indicated in Chapter 11. Unless specified otherwise, any links provided were last accessed in December 2023. Chuck Mingo and Troy Jackson (with Holly Crawshaw) published their own book in 2024 describing the Undivided curriculum called *Living Undivided: Loving Courageously for Racial Healing and Justice*. In some cases, the curriculum they describe was different from the iteration described in the book; in those cases, I described the version of the curriculum that was contemporaneous to the story being told, even if it subsequently evolved in different ways described in their book.

INTRODUCTION: Unlike *Anything* I've Ever Seen

3 **Trump spoke openly:** The quotation from Donald Trump's campaign launch speech in 2015 appeared in many places, including Amber Phillips's article in *The Washington Post*, " 'They're rapists.' President Trump's campaign launch speech two years later, annotated," published on June 16, 2017.

3 **According to the U.S. Census:** Data on Cincinnati demographics came from the U.S. Census Bureau. The 1940 data is available in

Table 36 in Working Paper No. 76 from the Population Division
of the U.S. Census Bureau, "Historical Census Statistics on Population Totals by Race, 1790 to 1990, and by Hispanic Origin, 1970
to 1990, for Large Cities and Other Urban Places in the United
States" by Campbell Gibson and Kay Jung, February 2005. The
2022 data is available on the U.S. Census Bureau website. For
easy access to this data, visit census.gov/quickfacts/fact/table/US
/PST045221.

4 **scarcity fueled racial resentment:** Research by Amy R. Krosch and
David M. Amodio (2014, "Economic scarcity alters the perception
of race," *PNAS: Proceedings of the National Academy of Sciences*,
111(25): 9079–9084) shows how economic scarcity can cause people to respond in discriminatory ways to outgroup members.

4 **The initiative passed by the largest margin:** The article "School
levy passes by wide margin" by Hannah Sparling and Rebecca
Huff, published in the *Cincinnati Enquirer* on November 6, 2016,
describes the initiative and its historic victory. The fact that Issue 44
won by the largest margin of any education levy in Cincinnati history was told to me by multiple interviewees involved in the campaign, as well as local city government officials. It is verified by data
maintained by the Cincinnati Public Schools in a document called
"History of School Tax Levies for Current Expenses in the Cincinnati School District," which tracks data from 1915 to 2020. Issue 44
passed with 62 percent of the vote, more than any other new education levy on record (the previous record was a new levy that passed
in 1948 with 61 percent of the vote). The document is available
online at cps-k12.org/cms/lib/OH50010870/Centricity/Domain
/99/TAXLEVY%20history%20REVISED%20110320%20revised
.pdf.

5 **The unexpected election outcome:** An account of the way the
Trump campaign was scrambling to make sense of his unexpected
victory in the immediate aftermath of the 2016 election appeared
in Michael Lewis's book *The Fifth Risk* (published in 2018 by W. W.
Norton & Company, New York).

6 **Even though Trump won the state:** The 2016 election results in
Hamilton County came from the Ohio Secretary of State's Office,
which makes statewide and county election results available on its
website.

6 **Given the documented ineffectiveness:** The most comprehensive studies on DEI programs are from Frank Dobbin and Alexandra Kalev, including their book *Getting to Diversity: What Works and What Doesn't*, published by the Harvard University Press (Cambridge, MA) in 2022. Earlier articles include "Why Diversity Training Doesn't Work: The Challenge for Industry and Academia," published in *Anthropology Now* in 2018 (10(2): 48–55); and "Why Diversity Programs Fail—And What Works Better," published in *Harvard Business Review* in 2016 (July–August). See also a summary of interventions designed to reduce prejudice from "Prejudice Reduction: Progress and Challenges" by Elizabeth Levy Paluck, Roni Porat, Chelsey S. Clark, and Donald P. Green, published in *Annual Review of Psychology* in 2021 (72: 533–560).

6 **Over the next seven years:** Two other articles from my research on Undivided have been published. My article with Maneesh Arora, "Igniting Change: An Evangelical Megachurch's Racial Justice Program," synthesized the survey data and was published in *Perspectives on Politics* in 2022 (20(4): 1260–1274). For analysis of the broader implications of the program on tackling racial injustice, see my article "Building a Bigger Tent: An Ohio Megachurch's Revival of Religious Community Activism," published in *The New Republic* in 2018.

7 **The story of so many:** For examples of the way many twenty-first-century social change efforts "[end] with a whimper," see Zeynep Tufekci's account and analysis of internet-fueled modern protest in *Twitter and Tear Gas: The Power and Fragility of Networked Protest*, published by Yale University Press (New Haven) in 2017. Read more about people's tendencies toward political hobbyism in Eitan Hersh's *Politics Is for Power: How to Move Beyond Political Hobbyism, Take Action, and Make Real Change*, published by Scribner (New York, 2020). "Five Years Later, Do Black Lives Matter?" by Keeanga-Yamahtta Taylor in *Jacobin* (2019) provides an account of the evolution of the Black Lives Matter movement in particular.

7 **Public opinion polls showed:** Research on the shift in public opinion after the outcry over George Floyd can be found in Jennifer Chudy and Hakeem Jefferson's 2021 article "Support for the BLM Movement Surged Last Year. Did it Last?," published in *The New York Times*. See also "In Pursuit of Racial Equality: Identifying the

Determinants of Support for the Black Lives Matter Movement with a Systematic Review and Multiple Meta-Analyses" by Flavio Azevedo, Tamara Marques, and Leticia Micheli, published in *Perspectives on Politics* (2022, 20(4):1305–1327), for a meta-analysis of the correlates of support for Black Lives Matter.

7 **the public response felt different:** An exploration of the ways some people considered the racial reckoning after George Floyd's murder a potentially pivotal moment of social change is *Politico*'s article "It Really Is Different This Time" (2020), published on June 4, 2020.

7 **One year later, many of the promises:** Research on how antiracist promises made by corporations and organizations after George Floyd's murder remained unfulfilled appeared in Janet Nguyen's *Marketplace* article "A Year Later, How Are Corporations Doing on Promises They Made to Fight for Racial Justice?" (2021) and Yume Murphy's *Vox* article "One Year After #BlackoutTuesday, What Have Companies Really Done for Racial Justice?" (2021). See also how Big Tech failed in their DEI strategy in "Big Tech promised to increase diversity after George Floyd's murder 2 years ago. Black employees say they've failed." The 2022 article by Diamond Naga Siu, Catherine Henderson, and Rachel DuRose was published in *Business Insider*.

7 **plummeted *below* the baseline level:** See data in Jennifer Chudy and Hakeem Jefferson's 2021 *New York Times* article cited earlier "Support for the BLM Movement Surged."

8 **"started in a bookstore":** The quote on how most Americans began their antiracism journey comes from a 2022 episode of the NPR podcast *Code Switch*, "They Came, They Saw, They Reckoned?" For more on the preferences and characteristics of liberal white people who are concerned about race, see Jennifer Chudy's work on racial sympathy, especially her 2021 article "Racial Sympathy and Its Political Consequences," published in *The Journal of Politics* (83(1): 122–136).

8 **Many resorted to buying swag:** For research on the consumerist turn in people's political action, see Eitan Hersh's book cited previously or Wendy Brown's *Undoing the Demos: Neoliberalism's Stealth Revolution,* published by Zone/Near Futures Books (New York) in 2015, and Theda Skocpol's 2004 book *Diminished Democracy: From*

Membership to Management in American Civic Life, published by the University of Oklahoma Press (Norman, OK). For a review of the consequences of political outsourcing for grassroots campaigns, read Dana R. Fisher's 2006 book *Activism, Inc.: How the Outsourcing of Grassroots Campaigns Is Strangling Progressive Politics in America,* published by the Stanford University Press (Stanford, CA). See Michael F. Maniates's article "Individualization: Plant a Tree, Buy a Bike, Save the World?," published in *Global Environmental Politics* in 2001 (1(3): 31–52), on the phenomenon of individualizing responsibility for environmental problems, which narrows possibilities of collective imagination and institutional responses.

9 **evangelicalism went into crisis:** On how evangelicalism entered into a crisis during the Trump years, see, for example, Peter Wehner's 2021 article "The Evangelical Church Is Breaking Apart," published in *The Atlantic;* Michelle Goldberg's 2021 *New York Times* article "The Christian Right Is in Decline, and It's Taking America with It"; and Timothy Dalrymple's commentary "The Splintering of the Evangelical Soul," which appeared in *Christianity Today* in April 2021.

9 **For centuries, scholars argued:** The argument that white supremacy was built into white Christian theology appeared in Anthea D. Butler's 2021 book *White Evangelical Racism: The Politics of Morality in America,* published by the University of North Carolina Press (Chapel Hill, NC), and Jemar Tisby's 2019 book *The Color of Compromise,* published by Zondervan (Grand Rapids, MI).

9 **A nationally representative study of congregations:** Data from Duke University's National Congregations Study about the extent to which congregations undertake programming related to questions of race appeared on page 64 of their 2021 report *Congregations in 21st Century America* by Mark Chaves, Joseph Roso, Anna Holleman, and Mary Hawkins.

9 **they focused it entirely:** Two prominent books examining how white evangelicals approached race based on interpersonal reconciliation instead of systemic injustices include Jesse Curtis's 2021 book *The Myth of Colorblind Christians,* published by NYU Press (New York), and Michael Emerson and Christian Smith's 2001 book *Divided by Faith: Evangelical Religion and the Problem of Race in America,* published by Oxford University Press (New York).

CHAPTER ONE: Podunk White People

19 **In 2016, Crossroads was among:** Data on the size of Crossroads Church comes from *Outreach* magazine, which keeps an annual list of the fastest-growing and largest churches in America. Their analysis is based on voluntary participation by churches. Crossroads is listed as the fastest-growing church in America in 2015 and 2017. In 2016, it was reported as having an attendance of 22,458. That grew to 35,253 by 2018 and stayed stable through 2022. See data online at outreach100.com/churches/crossroads-church. Data on its annual budget comes from its 2022 annual report, available online at assets.ctfassets.net/y3a9myzsdjan/Roap6IIk4oSyPdl6w g4Ul/4ac442d8a507c9cd6ccbcb463f99f307/08-31-2022_Audited _Financial_Statements_Crossroads_Community_Church-_Inc ._and_Subsidiary.pdf. Online attendance data is based on internal data reported to me from church staff.

21 **levels of partisan polarization:** The research on increasing partisan polarization in America is extensive. Some synthetic articles summarizing this work are listed here. On the origins and impact of partisanship, see "The Origins and Consequences of Affective Polarization in the United States" by Shanto Iyengar, Yphtach Lelkes, Matthew Levendusky, Neil Malhotra, and Sean J. Westwood, published in the *Annual Review of Political Science* in 2019 (22: 129–146). On the relationship between partisan animus and public opinion formation, see "Affective polarization, local contexts and public opinion in America" by James N. Druckman, Samara Klar, Yanna Krupnikov, Matthew Levendusky, and John Barry Ryan, published in *Nature Human Behaviour* in 2021 (5: 28–38). For an interdisciplinary exploration of political sectarianism and consequences for U.S. democracy, read Eli J. Finkel et al.'s "Political sectarianism in America," published in *Science* in 2020 (370(6516): 533–536).

21 **Multiple Fortune 500 companies:** An article by Alexander Coolidge describing the Fortune 500 companies in Cincinnati appeared in *The Cincinnati Enquirer* on June 5, 2023: "Cincinnati's Fortune 500 Companies Down to Five."

22 **Census data from 2020:** Data on the poverty rate by race in Cincinnati comes from the 2020 U.S. Census and is captured in a table at datausa .io/profile/geo/cincinnati-oh/?sexAgeRacePoverty=raceOption.

22 **Crossroads was 80 percent white:** Data on the racial diversity of Crossroads comes from internal data collected by the church and reported to me by church staff.

25 **"a cheap brand of Christianity":** The quotes about the Lausanne Convention, including Padilla's quotes, appeared on page 138 of Jesse Curtis's book *The Myth of Colorblind Christians,* published in 2021 by NYU Press (New York).

25 **a "definition-defying" amalgamation:** The quote about evangelicalism's "definition-defying" properties appeared on page 3 of Molly Worthen's book *Apostles of Reason: The Crisis of Authority in American Evangelicalism,* published in 2016 by Oxford University Press (New York). She also discusses the three questions that unite evangelicals in the first chapter.

26 **founded as a splinter organization:** The account of the racial history of the founding of the Southern Baptist Convention appeared in Robert P. Jones's 2021 book *White Too Long,* published by Simon & Schuster (New York). Other books documenting the history of whiteness in many Christian churches include: Anthea D. Butler's 2021 book *White Evangelical Racism: The Politics of Morality in America,* published by the University of North Carolina Press (Chapel Hill, NC), and Jemar Tisby's 2019 book *The Color of Compromise,* published by Zondervan (Grand Rapids, MI).

26 **The Lausanne Covenant recognized:** For an account of the way the Lausanne Covenant sought to bridge two sides, see Jesse Curtis's evaluation of it as a "committee-made compromise" that "embrac[ed] a series of qualifications" with respect to social justice (page 149 of his 2021 book *The Myth of Colorblind Christians,* published in New York by NYU Press). He then describes how "colorblind Christians" had "absorbed some tough criticism at Lausanne, but in the ensuing years they regrouped and spun the Congress in their favor" (page 150). Not all historians would agree, however. Other interpretations of Lausanne's history and legacy appear in Robert A. Hunt's 2011 article "The History of the Lausanne Movement, 1974–2010," *International Bulletin of Mission Research* (35(2): 81), and Brian Stanley's 2013 article "'Lausanne 1974': The Challenge from the Majority World to Northern-Hemisphere Evangelicalism," *Journal of Ecclesiastical History* (64(3): 533–51).

26 **Now, fifty years later:** Data on the world's largest megachurches is

available online through a spreadsheet compiled by Warren Bird at leadnet.org/world.

26 **In 2000, 21 percent of megachurches:** For data on diversity in megachurches, see Scott Thumma and Warren Bird's report *Megachurch 2020: The Changing Reality in America's Largest Churches,* published by the Hartford Institute for Religion Research in 2020; hartfordinstitute.org/megachurch/2020_megachurch_report.pdf.

26 **In 2008, Korie Edwards:** The challenges of building multiracial faith institutions in America are described in Korie L. Edwards's book *The Elusive Dream: The Power of Race in Interracial Churches,* published by Oxford University Press in 2008 (New York).

27 **According to 2018 polling data:** PRRI's 2018 survey data and racism index is reported in Figure 5.3 and pages 169–170 in Robert P. Jones's book *White Too Long.*

27 **"If you were recruiting":** The quote from Robert Jones about the prevalence of white supremacist views in religious groups comes from page 185 of his book *White Too Long.*

27 **They scorned the scourge:** Jesse Curtis's book *The Myth of Colorblind Christians* offers a comprehensive historical study of the pattern of white Christian churches' emphasis on diversity and interpersonal reconciliation instead of structural injustice in their efforts to combat racism. See also Michael O. Emerson and Christian Smith's book *Divided by Faith: Evangelical Religion and the Problem of Race in America,* or Kristin Kobes Du Mez's 2020 book *Jesus and John Wayne: How White Evangelicals Corrupted a Faith and Fractured a Nation,* published by Liveright (New York) on the way race intersects with gender.

29 **He called them the "other evangelicals":** See Wes Markofski's discussion of the "other evangelicals" in "The Other Evangelicals," published online at *Immanent Frame* in January 2018, and further work in his book *Good News for Common Goods: Multicultural Evangelicalism and Ethical Democracy in America,* published by Oxford University Press (New York) in 2023.

30 **"When I walked into that first meeting":** This quote from Troy Jackson also appeared in my article "Building a Bigger Tent: An Ohio megachurch's revival of religious community activism" in *The New Republic.*

30 **The idea of anti-bias:** This history of DEI programs is drawn from

Frank Dobbin and Alexandra Kalev's book *Getting to Diversity: What Works and What Doesn't,* published by the Harvard University Press (Cambridge, MA) in 2022.

31 **In 2021, Betsy Levy Paluck:** The quote about how research is "ill-suited to provide actionable, evidence-based recommendations for reducing prejudice" comes from Elizabeth Levy Paluck, Roni Porat, Chelsey S. Clark, and Donald P. Green's article "Prejudice Reduction: Progress and Challenges," published in *Annual Review of Psychology* in 2021 (72: 533–560).

31 **Nonetheless, nearly all big companies:** The statistic citing two-thirds of HR professionals comes from Frank Dobbin and Alexandra Kalev's article, "Why Diversity Training Doesn't Work: The Challenge for Industry and Academia," published in *Anthropology Now* in 2018 (10(2): 48–55).

CHAPTER TWO: Polished Concrete

34 **the entangled relationship:** For a history of the way race has historically evolved within Christian churches and how it has been embedded in the church from the outset, see Jemar Tisby's book *The Color of Compromise* (Grand Rapids, MI: Zondervan, 2019), Robert P. Jones's book *White Too Long* (New York: Simon and Schuster, 2021), Anthea Butler's book *White Evangelical Racism* (Chapel Hill, NC: University of North Carolina Press, 2021), Michael O. Emerson and Christian Smith's book *Divided by Faith* (New York: Oxford University Press, 2001), and Jesse Curtis's book *The Myth of the Colorblind Christian* (New York: NYU Press, 2021).

35 **"Old-fashioned racism":** For research on "old-fashioned racism" and how it evolved through history, see Michael Tesler's 2012 article "The Return of Old-Fashioned Racism to White Americans' Partisan Preferences in the Early Obama Era," from *The Journal of Politics* (75(1): 110–123). The quoted text comes from page 114.

35 **In 1945, pollsters asked:** The 1945 and 1972 survey data illustrating the decline of "old-fashioned racism" is quoted on pages 309–310 of Lincoln Quillian's "New Approaches to Understanding Racial Prejudice and Discrimination," published in the *Annual Review of Sociology* in 2006 (32: 299–328).

35 **Claiming the mantle of color blindness:** The quote on how white Americans' racial prejudice was hidden under the guise

of "traditional American values such as individualism and self-reliance" comes from page 416 of Donald Kinder and David Sears's 1981 article, "Prejudice and Politics: Symbolic Racism versus Racial Threats to the Good Life," published in the *Journal of Personality & Social Psychology* (40(3): 414–431).

36 **Some scholars called this "laissez-faire":** Scholars have a variety of terms for manifestations of racism that became expressed not as overt discrimination based on skin color but instead as intolerance of people who did not adhere to a set of values. These terms include *laissez-faire racism, modern racism, racial resentment, unconscious racism, symbolic racism,* and others. The *Annual Review of Political Science* has several articles synthesizing some of this research: for more on racial resentment, see Katherine Cramer's "Understanding the Role of Racism in Contemporary US Public Opinion" (2020, 23:153–169); for more on the impact of race on political attitudes, behaviors, and institutions, see Vincent L. Hutchings and Nicholas A. Valentino's "The Centrality of Race in American Politics" (2004, 7: 383–408). "Race and Authoritarianism in American Politics" (2019), by Christopher Sebastian Parker and Christopher C. Towler, discusses how authoritarianism drives racism; "On Assessing the Political Effects of Racial Prejudice" (2009, 22: 503–519), by Leonie Huddy and Stanley Feldman, provides an account of the nature and measurement of racial prejudice (2009, 12: 423–447). Moreover, in the *Annual Review of Sociology,* Hart Blanton and James Jaccard's "Unconscious Racism" (2008, 34: 277–297) investigates this concept and evaluates the method of implicit measurement; Lincoln Quillian's 2006 article "New Approaches to Understanding Racial Prejudice and Discrimination" reviews and critiques recent literature on prejudice, discrimination, and racism; Howard Winant's article "Race and Race Theory" expands on the idea of blindness to systems of oppression (2000, 26:169–185). Winant writes that at the turn of the twenty-first century, the challenge of fighting systems of racial subjugation was that we lived in "an era officially committed to racial equality and multiculturalism" yet still had to address the "persistence of racial classification and stratification." Other research documents the ongoing pervasiveness of racial subjugation in American life. Some recent pieces that provide overarching frameworks for con-

sidering how racism plays out in American life include Vesla M. Weaver and Gwen Prowse's *Science* article "Racial Authoritarianism in U.S. Democracy," published in 2020 (369(6508): 1176–1178); Elizabeth Hinton's 2021 book *America on Fire*, published by Liveright (New York); and Michael G. Hanchard's 2018 book *The Spectre of Race: How Discrimination Haunts Western Democracy*, published by Princeton University Press (Princeton, NJ).

39 **a core set of four beliefs:** The four distinctives that define evangelicalism are available on the website of the National Association of Evangelicals, on the page "What Is an Evangelical?" (nae.org/what-is-an-evangelical). Many credit David Bebbington with identifying these four principles. See, for instance, the book *Who Is an Evangelical?* by Thomas Kidd (New Haven: Yale University Press, 2019).

39 **The NAE was formed:** The dynamics of the founding of the National Association of Evangelicals appear in Molly Worthen's book *Apostles of Reason: The Crisis of Authority in American Evangelicalism* (New York: Oxford University Press, 2016), William Martin's 1996 book *With God on Our Side: The Rise of the Religious Right in America*, published by Broadway Books (New York), and Kristin Kobes Du Mez's 2020 book *Jesus and John Wayne* (New York: Liveright).

CHAPTER THREE: The Brave Journey

43 **The city erupted:** These historical details about the Over-the-Rhine neighborhood were drawn from *Cincinnati's Over-the-Rhine*, a book by Kevin Grace and Tom White, published in 2004 by Arcadia Publishing (Charleston, SC).

44 **analyzed the complexity of that choice:** Noel Ignatiev's book *How the Irish Became White* was published by Routledge Press (New York) in 1995. An article describing Ignatiev's past ("Noel Ignatiev's Long Fight Against Whiteness") by Jay Caspian Kang appeared on November 15, 2019, in *The New Yorker*.

44 **caused an estimated $3 to $5 million:** Walter C. Rucker and James N. Upton provide an overview of the uprising and estimates of damage on page 110 of their 2006 *Encyclopedia of American Race Riots* (Greenwood Press, Westport, CT).

45 **1,750 megachurches in the United States:** Data on the size, budgets, and attendees of megachurches comes from pages 2–3 of the

report *Megachurch 2020: The Changing Reality in America's Largest Churches,* by Scott Thumma and Warren Bird (Hartford Institute for Religion Research, 2020). Data on the skewed distribution of church attendance in the United States to large churches comes from page 10 of the 2021 report "Congregations in 21st Century America" by Mark Chaves, Joseph Roso, Anna Holleman, and Mary Hawkins with the National Congregations Study.

47 **Hybels had built Willow Creek:** To understand Willow Creek's place in the evangelical megachurch community, see the December 6, 2010, article in the magazine *Fast Company* by Jeff Chu. The article, titled "How Willow Creek Is Leading Evangelicals by Learning from the Business World," profiles Willow Creek's leader Bill Hybels, writing, "Evangelical Christianity proudly has no pope, and given its predilection for splintering, it can hardly be considered a single church. But if evangelicalism does have a global power center, it would have to be Willow Creek." The Willow Creek empire suffered a crisis when allegations of sexual abuse began to emerge around its head pastor. For more information about Bill Hybels's sexual abuse and his resignation refer to the following *New York Times* articles by Laurie Goodstein: "He's a Superstar Pastor. She Worked for Him and Says He Groped Her Repeatedly," which appeared on August 5, 2018; "How the Willow Creek Church Scandal Has Stunned the Evangelical World," which appeared on August 9, 2018; and "Willow Creek Church's Top Leadership Resigns Over Allegations Against Bill Hybels," published on August 8, 2018. Lynne and Bill Hybels's book *Rediscovering Church: The Story and Vision of Willow Creek Community Church* was originally published by Zondervan Press (Grand Rapids, MI) in 1995.

48 **this "seeker-sensitive" movement:** Descriptions of the origins of the seeker-sensitive tradition can be found in "The Father of Church Growth" by Tim Stafford, which appeared in *Christianity Today* on February 21, 1986; "The Legacy of Donald A. McGavran" by George G. Hunter III, which appeared in the *International Bulletin of Missionary Research* in 1992 (16(4)); "How Schuller Shaped Your Ministry," an interview with Robert Schuller featured in *Christianity Times* in 1997; and Lynne and Bill Hybels's book *Rediscovering Church.*

48 **McGavran challenged the iconic mission stations:** McGavran's

book *The Bridges of God: A Study in the Strategy of Missions* was originally published by World Dominion Press in 1955. His article "The Homogenous Unit in Mission Theory" also lays out his critique of the traditional mission station approach and articulates the homogenous unit principle, published by First Fruits, the open access press of the Asbury Theological Seminary. It is available online at oai:place.asburyseminary.edu:firstfruitspapers-1140.

49 **the pastor Robert Schuller extended:** See the article "How Schuller Shaped Your Ministry" published in *Christianity Today* in 1997 on the history of Schuller's contributions to the seeker-sensitive movement.

49 **the naked commodification:** Molly Worthen's book *Apostles of Reason* (New York: Oxford University Press, 2016) discusses the critique regarding commodification of faith, especially on pages 155–156. The response of church growth leaders to the critique, and its relationship to race, appears in Jesse Curtis's book *The Myth of Colorblind Christians* (New York: NYU Press, 2021), which discusses McGavran's dubious views on race.

50 **only one hundred congregants:** For data on declining membership in churches across the country, see the report *Congregations in 21st Century America*, published by the National Congregations Study. On page 10, they report that the median congregation had seventy regular participants. The chart on page 12 shows how participation is declining.

51 **were necessarily distinct:** For histories of the distinct evolution of Black and white churches, see work by Jemar Tisby (*The Color of Compromise*, Grand Rapids, MI: Zondervan, 2019), Robert P. Jones (*White Too Long*, New York: Simon and Schuster, 2021), Molly Worthen (*Apostles of Reason*), Michael O. Emerson and Christian Smith (*Divided by Faith*, New York: Oxford University Press, 2001), and Jesse Curtis (*The Myth of Colorblind Christians*). Research on the development of the Black church in particular appeared in Henry Louis Gates's 2021 PBS documentary *The Black Church: This Is Our Story, This Is Our Song*. Frederick Harris's 1999 book with Oxford University Press (New York), *Something Within: Religion in African-American Political Activism*, looks specifically at the relationship of the church to politics.

51 **When white evangelical leaders:** A description of the founding of the National Association of Evangelicals and the quotations from the president's opening speech comes from page 22 of Kristin Kobes Du Mez's book *Jesus and John Wayne* (New York: Liveright, 2020).

52 **Yet only white people attended:** William Martin's book *With God on Our Side* (New York: Broadway Books, 1996) chronicles the development of the religious right, including the NAE's early attempts to build unity. This theme also emerges in Jesse Curtis's book, Molly Worthen's book, and chapters 4 and 8 in Daniel Schlozman's 2015 book *When Movements Anchor Parties: Electoral Alignments in American History*, published by Princeton University Press (Princeton, NJ).

52 **In 1963, Black evangelicals:** A description of the founding of the NBEA is in Jesse Curtis's book *The Myth of Colorblind Christians*. The quotes from Howard Jones appear on page 29. Much of the history of the NBEA recounted in this chapter is drawn from Curtis's book.

52 **In January 1990, the NBEA:** The quotes from the 1990 statement of the NBEA appear on page 178 of Jesse Curtis's book *The Myth of Colorblind Christians*.

53 **In 1991, Bill McCartney:** Jesse Curtis's book *The Myth of Colorblind Christians* also chronicles the history of the Promise Keepers. The quote of the reporter at the Promise Keepers stadium rally comes from page 202.

54 **A *Chicago Tribune* headline:** For more on racial reconciliation efforts in Mississippi, read Joe Maxwell's *Chicago Tribune* article "Beating Racism, One Friendship at a Time," published on November 3, 1993.

54 **Edwards reports that once:** The story about Lydia is described in Chapter 1 of Korie L. Edwards's book *The Elusive Dream: The Power of Race in Interracial Churches* (New York: Oxford University Press, 2008).

55 **the ubiquity of the prosperity gospel:** For more information about the prosperity gospel, refer to the book *Blessed: A History of the American Prosperity Gospel* written by Kate Bowler and published in 2013 (New York: Oxford University Press), as well as the article

"Donald Trump's Prosperity Preachers" by Elizabeth Dias, which appeared in *Time* on April 14, 2016.

CHAPTER FOUR: The First Week

59 **an older white woman named Kathy Beechem:** Part of Kathy Beechem's history is chronicled in her autobiography, *So Far, So Good: A Memoir of a Brain Tumor Patient and His Caregiver*, published in 2011 by Strategic Book Publishing (Durham, NC). Her online obituary also records the career award she received: springgroveobituaries.org/obituaries/Kathleen-Kathy-Beechem?obId=28809892.

61 **Republicans, Sandra's dad thought:** For a history of Black Republicanism, see Leah Wright Rigueur's 2016 book *The Loneliness of the Black Republican*, published by Princeton University Press (Princeton, NJ).

62 **almost 97 percent:** Demographic data on Waynesville, Ohio, comes from the U.S. Census's Census Reporter website: censusreporter.org/profiles/16000US3982418-waynesville-oh/.

63 **some scholars argued:** For research on the way people's political beliefs shape their religious affiliations, see Michele F. Margolis's 2018 book *From Politics to the Pews*, published by the University of Chicago Press (Chicago, IL).

64 **When evangelicals first came together:** For estimates of the number of adherents when the National Association of Evangelicals first formed, see page 96 of the chapter "Pollsters as Pundits" in Robert Wuthnow's book *Inventing American Religion: Polls, Surveys, and the Tenuous Quest for a Nation's Faith*, published by Oxford University Press (New York) in 2015.

64 **White evangelicals reveled in Graham's popularity:** Kristen Kobes Du Mez's book *Jesus and John Wayne* (New York: Liveright, 2020) provides a history of the development of Billy Graham's orientation toward a masculine white politics focused on opposing the Cold War. Her book, along with *With God on Our Side* by William Martin (New York: Broadway Books, 1996), describes Graham's role in shaping evangelical Christianity in the twentieth century.

65 **The Christian Right:** See William Martin's book *With God on Our Side* and Daniel Schlozman's book *When Movements Anchor Parties* (Princeton, NJ: Princeton University Press, 2015) for a history

of the Christian Right and the rise of Pat Robertson. Schlozman's book in particular recounts the quintupling of their media platform on page 209.

65 **"God isn't a right-winger or a left-winger":** Pat Robertson's quote comes from page 211 of Daniel Schlozman's book *When Movements Anchor Parties*.

66 **a place of greater vulnerability:** An article I coauthored with Elizabeth McKenna and Michelle Oyakawa in 2021 titled "Habits of Courage: Reconceptualizing Risk in Social Movement Organizing" discusses the role of risk and vulnerability in activism and was published in the *Journal of Community Psychology* (49: 3101–3121). Sarita Srivastava's "'You're Calling Me a Racist?' The Moral and Emotional Regulation of Antiracism and Feminism" (2005), published in the *Journal of Women in Culture and Society* (3(1)), looks specifically at vulnerability and emotion in antiracist work. For research on the general role that emotions play in shaping people's political behaviors, see George E. Marcus's 2002 book *The Sentimental Citizen*, published by Penn State University Press (University Park, PA), or Davin L. Phoenix's 2020 book *The Anger Gap*, published by Cambridge University Press (New York). Robin DiAngelo's 2018 book *White Fragility: Why It's So Hard for White People to Talk About Racism*, published by Beacon Press Books (Boston, MA), addresses the question of the role of emotional burden in antiracism.

CHAPTER FIVE: His Head Is Burning

71 **the neuroscience of empathy:** For research on the neural basis of decision-making, see George E. Marcus's book *The Sentimental Citizen* (University Park, PA: Penn State University Press, 2002), as well as Antonio R. Damasio's 1994 book *Descartes' Error: Emotion, Reason, and the Human Brain*, published by Grosset/Putnam Books (New York); and Richard D. Lane and Lynn Nadel's 2020 book *Cognitive Neuroscience of Emotion*, published by Oxford University Press (New York).

72 **the poverty rate among Black families:** Data on the discrepancies between the poverty rate of Black families and that of white families comes from the Current Population Surveys. See page 8 of the report, "Socioeconomic Trends in Poverty Areas 1960 to 1968"

published by the Department of Commerce (Series P-60, No. 67, December 30, 1969).

73 **according to the 1960 Census:** Data on the discrepancies of college graduation rates between white persons and Black persons in 1960 are estimated from Figure 4.1 on page 160 of the U.S. Census Bureau's *Statistical Abstract of the United States,* published in 1999. These figures capture historical trends in educational attainment by race.

75 **Instead, as psychologists argue:** Research on the social dimensions of motivation and the importance of intrinsic motivation is summarized in a review article by Jacque Eccles and Allan Wigfield, "Motivational Beliefs, Values, and Goals," published in the *Annual Review of Psychology* in 2002 (53(1): 109–132).

CHAPTER SIX: Belonging

78 **Self-reflection could prompt:** See Sarita Srivastava's article " 'You're Calling Me a Racist?' " (*Journal of Women in Culture and Society,* 3(1)) on the possibility of people shutting down when engaging in antiracist work. For research on the ways DEI programs can potentially push people away from DEI work, see Frank Dobbin and Alexandra Kalev's book *Getting to Diversity: What Works and What Doesn't* (Cambridge, MA: Harvard University Press, 2022) and the article "Prejudice Reduction: Progress and Challenges" by Elizabeth Levy Paluck, Roni Porat, Chelsey S. Clark, and Donald P. Green (2021, *Annual Review of Psychology,* 72: 533–560).

79 **distinct from interactions:** An account of the distinction between relationships and interactions appeared in Kristin J. August and Karen S. Rook's chapter "Social Relationships" in Marc D. Gellman and J. Rick Turner's *Encyclopedia of Behavioral Medicine,* published by Springer (New York) in 2013.

79 **what psychologists called "social relationships":** On the difference between social relationships and transactional exchange relationships, see Karen S. Cook and Eric Rice's chapter "Social Exchange Theory," which appeared in the *Handbook of Social Psychology* (Hoboken, NJ: John Wiley) in 2006, and Peter Blau's 1986 book *Exchange and Power in Social Life,* published by Transaction Books (New Brunswick, NJ).

79 **a sense of acceptance, exchange, and growth:** For more on the way

social relationships can move people toward a "place of acceptance, exchange, and growth," see research on the way experiences of social connnectedness shape people's orientations toward generosity and expand their "circle of moral regard" in Daniel A. Yudkin, Ana P. Gantman, Wilhelm Hofmann, and Jordi Quoidbach's article "Binding Moral Values Gain Importance in the Presence of Close Others" (2021), published in *Nature Communications* (12: 2718).

82 **People's ability to enact change:** Research on the power of social relationships in recruiting others to activism and social change can be found in Betsy Sinclair's 2012 book *The Social Citizen: Peer Networks and Political Behavior,* published by the University of Chicago Press (Chicago, IL). To explore the social dimensions of voting behavior, read Todd Rogers, Craig R. Fox, and Alan S. Gerber's chapter "Rethinking Why People Vote: Voting as Dynamic Social Expression" in Eldar Shafir's 2013 book *The Behavioral Foundations of Public Policy,* published by Princeton University Press (Princeton, NJ); as well as Alan S. Gerber and Todd Rogers's 2009 article "Descriptive Social Norms and Motivation to Vote: Everybody's Voting and So Should You," published in *The Journal of Politics* (71(1): 178–191).

83 **helping people excavate their racial identities:** For research on the processes white activists undergo to embrace racial justice, see Mark R. Warren's *Fire in the Heart,* published by Oxford University Press (New York) in 2010.

CHAPTER SEVEN: Survey Week

88 **This practice evolved:** The idea of collective spaces for people with shared racial identities to gather—to define their own boundaries, build relationships with one another, articulate their collective interests, and reclaim space within organizations that have historically marginalized them—first emerged organically from labor organizing, when Black workers gained access to white-dominant unions and realized they needed their own collective space to articulate their collective interests. See, for instance, D. M. Lewis-Colman's book *Race Against Liberalism: Black Workers and the UAW In Detroit,* published by the University of Illinois Press (Urbana, IL) in 2008; Jennifer Bickham Mendez and James O'Neil Spady's 2007 article "Organizing Across Difference and Across Campus: Cross-Class

Coalition and Worker Mobilization in a Living Wage Campaign,"
from the *Labor Studies Journal* (32(4): 357–381). The concept of such
"free spaces" also spread to other kinds of groups navigating difference. See Francesca Polletta's 1999 article " 'Free Spaces' in Collective Action," published in *Theory and Society* (28(1): 1–38). See also
Lisa Blitz and Benjamin Kohl Jr.'s 2012 article "Addressing Racism
in the Organization: The Role of White Racial Affinity Groups in
Creating Change" in *Administration in Social Work* (36: 479–498);
Priscilla Douglas's 2008 article "Affinity Groups: Catalyst for Inclusive Organizations," published in *Employment Relations Today* (34:
11–18); and Ivuoma Onyeador, Sa-kiera T. J. Hudson, and Neil A.
Lewis Jr.'s 2021 article "Moving Beyond Implicit Bias Training: Pol-
icy Insights for Increasing Organizational Diversity," published in
Policy Insights from the Behavioral and Brain Sciences (8(1): 19–26).

88 **they substituted seemingly neutral symbols:** The story about DEI
programs that use shapes instead of racial categories appeared on
page 16 of Frank Dobbin and Alexandra Kalev's book *Getting to
Diversity* (Cambridge, MA: Harvard University Press, 2022).

89 **Stanford professor Hakeem Jefferson:** Hakeem Jefferson quotes
Higginbotham's definitions of respectability politics on page 1451
of the article "The Politics of Respectability and Black Americans'
Punitive Attitudes," published in the *American Political Science
Review* in 2023 (117(4): 1448–1464). The article extends Higginbotham's research to describe the way notions of respectability
impact politics. See also Cathy Cohen's 1999 book *The Boundaries
of Blackness: AIDS and the Breakdown of Black Politics,* published by
the University of Chicago Press (Chicago, IL), for more research
on respectability politics in the Black community.

89 **These definitions of "respectability politics":** The original definition of respectability politics comes from Evelyn Brooks Higginbotham's 1994 book *Righteous Discontent: The Women's Movement
in the Black Baptist Church, 1880–1920,* published by Harvard University Press (Cambridge, MA).

90 **Approximately 12 percent of Black Americans:** The data about
Black Americans' distribution on the Respectability Politics Scale
comes from figure 1 in Hakeem Jefferson's article, "The Politics of
Respectability."

92 **Describing the work:** Arlie Hochschild's work on emotional labor is

in her 1983 book *The Managed Heart,* published by the University of California Press (Berkeley, CA).

CHAPTER EIGHT: My Little Rebellion

99 **The gap between:** For research on the opinion-action gap in racial justice, see Jared Clemons's "From 'Freedom Now!' to 'Black Lives Matter': Retrieving King and Randolph to Theorize Contemporary White Antiracism," which appeared in *Perspectives on Politics* (20(4): 1290–1304) in 2022.

100 **In 2002, Yale professor:** For more on the individualization of responsibility, see Michael F. Maniates's "Individualization: Plant a Tree, Buy a Bike, Save the World?" published in *Global Environmental Politics* in 2001 (1(3): 31–52). This concept has subsequently been applied to a range of other policy areas, such as in Jennifer Hobbins's "Young Long-Term Unemployed and the Individualization of Responsibility" (2016), published in *Nordic Journal of Working Life Studies* (6(2): 43); Ellen Sweeney's 2014 article "The Individualization of Risk and Responsibility in Breast Cancer Prevention Education Campaigns," published in *Policy Futures in Education* (2014, 12(7)); Alison Reiheld's 2015 article "With All Due Caution: Global Anti-Obesity Campaigns and the Individualization of Responsibility," published in *The International Journal of Feminist Approaches to Bioethics* (2015, 8(2): 226–249).

100 **That's why former vice president:** A discussion of Gore's exhortation to change light bulbs appears in an article by Lance Newman titled "The inconvenient truth about Al Gore," in *Socialist Worker* on June 9, 2006.

100 **President George W. Bush similarly:** For examples of Bush's consumerist response to 9/11, see " 'Islam is Peace' Says President, Remarks by the President at the Islamic Center of Washington D.C.," on September 17, 2001. See also "At O'Hare, President Says 'Get on Board,' Remarks by the President to Airline Employees" on September 27, 2001. These speeches are available online at georgewbush-whitehouse.archives.gov/news/releases/2001/09/20010917-11.html and georgewbush-whitehouse.archives.gov/news/releases/2001/09/20010927-1.html, respectively.

100 **a sense of moral license:** For a review of research on moral licens-

ing, see Irene Blanken, Niels van de Ven, and Marcel Zeelenberg's 2015 article "A Meta-Analytic Review of Moral Licensing" in *Personality and Social Psychology Bulletin* (41(4)).

CHAPTER NINE: *The New Jim Crow*

108 **He knew that Alexander's book:** Read more about racial injustice in America's criminal justice system in Michelle Alexander's book *The New Jim Crow*, published by the New Press (New York) in 2012.

115 **Prominent evangelical pastors:** Many articles capture the depth and breadth of support for Trump among evangelical pastors. One example is Elizabeth Dias's article, "Evangelical Leaders Celebrate the Day Before Donald Trump's Inauguration," published in *Time* on January 19, 2017.

CHAPTER TEN: The Justice Team

119 **a "long-term vehicle for change":** Jane McAlevey's 2016 book *No Shortcuts: Organizing for Power in the New Gilded Age*, published by Oxford University Press (New York), and Elisabeth S. Clemens's 1997 book *The People's Lobby: Organizational Innovation and the Rise of Interest Group Politics in the United States, 1890–1925*, published by the University of Chicago Press (Chicago, IL), each discuss the importance of vehicles like the Justice Team in shaping people's ongoing action.

119 **A 2009 study randomly selected:** Data on the factors that predict the passage of policies in Congress that change the status quo comes from Frank Baumgartner, Jeffrey Berry, Marie Hojnacki, David Kimball, and Beth Leech's 2009 book *Lobbying and Policy Change: Who Wins, Who Loses, and Why*, published by the University of Chicago Press (Chicago, IL), page 208 and chapter 11.

120 **Reed had entered:** Details on Ralph Reed's background and evolution as a political strategist and his early work with Pat Robertson are drawn from an interview with Emma Green on the podcast *The Experiment*, in an episode titled "How the Evangelical Machine Got Made," which aired on May 13, 2021. William Martin's *With God on Our Side* (New York: Broadway Books, 1996) also recounts Robertson and Reed's founding of the Christian Coalition. Daniel Schlozman's book *When Movements Anchor Parties* (Princeton, NJ: Princeton

University Press, 2015) catalogues the history on pages 212–216. Quotes from Reed come from his interview with Emma Green.

124 **ISAIAH's intensive training:** For more background on the ISAIAH training, the history of faith-based community organizing, and the work of Faith in Action in particular, see Richard L. Wood and Brad R. Fulton's book *A Shared Future,* published by the University of Chicago Press (Chicago, IL) in 2015.

126 **Few things are more powerful:** Research on the power of an organized base of people appeared in Charles Payne's 1997 book *I've Got the Light of Freedom: The Organizing Tradition and the Mississippi Freedom Struggle,* University of California Press (Berkeley, CA); Jane McAlevey's *No Shortcuts;* Marshall Ganz's 2009 book *Why David Sometimes Wins: Leadership, Strategy and the Organization in the California Farm Worker Movement,* published by Oxford University Press (New York), and his chapter "Social Movement Leadership" in Nitin Nohria and Rakesh Khurana's *Handbook of Leadership Theory and Practice,* published by the Harvard Business School Press (Cambridge, MA) in 2010. Mark Warren's 2001 book *Dry Bones Rattling: Community Building to Revitalize American Democracy,* published by Princeton University Press (Princeton, NJ), provides in-depth guidance on rebuilding the social capital of American communities while encouraging racially inclusive democratic participation. Mark Warren and Karen Mapp's 2011 book *A Match on Dry Grass: Community Organizing as a Catalyst for School Reform,* published by Oxford University Press (New York), illustrates how organizing groups became powerful actors in school reform. See also my own research in *Prisms of the People: Power and Organizing in 21st Century America,* coauthored with Elizabeth McKenna and Michelle Oyakawa and published by the University of Chicago Press (Chicago, IL) in 2021; "The Organizational Roots of Political Activism: Field Experiments on Creating a Relational Context," published in 2016 in the *American Political Science Review* (110(2): 296–307); my 2014 book *How Organizations Develop Activists: Civic Associations and Leadership in the 21st Century,* published by Oxford University Press (New York); and a 2014 book coauthored with Elizabeth McKenna entitled *Groundbreakers: How Obama's 2.2 Million Volunteers Transformed Campaigns in America,* published by Oxford University Press (New York).

CHAPTER ELEVEN: I Told Them I Was Black

137 **Evangelical Christians often interpret:** A wonderful study of people's belief in coincidences and the role it plays in their faith is *When God Talks Back: Understanding the American Evangelical Relationship with God,* written by Tanya M. Luhrmann and published by Vintage Books (New York) in 2012.

138 **Often, speakers at Willow Creek:** The fact that speakers at Willow Creek had to have their outfits preapproved before speaking onstage came from an interview with a former staff member in the church.

141 **Psalm 86:11:** The version quoted here is the version that Chuck used in his speech, which was from a version of the Bible called The Message, and not the New Revised Standard Version of the Bible used elsewhere throughout this book.

141 **Anthea Butler, a Black professor of religion:** Anthea Butler's book discussing the way white supremacy is woven into evangelical Christian theology is *White Evangelical Racism* (Chapel Hill, NC: University of North Carolina Press, 2021).

CHAPTER TWELVE: Who Is in Charge of You?

144 **"Organization is sacrifice":** The W. E. B. Du Bois quotation comes from an article entitled "Opinion of W. E. B. Du Bois" that appeared in the NAACP's magazine *The Crisis* (20(1): 8), published in May 1920.

144 **small groups like the Justice Team:** Data on the prevalence of small groups in megachurches appeared in Scott Thumma and Warren Bird's report *Megachurch 2020: The Changing Reality in America's Largest Churches* (Hartford Institute for Religion Research, 2020), and in their book *The Other 80 Percent: Turning Your Church's Spectators into Active Participants,* published by Jossey-Bass (San Francisco, CA) in 2011.

145 **"the mother of all other forms of knowledge":** The Alexis de Tocqueville quote comes from his book *Democracy in America,* originally published in 1835. It appears on page 517 of the 1969 edition of the book published by Doubleday (New York).

145 **In a 2005 article:** *The New Yorker* article by Malcolm Gladwell about Rick Warren's Saddleback Church in California is called "The

Cellular Church," published on September 4, 2005. See also Curtiss Paul DeYoung, Michael O. Emerson, George Yancey, and Karen Chai Kim's 2003 book *United by Faith,* published by Oxford University Press (New York), on the power of small groups, specifically within multiracial congregations. Research on the relationship between small groups and giving is available in Scott Thumma and Warren Bird's report on megachurches and their book *The Other 80 Percent,* cited previously.

145 **Dave Ferguson, the leader:** Dave Ferguson's writing on small groups and leadership appeared in his 2018 book with Warren Bird *Hero Maker: Five Essential Practices for Leaders to Multiply Leaders,* published by Zondervan (Grand Rapids, MI). Ferguson's quote about Jesus spending 73 percent of his time with the apostles comes from a Zoom webinar he did with the Faith in Action network on May 20, 2020.

147 **Their relational bonds:** In addition to work already cited about the relational power of small groups, there is also research in other domains, such as workplaces, that illustrates how participatory practices can shape further action and general social attitudes: Sherry Wu and Elizabeth Levy Paluck's "Participatory Practices at Work Change Attitudes and Behavior Toward Societal Authority and Justice," published in *Nature Communications* (11: 2633) in 2020. Research cited in the fifth endnote of Chapter 6 captures the power of relational bonds in shaping political action.

149 **Sociologists Andrew Whitehead and Samuel Perry:** Whitehead and Perry's book on white Christian nationalism provides one of the most empirical accounts of the phenomenon. The data on white Christian nationalism from this chapter comes from their 2020 book *Taking America Back for God: Christian Nationalism in the United States,* published by Oxford University Press (New York), especially figure 1.1 on page 25.

CHAPTER THIRTEEN: Don't Talk to Me

160 **People learn habits:** A prominent theory about the way racism is reproduced is articulated in Michael Omi and Howard Winant's 1994 book *Racial Formulation in the United States: From the 1960s to the 1990s,* published by Routledge (New York). Brad R. Fulton, Michelle Oyakawa, and Richard L. Wood's article "Critical Stand-

point: Leaders of Color Advancing Racial Equality in Predominantly White Organizations," published in *Nonprofit Management and Leadership* in 2019 (30(4): 255–276), examines how organizations can address racial inequality.

160 **"Consequential human activity":** The quote from Nicholas Lemann appeared on page 52 of his 2021 article "A New Politics, A New Economics" in *Liberties: A Journal of Culture and Politics* (1(2)).

CHAPTER FOURTEEN: Who I Am Here

169 **The backlash:** For stories of the kind of backlash that people experience during the work of antiracism, see Mark R. Warren's *Fire in the Heart,* published by Oxford University Press (New York) in 2010, and the book *Everyday White People Confront Racial and Social Injustice: Fifteen Stories,* edited by Eddie Moore Jr., Marguerite W. Penick-Parks, and Ali Michael, published by Stylus Publishing (Sterling, VA) in 2015. For more on the way patterns of backlash play out at a societal level, see Ashley Jardina's book *White Identity Politics,* published in 2019 by Cambridge University Press (New York). The book *Protecting Whiteness,* edited by Cameron D. Lippard, J. Scott Carter, and David G. Embrace, recounts what the editors call the "rebirth of white resistance." It was published in 2020 by the University of Washington Press (Seattle, WA).

172 **Sociologist Mark Warren:** See Warren's book *Fire In the Heart* for the role that relationships play in helping people to navigate backlash.

CHAPTER FIFTEEN: No One Trusts Leadership

183 **Birdsall decided to organize a meeting:** Descriptions of Doug Birdsall's meeting in 2018 following Billy Graham's death appear in *The New Yorker* article "At a Private Meeting in Illinois, a Group of Evangelicals Tried to Save Their Movement from Trumpism" by Katelyn Beaty (April 26, 2018); and on pages 64–66 in Jack Jenkins's 2020 book *American Prophets: The Religious Roots of Progressive Politics and the Ongoing Fight for the Soul of the Country,* published by HarperOne (New York).

184 **Putting a point on the discussion:** The Charlie Dates quote, and the details about attendees leaving the meeting, come from Katelyn Beaty's article "At a Private Meeting in Illinois. . . ."

185 **A broader movement:** See citations in the sixteenth endnote of the introductory chapter for articles on the crisis in evangelicalism. Prominent books that have inspired a vibrant conversation about sexism and patriarchy in the church and the movement around deconstruction include Beth Allison Barr's 2021 book *The Making of Biblical Womanhood: How the Subjugation of Women Became Gospel Truth,* published by Brazos Press (Grand Rapids, MI); Rachel Held Evans's 2012 book *A Year of Biblical Womanhood: How a Liberated Woman Found Herself Sitting on Her Roof, Covering Her Head, and Calling Her Husband "Master,"* published by Thomas Nelson (Nashville, TN); and Kristin Kobes Du Mez's book *Jesus and John Wayne* (New York: Liveright, 2020).

CHAPTER SIXTEEN: Is This Martin's Dream for Me?

189 **"characteristics and competencies of Jesus":** The quotations about the purpose of the Huddle come from the curriculum guide for Huddle groups, downloaded from the Crossroads website: crossroads.net/huddle/.

190 **aggression became equated with masculinity:** See Kristen Kobes Du Mez's book *Jesus and John Wayne* (New York: Liveright, 2020) for a discussion of historical patterns of masculinity in the church.

CHAPTER SEVENTEEN: Someone Call Chuck

197 **The Don't Panic series:** Descriptions of the Don't Panic series are available on the Crossroads website. Quotes are taken from their description of "The Kingdom Truth" in their "Election Survival Guide" on the website at: crossroads.net/dontpanic/election -survival-guide/.

198 **According to *The Washington Post*:** Statistics on the rates of homicides of Black men come from *The Washington Post*'s Fatal Force Database, available online. The numbers reported here come from a Github download of their database on January 2, 2024: washing tonpost.com/graphics/investigations/police-shootings-database/.

199 **Political scientist Albert Hirschman:** Hirschman's canonical work *Exit, Voice, and Loyalty* was published in 1970 by Harvard University Press (Cambridge, MA).

200 **They identified forty-six associations:** Data on the prevalence of large, federated membership associations at the turn of the twenti-

eth century comes from a 2000 article by Theda Skocpol, Marshall Ganz, and Ziad Munson, "A Nation of Organizers: The Institutional Origins of Civic Voluntarism in the United States" in *The American Political Science Review* (94(3): 527–546).

CHAPTER EIGHTEEN: Finding My Power

208 **The American Family Survey found:** Statistics on marriage during the COVID-19 pandemic come from the American Family Survey, a nationally representative YouGov survey of three thousand Americans sponsored by the *Deseret News* and the Center for the Study of Elections and Democracy. W. Bradford Wilcox, Lyman Stone, and Wendy Wang report the results in an Institute for Family Studies blogpost entitled "The Good and Bad News About Marriage in the Time of COVID" from September 22, 2020.

209 **A 2021 survey:** Data on the relationship between evangelicalism and disinformation comes from the American Enterprise Institute survey reported in the article "Rise of Conspiracies Reveals an Evangelical Divide in the GOP," written by Daniel A. Cox on February 12, 2021 (aei.org/articles/rise-of-conspiracies-reveals-an-evangelical-divide-in-the-gop/).

CHAPTER NINETEEN: The Bitch at the Protest

217 **Social identities had become:** Data demonstrating the layering of political and social identities in twenty-first-century American politics can be found in Lilliana Mason's book *Uncivil Agreement: How Politics Became Our Identity,* published in 2018 by the University of Chicago Press (Chicago, IL).

CHAPTER TWENTY: I Knew You'd Be Here Today

223 **Bethel was a small town:** Demographic data on Bethel, Ohio, comes from DataUSA.io and is available online here: datausa.io/profile/geo/bethel-oh#:~:text=In%202021%2C%20Bethel%2C%20OH%20had,%2438%2C708%2C%20a%208.55%25%20increase. It draws on Census data from 2021.

223 **On the day of the protest:** Hannah Knowles's June 16, 2020, article in *The Washington Post,* "A Tiny Ohio Town's Black Lives Matter Event was Overrun by Counterprotestors," and Dan Horn's June 17, 2020, article in *USA Today,* " 'It Got Ugly': What Happened When

Black Lives Matter Protests Came to Small Town Ohio," chronicle the events in Bethel, Ohio.

224 **nothing was more effective:** Evidence for the power of personal experience in shaping people's reactions to disinformation can be found in Emily Kubin, Curtis Puryear, Chelsea Schein, and Kurt Gray's article "Personal Experiences Bridge Moral and Political Divides Better than Facts" in the *Proceedings of the National Academy of Sciences,* January 25, 2021 (118(6)).

CHAPTER TWENTY-ONE: Ordinary People

229 **By 2021, half a million people:** Data on the growth and size of Crossroads came from information collected by the church and reported to me by church staff.

229 **"Give it up":** The quote from the insurrection at the U.S. Capitol appeared in the article "Mass Delusion in America" by Jeffrey Goldberg, published in *The Atlantic* on January 6, 2021.

EPILOGUE: Radical Grace

237 **"A Peek Behind the Curtain":** The document is available online at express.adobe.com/page/WfntehdotQrAH/. It was last accessed on January 2, 2024.

239 **Liberating Evangelicalism:** A description of Evangelicals 4 Justice and the conference they organized in 2019 can be found at their website online: liberatingevangelicalism.org/about/. It was last accessed on January 2, 2024.

240 **A scholar observing the conference:** The phrase "revolution by trial and error" comes from Andrea Smith's 2019 book *Unreconciled: From Racial Reconciliation to Racial Justice in Christian Evangelicalism,* published by Duke University Press (Durham, NC).

INDEX

Ohio Safe and Healthy
  Communities Campaign
  support, 178–79
Over-the-Rhine march, 119
relationship building, 225
Tensing trial prayer guides, 127
universal preschool education
  ballot initiative, 127–28, 178

Kenosha, Wisconsin, 227
Ku Klux Klan, 34
kujichagulia (self-determination),
  234

Lagos, Nigeria, 26
Lausanne Covenant, commitment
  to social justice, 25–26
Lausanne I, 24–26
Lausanne Movement, 183–85
Legacy Museum, 232
Lemann, Nicholas, 160
LGBTQIA+ community, 237–38
Liberating Evangelicalism:
  Decentering Whiteness
  conference, 239–40
Lincoln Heights Missionary
  Baptist Church, 50
Living Faith Church, 26
Longfellow, Henry Wadsworth, 21
Lowery, Lynda Blackmon, 230

Maniates, Michael, 100
Markofski, Wes, 29
marriage, patterns of patriarchy
  in, 190–91
Martin, Trayvon, 23–24
McCartney, Bill, 53
McGavran, Donald, 48
media, imbalanced portrayals of
  Black/white communities, 85

media stereotypes of the Black
  community, 85
megachurches
  attendance for, 45–46
  Crossroads (*See* Crossroads)
  service production value, 138
  small group practice, 144–46
  as white dominant, 27
  world's largest, 26
Michelle, 111–16
Mills, Mike, 236
Mingo, Chuck
  at Abbey of Gethsemani,
    136–37
  attending Crossroads, 55
  background, 45
  Black pride of, 135
  commitment to race issues, 57
  controversy over Spark Talk,
    141–43
  negotiating power and
    compromise, 176
  offered to preach, 56
  as pastor, 56–57
  personal growth focus, 56
  on police brutality, 118
  questioning his calling, 182–83,
    186–87
  racial injustice declaration, 12,
    22, 28–29
  racial justice video recordings,
    230–31
  on sabbatical, 133–36
  Sandra and, 180–81
  speaking on injustice, 138–41
  on starting Undivided, 21
  wanting a traditional Black
    church, 50
missionaries, 48
Montgomery, Alabama, 232

Hahrie Han is the Stavros Niarchos Foundation Professor of Political Science and director of the SNF Agora Institute and the P3 Research Lab at Johns Hopkins University. An elected member of the American Academy of Arts and Sciences, she has published four previous books: *Prisms of the People, How Organizations Develop Activists, Groundbreakers,* and *Moved to Action.* Her most recent book was awarded the 2022 Michael Harrington Book Award from the American Political Science Association for "scholarship contributing to the struggle for a better world," and she was also named a 2022 Social Innovation Thought Leader of the Year by the World Economic Forum's Schwab Foundation. She has written for *The New York Times, The Washington Post,* and *The New Republic,* among other national publications. She lives in Baltimore, Maryland.

A NOTE ON THE TYPE

This book was set in Scala, a typeface designed by the Dutch designer Martin Majoor (b. 1960) in 1988 and released by the FontFont foundry in 1990. While designed as a fully modern family of fonts containing both a serif and a sans serif alphabet, Scala retains many refinements normally associated with traditional fonts.

Composed by Westchester Book Composition,
Danbury, Connecticut

Printed and bound by Berryville Graphics,
Berryville, Virginia

Designed by Betty Lew